Spanish Dishes from the Old Clay Pot

Olla Podrida

by

Elinor Burt

ROSS BOOKS

P.O. BOX 4340
BERKELEY, CALIF.
94704

Library of Congress Cataloging in Publication Data

Burt, Elinor
  Spanish dishes from the old clay pot-olla podrida.

  1. Cookery, Spanish. I. Title.
TX723.5.S7B87 1977 641.5'946 77-2299
ISBN 0-89496-002-4 lib. bdg.
ISBN 0-89496-001-6 pbk.

Dedicated to my former
students who helped me
collect this material

The Old Clay Pot

Olla Podrida . . .

I have compiled this book for you, the people of the Americas, so that you may understand how Spanish food and crockery cooking has influenced the present-day tastes of the world. There is no extensive book, to my knowledge, that deals in depth with this particular subject, and so I take great pleasure in presenting this contribution to you.

I have subtitled this book *Olla Podrida* for two reasons: first, we might say that the "olla," or the old earthen clay pot, is the "mother" of our present-day casserole. "Podrida" means continually full of good things — rich and spicy. In the Spanish countries, we find suitable recipes for the "olla Podrida" that have been the glory of their hospitable tables for centuries. The dish that bears this name is one that is continually on the stove and can be found at any Spanish meal, especially luncheon. Variations, too, are found in the name of this dish both in Spain and in the Americas, such as the South American *Puchero* and the Mexican *Cordero*. Occasionally, a hodgepodge dish made up of bits of everything is served either hot or cold, and called "olla podrida."

My second reason for calling the book *Olla Podrida* is that the name is so dear to the group of students who helped me gather many of my choicest recipes, and to whom I am dedicating this book.

It is only fitting that I should dedicate this book to that group of students who, six years ago, helped me to organize this material. When I began to teach this subject, I soon discovered that there was practically no information available for our use. My students and friends co-operated with me by translating and bringing recipes from their homes.

From that small nucleus, the book has grown. It is the outgrowth of consistent research from the kitchens of homes here and abroad, from

Americanization groups, from numerous classes of students, from friends, and of personal travel into the countries themselves.

I am particularly grateful to those who helped me so materially with the early part of this study. Among the students whom I wish to thank are Angelina Granados, Marie Dieguez, Zola Hoskins Williams, and scores of others who contributed their recipes and translations. There were also three Spanish teachers, Helen Jewett French, Violet Rhein Warren, and Evelyn Higgins Powell, who were able to give me invaluable assistance because they had studied in Mexico, Cuba, and Spain. I am also grateful to Miss Elsie Brown of the Pan American Union in Washington, D.C., and the consuls in San Francisco for their kindness and help.

Recently, I had the privilege of working on a project at the Bureau of Home Economics in Washington, D.C., on "Low Cost Diets for Racial Groups," and the next year I had the good fortune to make a trip around the world. From both of these experiences I gathered additional material to complete this book, so that you, too, might become acquainted with these recipes.

Sometimes I had a recipe without a name; sometimes I had the ingredients without a recipe; and sometimes I ate the Spanish dish itself and had to guess what it contained. But I have tried to put them together in the best form that I could, so that they would not be lost to you for all time.

May the olla podrida always be sizzling and bubbling for you.

ELINOR BURT

Acknowledgments

I wish to thank Angelina Granados, Marie Dieguez, Zola Hoskins Williams, and the scores of other students who contributed their recipes and translations. I am also grateful to Helen Jewett French, Violet Rhein Warren, and Evelyn Higgins Powell, whose studies in Mexico, Cuba, and Spain enabled them to give me valuable assistance. I am additionally indebted to Miss Elsie Brown, of the Pan American Union in Washington, D. C., and the consuls in San Francisco for their kindness and help.

Contents

Spain and Latin America

Spanish foods may well be divided into three classes, Spanish, Mexican, and Latin-American, to say nothing of the Spanish influence in our own South and West.

Spain markets sardines packed in the finest olive oil; also the unusually large Jordan almonds so delicately salted. Great green olives and green peppers, oranges, grapes, and pimientos come in the cargoes from Spain.

But we must not confuse Spain with Mexico or Latin America. Mexico, the sunny land to our south, has trains laden with chili, scarlet pimientos, green avocados, and yellow bananas. Many people express surprise when they discover that Mexican food doesn't blaze with pepper. Mexico has developed a distinct flavor of her own, more highly seasoned than the Spanish, yet not so hot as we sometimes suppose. Can't you almost taste her tortillas, enchiladas, and frijoles?

Latin America, or Central and South America, has inherited many recipes from Spain and Portugal, but they have been altered considerably by the products on hand. Coffee, aromatic and spicy, delicious game, alligator pears, melons, and Brazil nuts all lend individual zest to the Latin-American meals.

If you want good food, well blended, serve a real Spanish dinner, but if you want something distinctive, call on Mexico.

The colors should always be red and yellow. Therefore, the fall is the time of year for this party. Gourds, pumpkins, or fresh fruits make desirable centerpieces for Spanish dinners, but flowers such as tulips, marigolds, carnations, poppies, chorizemas, bittersweets, orange lantanas, berries in variety, chrysanthemums, autumn leaves, dahlias, or roses are quite suitable and in keeping as to color.

Guest Menus

Spain

Peach Salad
with Cheese Balls and Pimiento
Paella à la Valencia
Carrots   Tomatoes
Caramel Custard
Pasteles
Coffee

Orange Salad
Olla Podrida
Fried Peppers   Tomatoes
Spanish Cream
Pasteles
Coffee

Mexico

Avocado and Melon Salad
Enchiladas
String Beans   Corn
Mantecado
Pralines
Coffee

Mixed Vegetable Salad
Tamales
Colache   Tomatoes
Leche de Piña
Penocha
Coffee

Latin America

Brazilian Salad
Paella
Yellow Tomatoes   Squash
Butterscotch Tapioca
Mocha Cake
Coffee

Avocado and Tomato Salad
Pescado Papillot
String Beans   Potatoes
Mousse Café
Coconut Cake
Coffee

Creole Cookery

Melon Ball Cocktail	Crab Cocktail
Okra Salad	Melon Salad
Creole Chowder	Corn Creole
Spinach　　Squash	String Beans　　Tomatoes
Strawberry Shortcake	Gingerbread
Coffee	Coffee

NOTE: With any of these menus one may serve French bread or tortillas; any tropical or subtropical fruit, and crackers and cheese. Orange marmalade, candied orange peel, and glacé fruits, although not always typical, are in keeping with this type of meal.

Spanish Quick Meals

Serve with these quick meals: lettuce with French dressing, French bread, a bowl of fruit, and crackers and cheese. A vegetable may be served if desired.

1. CORN TAMALE PIE—Mix 1 can corn, 1 can tamales, 1 can tomatoes, 2 eggs, and salt and pepper. Cook in a casserole thirty minutes. 400 degrees.

2. CORNED BEEF TAMALE—Mix 1 can corn, 1 can tamales, and 1 can corned beef. Heat and serve.

3. CHILE CON CARNE—Mix 1 can chile con carne, and 1 can spaghetti. Heat and serve.

4. CHILE CON CARNE WITH RICE—Mix 1 can chile con carne, and 1 cup cooked rice. Heat and serve.

5. SPANISH SPAGHETTI—Mix 1 can of vegetable soup, 1 can spaghetti, and 1 can corn. Heat and serve.

6. FRIJOLES—Mix 1 can corn, 1 can beans (string, lima, Boston baked or any red beans), and 1 can tomatoes. Heat, and if it is too thin, add an egg.

7. VEGETABLE DISH—Mix 1 can peas, 1 can corn, 1 can tomatoes, and 1 can salmon. Season. Cover with cracker crumbs. Bake in a casserole thirty minutes. 400 degrees.

8. STEW—1 can beef (plain or corned), 2 onions chopped, 2 tomatoes peeled and cut in pieces, water to cover, and seasonings. Simmer thirty minutes. Thicken gravy with 2 tablespoons flour mixed with a little cold water.

Suitable Garnishes

COCKTAILS—Parsley, stuffed olives, mint, catsup, or celery, for fish.
Cherries, tangerine oranges, colored pears or pineapple, crystallized candy, dates, and avocado, for fruit.

SOUP—Brown crackers, croutons, shirred eggs, paprika, parsley, olives, whipped cream, diced vegetables, and pimiento.

MEATS OR ENTREES—Parsley, celery tops, lettuce, water cress, mint, cloves, lemon for fish, spiced pickles, tomatoes sliced or quartered, halves of small yellow or red tomatoes, radishes, hard-cooked eggs (sliced or put through a sieve or chopped), chopped pickles and pimiento, vegetables cut in fancy shapes or diced, paprika, red or green pepper strips or rings, cheese balls, grated cheese, stuffed olives, sliced or whole, and jelly.

VEGETABLES—Grated cheese, browned crumbs, paprika, pimiento, green pepper strips, chopped parsley, tomato and various sauces.

SALADS—Lettuce, olives, hard-cooked eggs, radishes, pickles, nuts, cheese balls, crackers, cherries, dressing, paprika, pimiento or green pepper strips, and colored fruits.

DESSERTS—Sauces such as chocolate, marshmallow, caramel, cherries, rubyettes, emeraldettes, candied fruit, fresh crushed fruits, fresh whole fruits, candies, nuts, whipped cream, and fancy cakes and cookies.

Helps and Hints

The Spanish entree is the feature of the Spanish meal. Many interesting and tasteful accompaniments may be served, but one should always remember that the green salad or salad bowl, French bread or rolls, fruit, crackers, and cheese are always good and suitable. Fancy salads and desserts are creations of the United States, but I have added a few recipes in these pages for variety.

In cooking these entrees, it might be well to note the following:

1. A real Spanish recipe requires a little imagination. Seasonings and vegetables may be used in these entrees according to tastes and conditions. The proportions, except liquids, rarely alter the recipe. Recipes which are too large may be decreased.

2. A bouillon cube, canned soup, or soup stock often adds materially to the flavor of many of the entrees.

3. Canned tomato paste may be used.

4. Chili powder, prepared commercially, may be substituted for some or all of the seasonings.

5. Saffron may be purchased at any drugstore.

6. Curry powder, although not a substitute, may be used in place of saffron.

7. Spanish foods are rather oily. The fat is put into the food, rather than on it. Butter is rarely used. If less oil is desired, it will not alter the recipe unless the fat replaces the meat.

In the following pages, I have tried to give you a collection of Spanish and Latin-American foods. The so-called Spanish meal is always popular. Try it on your friends!

Peppers, Nightshade Family

1. Anaheim Chili, the best-known hot pepper. Long pods. Used for chile con carne and tamales.
2. Bell, a red or green pepper used for seasonings, salads, and stuffing.
3. Cayenne, a hot variety from which cayenne pepper is made.
4. Mexican Chili, a long hot pepper similar to Anaheim.
5. Pimiento, a mild sweet pepper.
6. Tabasco, a hot seasoning made from small, red, pungent "bird peppers."

Wines (Spain)

Amontilliado, a first-class sherry.
Manzanilla, a light, delicate wine.
Solera Wines, Olorosos, the Finos, the Amorosor, the Amontillados. All dry types of sherry.
Tio Pepe, fine, dry, delicate sherry.
Xeres, dry and rich sherry.
Montilla, dry, good flavor and odor.
Pedro Ximenes, fine delicate wine.
Malaga, rich dessert wine, light in alcohol.

Rioja Wines

Bilbainas: "Villa Poceta," Claret. 1904-1910 finest. 1917 delicate.
Burgundies, Bilbainas, "Castle Pomal" 1912. 1926 soft wine.
White Wines, "Dry England," 1910 and 1917. Sauternes— 1912—1914—1926.

Bebida (Beverages)

Café, or Mexican coffee, is served continental fashion with hot milk or cream. The coffee is made very strong and is poured into a fancy bottle. A small amount of the coffee extract is needed for each cup of milk. This is the most appropriate beverage to serve with Mexican or Spanish meals.

Chocolate is commonly used among the Spanish and Mexicans, especially for breakfast. It is generally made very thick, and is scooped up by dipping bread into it.

Café de Mexicano (Mexican Coffee)

1 cup finely ground coffee   3 cups boiling water

6 cups hot milk

1. Place coffee grounds in a drip pot and pour boiling water over them.
2. Keep the pot warm and pour coffee through from ten to twenty times.
3. Serve a few spoonfuls of coffee extract to a cup of hot milk.

Cocoa

1 cup sugar	6 cups milk
2 eggs	2 teaspoons vanilla
8 to 10 teaspoons cocoa	Cinnamon

1. Beat eggs, add sugar, and cream well.
2. Dissolve cocoa in 1 cup of milk, and steam in a double boiler twenty minutes. Stir into the sugar and egg mixture. Heat the rest of the milk, but do not boil, and add to the cocoa mixture.
3. Add vanilla and beat until it is frothy.
4. Sprinkle each cup with cinnamon.

Chocolate

4 squares sweet chocolate	3 eggs
1 quart milk	½ teaspoon vanilla

1. Melt chocolate over hot water. When melted, add the milk and heat the mixture in a double boiler.
2. Beat egg yolks. Stir some of the hot chocolate mixture into them. When well blended, add remaining chocolate mixture and return all to the double boiler. Heat.
3. Add the stiffly beaten egg whites and vanilla. Serve at once.

French Creole Drink

1 fresh pineapple	Sugar
1 lemon	Ice
1 quart milk	

1. Crush pineapple and lemon. Strain through a sieve or piece of linen.
2. Add milk and sweeten to taste. Add ice and serve.

Mint Julep No. 1

1 cup sugar	½ cup strawberry juice
2 cups cold water	½ cup raspberry juice
6 sprigs mint	Juice of 4 lemons
1 cup boiling water	Cracked ice

1. Boil sugar in cold water for twenty minutes.
2. Crush mint and pour boiling water on it. Let stand ten minutes, strain, and add to syrup. Cool.
3. Add other ingredients and serve.

Mint Julep No. 2

8 sprigs mint	Dash of Seltzer
½ teaspoon powdered sugar	Cracked ice
	¼ cup whisky or brandy

1. Crush two sprigs of mint and put into a mixing glass. Add sugar and Seltzer.
2. Fill mixing glass with cracked ice, add brandy or whisky, and shake well.
3. Pour into individual glasses, and decorate with a sprig or two of mint.

Orange Cocktail

Juice of 3 large oranges   Sugar
Juice of 1 lemon   Water if desired
1 wineglass of sherry   Cherries

1. Mix first five ingredients. Strain.
2. Serve with a cherry in each glass.

Purple Fruit Juice (Peru)

6 ears purple corn   2 three-inch sticks cin-
1 pineapple   namon
10-12 whole cloves   Sugar
Cherries   Ground cinnamon

1. Cut corn from cob and pare pineapple.
2. Place corn, pineapple parings, and two of the corncobs in a kettle. Add cloves and two sticks of cinnamon. Cover with cold water, bring to a boil, and simmer twenty to thirty minutes. Strain and cool.
3. Grate pineapple.
4. Just before serving, add grated pineapple, cherries, ground cinnamon, and sugar to taste. Chill.
5. Serve ice-cold with wafers.

Pisco Punch
(Peru)

(Recipe for one glass)

1 teaspoon powdered sugar   1 jigger pisco (Peruvian
3 teaspoons lemon or lime   white wine)
   juice   1 cube pineapple
¼ glass water   2 teaspoons sirup
Tumbler of crushed ice

1. Stir sugar and lemon juice until dissolved. Add water.
2. Fill tumbler with ice and pour pisco over it.
3. Add cube of pineapple and sirup.

SIRUP

1 cup sugar   1 cup boiling water

1. Dissolve sugar in boiling water. Boil twenty minutes. Cool.

Piña Fría (Pineapple Drink)
(Cuba)

2 cups pineapple juice   Sugar or sirup to sweeten
½ cup Bacardi or more as   Crushed ice
    desired

1. Mix first three ingredients.
2. Fill glasses with crushed ice, add juice, and serve.

Jugo de Piña (Juice of Pineapple)
(Cuba)

Pure juice of fresh pine-   Sugar to sweeten
    apple

1. Serve cold in small glasses.

Iced Tea

6 glasses strong hot tea   Mint, lemon, orange, cloves,
Ice   or orange marmalade as
Sugar to taste   desired

1. Pour tea over ice.
2. Fill the glasses with ice and add flavorings. Crush the mint if it is used.
3. Pour tea into glasses and serve.

Eggnog No. 1
(Individual)

2 teaspoons sugar   ½ wineglass rum
1 egg   1 wineglass rich cream,
½ wineglass brandy   whipped
     Salt if desired

1. Separate egg and beat yolk and white.
2. Mix well-beaten yolk with sugar. Add liquors slowly.
3. Add the stiffly beaten egg white, whipped cream, and salt if desired.

Eggnog No. 2
(Individual)

2 teaspoons sugar   Vanilla
1 egg   2 tablespoons cream
Salt if desired   1 glass cold milk

1. Mix sugar, egg yolk, salt, and vanilla. Add cream and stiffly beaten egg white.
2. Pour the mixture into a glass, add milk, mix well, and serve.

Eggnog No. 3

2 cups pastry cream
6 eggs
1/8 teaspoon salt

4 tablespoons confectioner's sugar
1/4 teaspoon vanilla

1. Whip cream and combine with beaten egg yolks, salt, sugar, and vanilla.
2. Fold in stiffly beaten egg whites, and serve in glass or from a bowl.

Note: Three wineglasses rum and three wineglasses brandy may be added if desired.

Planter's Punch
(Individual)

1 tablespoon sugar
1 wineglass Jamaica rum
1/2 wineglass brandy
Juice of 1/2 lemon

Pineapple and orange juice
to taste
Crushed ice
Slice of orange or pineapple

1. Dissolve sugar in rum and add brandy.
2. Add fruit juices and pour into a tall glass.
3. Fill with crushed ice and mix thoroughly with a spoon.
4. Garnish with slice of orange or piece of pineapple.

Southern Punch

Juice of 12 oranges
Juice of 4 lemons
1 cup grape juice
1 cup sugar

1 can grated pineapple
1 quart strong tea
4 pints ginger ale
Ice

1. Mix all ingredients except ginger ale and ice. Chill.
2. Add ginger ale and ice just before serving.

Note: Jelly dissolved in hot tea may replace some of the sugar, and adds a delicious flavor. Fruit gelatins may also be added.

Spiced Cider

1 quart cider
1/4 cup sugar
1/8 teaspoon salt

8 short pieces stick cinnamon
12 whole cloves
8 whole allspice berries

1. Mix all ingredients and bring to a boiling point. Cool.
2. Let stand several hours and remove the spices.
3. Reheat to serve.

Miscellaneous Drinks

Cider, grape juice, grape juice and Shasta water, lemon
and orangeade, lemon and orangeade with Shasta water, eggnog, crushed and strained tropical fruits of various kinds.

Spanish Food

'Tis Spain that blends
The hearts of friends.

Spain

~~~~~~

In the land across the sea where the Señoras and Señoritas hold sway, many tempting dishes are made. The Spanish love good things to eat—well flavored and well blended.

And contrary to general opinion, Spanish foods are not fiery and hot, but colored with saffron and mildly flavored with pimientos, bell peppers, onions, and a little garlic. The Spanish use a great deal of oil in their food, and it is rich and greasy. Foods must be cooked both slowly and long to develop the characteristic Spanish flavor.

The continental breakfast is eaten by most of the people. This consists of an enormous hard French roll or solid Spanish bread with butter or cheese, and coffee, or perhaps fried sticks of doughnut dough with coffee, chocolate, or eggnog. The other meals vary in size with the location and class and needs of the people. We find all sorts of foods consumed, from the hard bread with blood sausage and cheese to the more formal type of meal just across the French border. But the recipes that we shall consider here are the foods most characteristically Spanish and used by the greatest number of people.

The formal noon meal and dinner are very much the same, and generally include a fish course, an entree, a vegetable, a meat course, a sweet, and a fruit. Tea and coffee are rarely served; wine accompanies most of the meals.

The noon meal may begin with the hors d'oeuvres (olives, pickles, sardines, small salads, and pickled vegetables), but most of the time this meal commences with a stuffed omelet or eggs fried with vegetables such as potatoes, asparagus, or tomatoes. For variation, too, a salad bowl, consisting of olives, radishes, bits of tomato and lettuce, is served.

This is often followed by fish, either fried or boiled, served with a tomato or herb sauce.

Then the unvaried pot of the day—the *garbanzo* beans or

rice served with meat and vegetables. The foundation is nearly always *garbanzos* (the large chick-pea), or rice. All available vegetables are put into the pot, and sometimes a piece of meat, sausage, baby clams or other fish. The most common vegetables are tomatoes, spinach, carrots, artichoke hearts, and any leftover tidbits. A variety of dishes are made in this way, from the simple *Cocido* to the famous olla podrida.

Soup is the substitute for the omelet at the evening meal. For dinner, the fish is usually fried. Then comes the meat, which is chicken, beef, veal, or mutton made into stew or pot roast, and served with gravy. The vegetables are often served before the meat, and the meat is served alone with potatoes and carrots.

Lettuce with French or Spanish dressing appears at almost every meal, along with the hard bread or rolls. A single cold, marinated vegetable, such as cauliflower, often takes the place of a salad.

Both the noon and evening meals end with a sweet or fruit, or a bit of cheese. The sweet may be a custard (the most common) or round doughnut balls full of fruit or currants, jellied quince, dates, dried figs, nuts (almonds), and raisins, or *pasteles,* which are cakes and pastries of all sorts and descriptions.

Eight-thirty seems to be the earliest one can dine in Spain. The formal meals are large, but in private homes many courses are omitted. If the noon meal is considerably smaller, an in-between snack is often appropriate in the late afternoon.

Sopas (Soups)

Sopa Española (Spanish Soup)

1 green pepper, chopped
1 onion, chopped
1 tablespoon butter
½ cup cooked rice
4 cups brown stock
2 cups canned tomato

5 tablespoons flour
2 tablespoons horse-radish
½ tablespoon Worcester-
   shire sauce
Salt, pepper, cayenne, and
   tabasco sauce

1. Cook the green pepper and onion in butter until soft but not brown.
2. Add rice, stock, and tomato. Blend flour with a little cold water and add. Simmer twenty minutes.
3. Rub through a sieve and add seasonings to taste.
4. Reheat and serve.

Andalusian Consommé

1 quart consommé	½ cup tomato purée
	¼ cup vermicelli

1. Heat consommé and tomato purée. Add vermicelli and cook until tender.

Purée of Crab

1 dozen crabs	1 stick celery, chopped
1 halibut head	1 bay leaf
1 onion, chopped	Fried bread
1 carrot, chopped	Salt and pepper

1. Cook crabs, halibut head, onion, carrot, celery, and bay leaf.
2. When head is cooked, strain the mixture.
3. Remove meat from claws of crab. Pound and return to broth. Season, and cook ten minutes.
4. Put fried bread in soup and serve.

Sopa de Pescado (Fish Soup)

1 pound fish	⅛ teaspoon cayenne
1 tablespoon flour	Salt and pepper
3 cups tomato purée	½ cup minced onion
3 cups fish stock	1 tablespoon butter or oil
3 bay leaves	1 teaspoon minced parsley

1. Place fish in saucepan, cover with boiling water, and boil thirty minutes. Drain off stock and save. Cool fish.
2. Remove the skin and bones and shred fish.
3. Mix flour and tomato purée. Add fish stock and seasonings.
4. Brown onions in butter, and add. Simmer slowly for thirty minutes.
5. Remove bay leaves and add fish five minutes before serving.
6. Sprinkle each dish with parsley and serve.

Sopa de Garbanzo (Pea Soup)

3 cups fresh peas	1 tablespoon minced carrots
1 cup olive oil	1 teaspoon onion juice
1 can tomato sauce	Salt and pepper
2 cups water	Pinch of soda
1 tablespoon minced parsley	2 tablespoons flour

1 quart milk

1. Cook peas in oil until tender.
2. Add tomato sauce, water, parsley, carrots, onion juice, salt, pepper, and soda.
3. Mix flour with a little of the milk, adding remainder to soup. Heat the soup and thicken with flour mixture.

Sopa de Garbanzos y Espiñacas
(Pea and Spinach Soup)

1 pound garbanzos	Few sprigs parsley, minced
1 pound dry salt cod	2 tomatoes, chopped
2 onions, chopped	Salt and pepper
1 carrot, sliced	Mixed herbs
2 pounds spinach, cooked	2 hard-cooked eggs,
1 clove garlic, minced	chopped

1 bay leaf

1. Soak garbanzos overnight. Drain.
2. Soak codfish overnight. Drain.
3. Cover peas with fresh water. Shred codfish into small pieces and add to peas along with one onion, carrot, salt, pepper, bay leaf, and herbs. Simmer until the peas are tender.
4. Chop spinach. Drain and add to soup.
5. Fry the second onion with garlic, parsley, and tomatoes. Add some liquid from peas, salt, pepper, bay leaf, and herbs. Cook forty-five minutes.
6. Combine the two mixtures, add chopped eggs, and serve.

Potaje de Lentejas Oscuras (Lentil Soup)

1 tablespoon minced onion	1 tablespoon oil
Minced garlic to taste	2 cups cooked lentils
2 tablespoons minced parsley	

1. Cook onion, garlic, and parsley in oil.
2. Add lentils and moisten with water in which they were cooked.
3. Reheat and serve.

Sopa de Legumbres (Vegetable Soup)

3 tablespoons oil
1 onion, chopped
Vegetables: artichoke bottoms, string beans, peas, chopped lettuce, and vegetable marrow

1 slice pork or ham, cut in small pieces
Salt, pepper, nutmeg
½ cup white wine
3 tablespoons tomato sauce
Tiny new potatoes

1. Heat oil in saucepan. Add onion, meat, and as many vegetables as possible. Season. Add wine and tomato sauce.
2. Simmer until vegetables are almost done. Add potatoes and cook until tender.
3. Serve with chicken.

Sopa Mezclada (Thick, Mixed Soup)

4 to 6 cups veal stock
2 potatoes, sliced
2 turnips, sliced
2 sticks celery, shredded
1 cup shredded cabbage

½ cup cooked kidney beans
¼ teaspoon saffron
Salt and pepper
3 tablespoons rice
¼ cup vermicelli

1. Heat stock and add vegetables, seasonings, rice, and vermicelli.
2. Simmer until all are tender.

Imperial Soup

Cooked chicken
2 ounces ham
Bread crumbs

4 eggs, beaten
1 pint broth

1. Cut chicken and ham in small pieces. Add eggs and broth, and heat all together.
2. Grease a mold and sprinkle with crumbs. Add mixture and cook as a custard, over warm water.
3. When done, dice and put in soup.

Tourin de Catalonia

2 onions	1 bay leaf
2 tablespoons oil	Salt, pepper, nutmeg
½ cup ham, chopped	½ cup white wine
1 stick celery, chopped	6 cups hot stock
Sprig thyme	2 egg yolks, beaten

1 teaspoon vinegar

1. Slice onions and place in saucepan with oil, ham, celery, herbs, salt, pepper, and nutmeg.
2. When mixture is browned, add wine and hot stock.
3. Simmer fifteen minutes.
4. Put egg yolks and vinegar in a tureen and pour hot soup over them.

Sopa de Albondiguillas (Soup with Meat Balls)

¼ pound lean mutton	Salt, pepper, red pepper
¼ pound lean pork	1 egg, beaten
1 clove garlic, minced	¼ cup tomato sauce
Few sprigs parsley and	Bread crumbs
chervil, minced	6 cups hot stock

1. Chop meat, garlic, parsley, and chervil. Add salt, pepper, red pepper, egg, and tomato sauce.
2. Shape into very small balls. Roll in crumbs and fry in butter or fat.
3. Add meat balls to soup stock and simmer fifteen minutes.

Sopa de Cebolla (Onion Soup) No. 1

2 large onions, shredded	2 egg yolks
2 tablespoons oil	1 teaspoon vinegar
4 cups stock or water	4 slices toasted bread, cut
Salt and pepper	in pieces

1. Fry onion in oil. When brown add either the stock or water. Season with salt and pepper and cook ten minutes.
2. Beat egg yolks and vinegar, and place in tureen with bread.
3. Pour onion broth over all.

Sopa de Cebolla (Onion Soup) No. 2

2 or 3 onions, shredded	4 cups water
1 sprig parsley, minced	Salt and pepper
Herbs and 1 clove garlic	Thinly shaved slices bread
2 or 3 tablespoons olive oil	or crackers

Eggs

1. Fry onions, parsley, herbs, and garlic in oil. Add water, salt, and pepper, and simmer in a casserole one-half hour.
2. Add shaved bread to soak up juice.
3. Serve in casserole with poached eggs.

Sopa de Sevilla (Seville Soup)

24 shelled almonds
5 cups beef stock
½ cup raw white fish, cut in small pieces
1 cup cooked lobster, cut in small pieces
½ cup cooked peas
½ cup cooked ham, minced
2 hard-cooked eggs, sliced
Salt
¼ teaspoon white pepper
1 teaspoon saffron
⅓ cup raw rice
Parsley

1. Place almonds in a saucepan and add barely enough cold water to cover them. Bring them to a boil and simmer until skins are loosened.
2. Drain, reserving liquid. Remove skins.
3. Pour stock into a large kettle, and add one cup of water in which almonds were cooked. Then add fish, lobster, peas, ham, eggs, salt, pepper, and saffron.
4. Pound almonds to a paste or grind very fine and add to soup.
5. Bring soup to boiling point, and add rice. Cook all until rice is soft.
6. Place a sprig of parsley in each plate when serving soup.

Note: Shrimps or crab may be substituted for lobster. Drained canned peas may be used instead of fresh-cooked peas.

Salsas (Sauces)

Salsa Español (Brown or Spanish Sauce)

1 small onion, chopped
3 tablespoons butter
3 tablespoons flour
1½ cups brown stock
5 or 6 slices of carrot
1 stalk celery, chopped
1 sprig thyme (a pinch of powdered thyme may be used)
½ bay leaf
Salt and pepper

1. Fry onion in butter until brown. Add flour and blend. Add stock, stirring constantly until mixture thickens. Then add other ingredients.
2. Cook slowly for as long as possible. The longer the cooking, the better the flavor.
3. Strain and serve.

Salsa Señora

2 tablespoons chopped raw
ham
¼ cup butter

¼ cup flour
½ teaspoon salt
1½ cups brown sauce

1. Cook ham in butter until brown. **Add** flour and salt. Stir until well blended and add brown sauce.
2. Heat to the boiling point. **Strain sauce if desired.**

Rábano Picante (Horse-radish Sauce)

3 tablespoons horse-radish
1 tablespoon prepared mustard

½ teaspoon Worcestershire
sauce
1 cup whipped cream

Salt and pepper

1. Combine horse-radish, mustard, and Worcestershire sauce with whipped cream. Add salt and pepper to taste.
2. Let mixture chill one hour before serving.

Note: Serve with cold meats.

Salsa de Alcaparrado (Caper Sauce)

½ cup olive oil
1 teaspoon flour
½ cup stock

½ cup vinegar
½ cup minced capers
Salt and pepper

1. Heat oil in a saucepan over a slow heat, add flour, and stir until brown. Add stock and vinegar, and bring to boil.
2. Add capers, salt, and pepper.

Note: Serve with fish or strong meats.

Salsa de Aceite (Olive Sauce)

½ cup olive oil
1 tablespoon flour
1 tablespoon peanut butter

2 tablespoons vinegar
½ cup white wine or stock
Salt and pepper

1 cup minced olives

1. Heat oil in saucepan, add flour and peanut butter, and mix well.
2. Add vinegar, wine, salt, and pepper, and then olives.
3. Simmer a few minutes to let flavors blend.

Note: Serve with fish.

Salsa de Andrajos (Giblet Sauce)

6 chicken gizzards
1 cup chicken broth
1 tablespoon minced parsley
1 teaspoon sage

1 tablespoon chili powder
½ cup minced onion
1 tablespoon butter or oil
3 cups tomato purée

Salt and pepper

1. Boil gizzards until tender. To broth add minced parsley, sage, and chili powder.
2. Fry onions in butter until light brown. Add tomato and boil five minutes.
3. Combine two mixtures and boil five minutes longer. Season.

Note: Serve on eggs, chicken, or any Spanish entree.

Tomato and Herb Sauce

1 tablespoon minced onion
1 tablespoon butter or oil
1 tablespoon flour
2 cups tomatoes or tomato purée

Minced herbs as desired
(parsley, chives, onion tops, mint, thyme, sage, laurel, chervil, nasturtium seeds)

Seasonings: sugar, salt, paprika, pepper, or pimientos

1. Brown onion in butter or oil, then add flour.
2. Stir in tomatoes, herbs, and seasonings.
3. Add a little lemon juice when sauce is served with fish.

Salsa Sabayona (Sabayon Sauce)

2 egg yolks
2 tablespoons sugar

1 cup milk, scalded
4 tablespoons sherry

1. Beat egg yolks with sugar and add scalded milk very slowly.
2. Turn into a double boiler and add sherry. Stir quickly until it thickens. Remove immediately. Serve hot.

Salsa Espagnole (Spanish Sauce)

¼ pound carrots
¼ pound onions
¼ pound lean bacon or ham
½ cup butter or oil
½ cup flour
2 tablespoons Madeira
Few sprigs parsley, minced

½ cup white wine
1½ quarts stock
A few mushrooms
3 tablespoons tomato purée
1 bay leaf
Sprig of thyme, minced

1. Dice vegetables and bacon and simmer in oil until vegetables are colored.
2. Add flour and mix until brown.
3. Add wine and stock. Bring to boiling point and add mushrooms, tomato purée, and seasonings.
4. Simmer one hour.

Huevos (Eggs)

Huevos Españolos (Spanish Eggs) No. 1

Bread—4 slices cut in rounds
Drippings
2 Spanish onions, sliced

Salt and pepper
4 eggs

1. Fry rounds of bread in drippings, browning nicely on both sides. Remove from pan and keep warm.
2. Fry onions in same pan until tender, adding salt and pepper as they cook.
3. Poach eggs.
4. Pile onions on the croutons. Place on each a nicely poached egg.

Huevos Españolos (Spanish Eggs) No. 2

6 hard-cooked eggs
1 tablespoon bread crumbs
1 tablespoon cracker
    crumbs
6 stuffed olives

2 tablespoons butter, melted
1 teaspoon minced onion
Salt and pepper
⅛ teaspoon cayenne

1. Cut eggs in half lengthwise. Remove yolks and mash them. Place whites in a casserole.
2. Moisten bread and cracker crumbs in a little water and mix with egg yolks, butter, onion, salt, pepper, and cayenne.
3. Fill the whites and place half a stuffed olive on each.
4. Bake in a moderate oven (375°) until heated through.
5. Serve with red chili or Spanish sauce.

Huevos Españolos (Spanish Eggs) No. 3

1 raw egg	6 hard-cooked eggs
Salt and pepper	Corn meal

Fat for frying

1. Beat raw egg, and add salt and pepper.
2. Split hard-cooked eggs lengthwise. Dip each half in beaten egg, then in corn meal.
3. Fry in deep fat until brown.

Huevos Españolos (Spanish Eggs) No. 4

6 hard-cooked eggs	2 raw eggs
1 tablespoon mashed potato	Salt and pepper
1 tablespoon minced parsley	⅛ teaspoon cayenne
¼ cup minced chicken	1 cup cracker crumbs

Fat for frying

1. Cut eggs lengthwise and remove yolks.
2. Mash yolks and add potato, parsley, chicken, beaten yolks of raw eggs, salt, pepper, and cayenne. Mix well and fill whites.
3. Beat egg whites stiff. Dip the stuffed eggs in egg whites and then in cracker crumbs. Let stand twenty minutes.
4. Fry in deep fat until golden brown.
5. Serve with tomato or white sauce.

Tortilla Española (Spanish Omelet) No. 1

4 eggs	½ teaspoon salt
4 tablespoons milk	⅛ teaspoon pepper

2 tablespoons butter

1. Beat eggs slightly, and add milk, salt, and pepper.
2. Heat omelet pan, and butter sides and bottom. Turn in mixture, and spread evenly. Cook over a low heat. As it cooks, prick and pick up with a fork until the whole is of a creamy consistency. Increase heat and brown quickly on bottom.
3. Just before serving, pour the following sauce over it.

SAUCE

2 tablespoons butter	½ teaspoon salt
2 tablespoons minced onion	1 bell pepper, cut fine
1 to 2 teaspoons chili powder	1 tablespoon flour

2 cups tomato purée

1. Heat butter, add minced onion, and brown. Add chili powder, salt, green pepper, flour, and tomato purée.

2. Let simmer ten minutes and pour over omelet.

Tortilla Española (Spanish Omelet) No. 2

4 egg yolks	1 tablespoon hot water
½ teaspoon salt	4 egg whites
Few grains pepper	1 tablespoon butter

1. Beat egg yolks, salt, pepper, and hot water until thick.

2. Beat whites until stiff. Fold into first mixture.

3. Heat omelet pan, and butter sides and bottom. Turn in mixture and spread evenly. Cook over a low heat until well puffed and delicately browned on bottom. Place in slow oven (300°) to finish cooking top.

4. Place a few spoonfuls of the following sauce on one half of omelet, fold the other half over, remove to serving dish, and pour the remaining sauce on top.

5. Garnish with parsley and points of toast.

SAUCE

2 green peppers, minced	1 tablespoon sugar
1 sweet red pepper, minced	1 teaspoon salt
1 onion, minced	Pepper
3 tablespoons butter	Cayenne
1 quart tomato purée	1 tablespoon flour

2 or 3 mushrooms, chopped

1. Sauté peppers and onion in two tablespoons butter. Add tomato purée, sugar, salt, pepper, and cayenne. Cook until smooth.

2. Melt one tablespoon butter, add flour, blend, and add to sauce.

3. Add mushrooms and simmer fifteen minutes.

Note: For variations, minced ham, a half-dozen cooked oysters, or leftover vegetables may be used.

Tortilla Española (Spanish Omelet) No. 3

2 eggs
2 tablespoons milk
Salt and pepper
1 cup cold boiled potatoes, diced
¼ to ½ cup olive oil

2 tablespoons cooked green peas
1 cup tomato sauce
1 tablespoon grated cheese
1 tablespoon minced parsley
Dash of cayenne or paprika

1. Beat eggs, and add milk, salt, and pepper.
2. Fry potato in oil. Drain and mix with peas and two tablespoons tomato sauce.
3. Fry egg mixture slowly. When set, add potato mixture.
4. Fold over, remove to serving dish and sprinkle with cheese and parsley.
5. Heat tomato sauce, pour over all, sprinkle with cayenne, and serve.

Huevos de Caracas (Caracas Eggs)

2 ounces chipped beef
2 tablespoons butter
1 teaspoon chili powder

¼ pound mild cream cheese
1 cup cooked tomatoes
3 eggs

1. Shred the chipped beef quite fine and heat in butter.
2. Add chili powder, cheese, and tomatoes. Simmer twenty minutes.
3. Stir in beaten eggs and cook slowly until it sets, something like scrambled eggs.

Huevos de Barelas (Baked Eggs)

Eggs   2 tablespoons Spanish or Mexican sauce for each egg

1. Break egg into well-greased ramekin or custard cup.
2. Pour sauce over egg and bake in a moderate oven (375°) until white is set.

Note: Cooked vegetables such as asparagus, tomatoes, potatoes, peas, or carrots may be chopped and sprinkled over eggs before adding sauce.

Huevos à la Flamenca (Flaming Eggs)

2 sweet red peppers, chopped
Butter

1 slice ham
6 hard-cooked eggs, sliced lengthwise

1 cup cooked string beans

1. Sauté peppers in butter.
2. Fry ham and chop.
3. Combine all ingredients and heat.

Huevos en Toledo (Fried Eggs à la Toledo)

3 tablespoons butter	2 to 3 tablespoons butter
1 cup minced cooked ham	6 eggs
2 cups cooked peas	1 sweet red pepper, cut in
2 tablespoons minced fresh	rings
mushrooms	12 ripe olives, pitted

1. Melt butter in frying pan, and add ham, peas, and mushrooms. Cook slowly until mushrooms are slightly browned.
2. In another frying pan, melt butter and add eggs. Fry slowly until white is set, spooning hot butter over eggs as they cook.
3. Place ham mixture in center of a hot platter and lay eggs around it.
4. Garnish with pepper rings and olives.

Tortilla de Barcelona (Macaroni Omelet)

1 pound macaroni, broken	1 cup grated Parmesan
in 1-inch pieces	cheese
1 teaspoon salt	Salt
1 tablespoon oil	3 eggs, well beaten

3 tablespoons olive oil

1. Place macaroni in a saucepan, cover with boiling water, and add salt and oil. Cook until tender. Drain.
2. Sprinkle macaroni thickly with cheese, and add salt to taste. Add eggs and mix well.
3. Pour oil onto a hot griddle. Drop macaroni mixture onto griddle by spoonfuls, and cook like pancakes.

Note: When in Barcelona, I was fascinated by the colored macaroni in the markets, and I suggest using the colored product found in our markets for this dish.

Pescado (Fish)

Bouillabaisse (Mediterranean Special)

1 onion	1½ dozen whole clams with
1 clove garlic	shells
1 cup olive oil or less	1 large crab, cooked
1 can tomatoes	1 lobster
1 can pimientos	2 slices white fish
Bay leaves	Fish stock made from head,
1 bunch parsley	bones, and trimmings

Salt and pepper

1. Mince onion and garlic and fry in oil. Add tomatoes, pimientos, bay leaves, parsley, and other seasonings. Cook twenty minutes.
2. Put clams, shells and all, in bottom of deep saucepan. Clean and crack crab, but leave meat in legs and claws. Spread crab over clams, then lobster in sections. Over this put fish, which has been washed, boned, skinned, and cut into two-inch squares. Fish should not touch the bottom of the pan.
3. Add hot tomatoes and enough fish stock to cover. Place a lid on pan and cook half an hour. Add more stock or water, if necessary.

Note: This should be eaten with both a fork and spoon.

Bacalao (Spanish Codfish)

⅔ cup salt codfish	Pepper
4 boiled potatoes	1 cup tomato sauce
3 pimientos	Buttered crumbs

1. Pick over codfish and separate into small pieces. Cover with luke-warm water and soak several hours until soft. Drain.
2. Cut potatoes in slices and arrange a layer in buttered baking dish. Cover with layer of fish. Add strips of pimiento and sprinkle with pepper. Repeat until all ingredients are used.
3. Pour tomato sauce over this and cover with buttered crumbs.
4. Bake one-half hour, or until crumbs are nicely browned. (400°.)

Ostras à la Española (Spanish Oysters) No. 1

1 quart oysters	1 teaspoon salt
2 cups cracker crumbs	Chili powder
4 tablespoons butter	Milk

1. Place alternate layers of oysters and crumbs in well-buttered casserole.
2. Over each layer of oysters, dot butter, and sprinkle seasonings.
3. Pour just enough milk over the whole to cover.
4. Bake in moderate oven thirty to forty minutes. (400°.)

Ostras à la Española (Spanish Oysters) No. 2

24 oysters	2 tablespoons cream
2 pounds spinach	1 teaspoon salt
2 tablespoons chopped onion	Pepper
1 clove garlic, minced	1 whole egg and 1 yolk
1 cup butter	Buttered bread crumbs

1. Scald twelve oysters in their own liquor. Do not boil. Chop the other twelve oysters raw.
2. Cook spinach in boiling, salted water for three minutes. Drain, press out water, and chop very fine.
3. Add onion, garlic, butter, chopped oysters, cream, and seasonings. Cook for five minutes and add beaten eggs.
4. Put whole oyster in bottom of ramekin or custard cup. Fill with spinach mixture. Sprinkle with bread crumbs.
5. Bake until set, about twenty minutes. (350°.)

Ostras à la Catalan (Oysters à la Catalan)

1 tablespoon butter	1 teaspoon Worcestershire
2 tablespoons grated Edam	sauce
or Parmesan cheese	2 tablespoons cream
4 tablespoons catsup	1 crab
Salt and pepper	2 dozen oysters

Buttered toast

1. Put butter and cheese in double boiler. Add catsup and sauce. Mix well.
2. Add cream and meat from crab. When boiling hot, drop in oysters and add seasoning. Cook until oysters are crinkled.
3. Serve on hot buttered toast.

Langostinos Salteados (Sautéd Lobster)

Meat of 2 lobsters	2 tablespoons chopped parsley
2 tablespoons oil	Salt and pepper
1 small onion, minced	½ cup white wine
1 clove garlic, minced	3 tablespoons tomato sauce

1. Fry lobster meat in oil. Add onion, garlic, and parsley. Season with salt and pepper.
2. Add wine and tomato sauce. Heat and serve.

Pescado con Tomates (Baked Fish with Tomato)

3 or 4 pounds fish	2 teaspoons chili powder
Bread or dressing	2 cups tomato juice
1 teaspoon salt	¼ cup butter

1. Wash and wipe whole dressed fish carefully. Fill with moist bread or dressing to hold shape. Rub salt and chili powder on fish.
2. Place in baking pan, pour the tomato juice over it, add butter, and bake thirty minutes covered. Uncover and brown under broiler. (450°.)

Bacalao con Patatas (Codfish and Potatoes)

1 pound dry salt cod
2 pounds potatoes, sliced
1 pound onions, chopped
1 clove garlic, minced

¼ teaspoon saffron
Pepper
2 or 3 tablespoons oil
2 tomatoes, quartered

1 tablespoon chopped parsley

1. Soak cod twelve hours, changing water frequently.
2. Put in pan of cold water and bring to boil. Drain, and remove bones from fish.
3. Put potatoes, onions, garlic, and parsley in codfish pan. Cover with boiling water.
4. Simmer until potatoes are done. Add saffron and pepper.
5. Roll codfish in flour and fry in oil. Add tomatoes.
6. Place fish on a hot platter, and pour tomatoes on top. Surround with potatoes.

Stuffed Trout

2-pound trout
2 ounces truffles
2 ounces mushrooms
Salt and pepper

1 small onion, sliced
2 or 3 carrots, sliced
Flour
1 egg, beaten

Fat for frying

1. Cut head off fish.
2. Chop truffles and mushrooms, season with salt and pepper, and stuff fish with them.
3. Place fish in a saucepan, add onion and carrots, cover with water, and simmer half an hour.
4. Cool fish and roll in flour and egg.
5. Fry in oil.

Ollo Podrido de Pescado (Fish Casserole)

Any white fish, cut in equal pieces
1 sprig each of fennel, sweet basil, thyme
1 carrot, diced
2 sticks celery, diced
2 onions, diced

Oil
2 cloves garlic, minced
2 tablespoons minced parsley
Salt and pepper
1 pound tomatoes
1 cup rice

1. Make a stock of head, tail, and bones of fish. Strain, and add herbs, carrot, celery, and onions.
2. Put oil in frying pan and brown fish.
3. Place fish in baking dish, and cover with oil, garlic, and parsley. Season with salt and pepper. Bake in a slow oven (375°) thirty to forty minutes.
4. Slice tomatoes and fry in oil.
5. Put rice in pan in which fish was cooked. Moisten it with fish stock. Season. Cook until rice is soft and water absorbed.
6. Serve rice piled on plate, with tomatoes and fish around it.

Lenguados Español (Spanish Sole)

3 sole
Salt and pepper
1 teaspoon lemon juice
4 shallots, chopped
½ cup white wine
½ pound mushrooms, chopped
1 tablespoon minced parsley
1 tablespoon oil
Bread crumbs

1. Season fish with salt and pepper. Rub on lemon juice. Place in baking dish.
2. Cover with shallots, mushrooms, and parsley. Add oil and wine. Cover with crumbs.
3. Bake twenty-five minutes, or until fish is tender. (400°.)

Merluza al Horno (Baked Haddock)

2 tablespoons oil
2 pounds haddock
6 tablespoons white wine
1 cup tomato purée
Salt and pepper
¼ cup bread crumbs
1 clove garlic, minced
1 tablespoon minced parsley

1. Put oil in baking dish, and then haddock.
2. Pour wine over this, and then tomato. Season.
3. Sprinkle with crumbs, garlic, and parsley.
4. Bake fifteen minutes in a hot oven. (475°.)

Meluza en Salsa
(Fresh Codfish in Spanish Sauce)

2 tablespoons olive oil
1 clove garlic
1 onion, minced
1 teaspoon minced parsley
2 tomatoes, chopped
¼ cup boiling water
2 pounds fresh cod, cut in four or five slices
2 peppercorns
2 tablespoons chopped roasted almonds
2 tablespoons chopped unroasted almonds
2 tablespoons soft bread crumbs
2 tablespoons milk

1. Heat oil in a saucepan, add garlic, onion, and parsley, and fry until slightly browned. Remove garlic, and reserve.
2. Add tomatoes and water. Bring to boil, add fish, and simmer until tender.
3. Put garlic, peppercorns, and almonds in a mortar. Pound to a paste. Add bread crumbs, which have been soaked in milk. Work to a paste with fingers.
4. When ready to serve, remove fish to hot platter, add paste to sauce, and cook two minutes. Pour sauce over fish, and garnish with parsley.

Entradas (Entrees)

Olla Podrida (Old Spanish Way) No. 1

2 cups garbanzos (chick-peas)	¼ pound Spanish dry sausage
3 or 4 slices bacon	1 clove garlic, minced
2 quarts water	Red pepper
1 chicken, disjointed	Salt

1. Cover garbanzos with water and soak several hours or overnight. Drain.
2. Cover bacon with water and simmer gently for two hours.
3. Add garbanzos to bacon and simmer two hours longer.
4. Add chicken, sausage cut in pieces, garlic, red pepper, and salt. Simmer until all water is absorbed.

Note: Fresh pork, turkey, duck, or rabbit, or a mixture of several, may be used in place of the chicken.

Olla Podrida No. 2

1 pound garbanzos	1 bay leaf
½ pound raw ham or bacon, cut in pieces	1 clove garlic
4 pounds beef, sliced	2 teaspoons minced sweet red pepper
1 quart stock or water	4 carrots, diced
Sprig of parsley	1 stalk celery, diced
Sprig of thyme	Salt and pepper

1. Soak beans overnight. Drain, cover with fresh water, and boil until tender.
2. Place ham and meat in a deep saucepan, and add stock. Tie herbs in a muslin bag and add to meat. Simmer for two hours.
3. Add beans, red pepper, carrots, celery, salt, and pepper, to meat. Boil gently until vegetables and meat are tender.

Catalan Olla Podrida (Escudille) No. 3

1 cup garbanzos
1 fowl
½ pound mutton or beef
¼ pound salt pork
6 tablespoons lard
¼ pound Spanish red
    sausage
¼ pound Spanish white
    sausage

½ pound ground beef
Salt and pepper
Saffron or curry powder
2 sprigs parsley, minced
1 egg, beaten
2 onions, chopped
4 potatoes, sliced
6 cabbage leaves, shredded
½ pound egg noodles

1. Wash garbanzos, cover with water, and soak several hours or overnight. Drain.
2. Disjoint the fowl, and cut mutton or beef and salt pork in pieces. Brown in lard.
3. Remove skin from sausage, cut in pieces, place in a large kettle. Add browned meat and four quarts of water. Bring to a boil, and simmer two hours.
4. Add garbanzos and simmer one hour longer.
5. Mix ground beef with salt, pepper, saffron, parsley, and egg, and mold into balls.
6. Add meat balls, onions, potatoes, and cabbage to first mixture, and boil one hour longer.
7. Drain, cook noodles in broth, and serve as a soup.
8. Heat a little oil or lard in a frying pan. Brown meat and vegetables. Serve as main course.

Olla Podrida No. 4

1 rabbit
2 bay leaves
1 sprig parsley

Thyme, sage, mace, salt, pepper
Cooked vegetables (onions, peppers, cauliflower, carrots)

1 to 2 dozen oysters

1. Clean rabbit and cut into pieces. Boil one hour in a quart of water with seasonings. Five minutes before it is done, add oysters.
2. Remove rabbit and oysters to a platter. Garnish with the vegetables, which have been cooked together.
3. Thicken the liquor with a little flour. Add a little milk. Pour over all.

Olla Podrida No. 5

½ cup garbanzos
Leftover meat, bones, ham, poultry, or game
Water
Soup greens
1 Spanish pepper
1 clove garlic, minced
1 small cabbage, shredded
½ cup strained tomato
3 or 4 button onions, scalded
2 tablespoons rice
1 scant teaspoon chili powder dissolved in water
A few cumin seeds
Salt

1. Soak garbanzos overnight. Drain and tie in a cheesecloth bag.
2. Cook meat and bones in water with soup greens. Add pepper, garlic, and beans. Simmer until the meat falls to pieces. Skim and strain.
3. Put broth, pieces of meat, and garbanzos in a kettle. Add other ingredients. Season well with salt and simmer another hour. Remove grease.

Olla Podrida No. 6

1 chicken
½ pound Spanish sausage
1 cup hot water
1 tablespoon butter
2 small onions, chopped
2 green peppers, shredded
4 tomatoes, cut in pieces
Salt and pepper
1 cup rice
4 hard-cooked eggs

1. Cut chicken and sausage in pieces. Place in a saucepan, add water, and cook fifteen minutes.
2. Melt butter in a frying pan, add onions and brown, then add green peppers and cook a few minutes. Add tomatoes, salt, and pepper, and cook ten minutes. Add to chicken.
3. Wash rice and add to chicken mixture. Cook until rice is tender.
4. Pour onto a hot platter and garnish with hard-cooked eggs, cut in quarters.

Chuletas de Ternera (Veal Cutlets)

6 veal cutlets
2 tablespoons oil
½ cup minced ham
½ cup chopped mushrooms
1 onion, chopped
½ cup white wine
½ cup tomato purée
¼ cup stock
Salt and pepper
¼ cup almonds or hazelnuts
¼ teaspoon saffron
1 tablespoon chocolate
Mixed spices to taste

1. Fry cutlets in oil until brown. Place in a casserole.
2. Cover with ham and mushrooms.
3. Fry onion in pan in which cutlets were browned. When brown, add wine, tomato purée, stock, salt, and pepper. Simmer.
4. Mix nuts, saffron, chocolate, and spices. Moisten with boiling water and add to sauce.
5. Pour over cutlets, cover casserole. Place it in a slow oven and bake thirty to forty minutes. (350°.)

Arroz y Riolapin (Rice Rabbit)

½ rabbit
2 tablespoons lard
1 clove garlic, minced
2 onions, chopped
2 tablespoons ground
   almonds

½ cup boiling water
1 small bunch parsley,
   minced
¼ teaspoon cinnamon
6 small artichokes
2 cups raw rice

Salt and pepper

1. Brown rabbit in lard and add other ingredients.
2. Simmer until tender, adding more water if needed.

Estofado de Madrid (Pork and Vegetable Stew)

1 pound fresh pork, sliced
   thin
1 cup finely chopped onions
1 cup finely chopped mixed
   vegetables

Garlic
1 green pepper, chopped
2 tomatoes, sliced
Salt to taste
1 pint hot stock or water

1. Remove the fat from meat and fry fat with the onions and mixed vegetables. Skim out fat when brown.
2. Rub the meat with garlic, and brown.
3. Place both meat and vegetables in a casserole with green pepper, tomatoes, salt, and stock.
4. Cover closely and cook one hour or more.

Solomillo (Loin of Pork)

Loin of pork
6 or 8 potatoes
2 tablespoons oil
2 tablespoons chopped
   parsley

12 very large olives
¼ to ½ cup chicken or
   other cooked meat
6 globe artichokes, cooked
2 pimientos

1 cup tomato sauce

1. Roast loin of **pork.**
2. Cut potatoes into small balls the size of marbles. Cover with boiling, salted water and cook until done. Roll in oil and parsley.
3. Remove stones from olives and fill with cooked meat. Put six of these on the bottoms of globe artichokes.
4. Pour meat drippings over both potatoes and olive-artichoke combination.
5. Chop pimiento and add to tomato sauce. Heat and serve with meat.
6. Place meat on a large platter. Arrange potatoes and olive-artichoke combination around meat. Place the other six olives on top of potatoes.

Chorizo (Pork Sausage)

2 pounds fresh lean pork	1 sprig parsley, minced
1 pound fat pork	1 clove garlic, minced
2 onions, minced	1/2 teaspoon cayenne pepper
1/2 teaspoon black pepper	2 teaspoons salt
1/2 teaspoon chili pepper	1 bay leaf
1 sprig thyme, minced	1/4 teaspoon allspice

1. Grind meat and add other ingredients.
2. Mix thoroughly and fill casings.
3. Fry slowly.

Pisto Manchego (Pork Stew)

1/2 pound pork	2 tomatoes, cut in pieces
2 or 3 onions, chopped	Few pimientos, chopped
Lard	Stock or gravy
Small marrows (squash), cut in chunks	Salt and pepper
	Eggs

1. Fry pork and onions in lard.
2. Add marrows, tomatoes, and pimientos.
3. Moisten well with the stock or gravy. Season.
4. Serve with scrambled eggs.

Pollitos Salteados (Fried Chicken)

3 small chickens	Mixed herbs to taste
1 tablespoon each, butter and oil	3/4 cup sherry
3/4 cup diced ham	3/4 cup tomato purée
2 onions, chopped	1 cup stock, or more
	Salt and pepper

1. Brown chickens in butter and oil. Add ham, onions, and herbs.
2. When brown, add wine, tomato purée, stock, salt, and pepper. Cover pan.
3. Bake in oven until tender. (400°.)
4. Serve with artichokes and fried potatoes.

Paella de Valencia (Chicken and Rice) No. 1

2 cups raw rice
1 cup olive oil or chicken fat
2 large onions, sliced
Garlic, minced
1 fat chicken
1 cup tomatoes

1 cup string beans
1 cup shrimps
½ cup ground parsley
Salt and pepper
Spanish saffron or curry
powder

1. Fry rice in oil until a light brown. Add onions and garlic, after draining off most of the oil.
2. Boil chicken until tender. Skim off fat, reduce the liquor to three cups, and add rice. Cook until tender, adding more water if necessary.
3. Cut chicken in large pieces, place in a casserole, and add rice and other ingredients. Cover tightly and bake two hours or more in a slow oven. (350°.) This may be cooked in a tightly covered kettle on top of stove.
4. Serve with ripe olives.

Note: A mixture of veal and pork can be used in place of chicken.

Paella (Chicken and Rice) No. 2

1 onion, chopped
1 clove garlic, minced
2 tablespoons oil or chicken
  fat
1 chicken, boiled and cut in
  pieces

1 cup broth
1 cup shrimps
1 cup rice
1 ripe tomato, chopped
6 artichoke hearts, split
2 pimientos, chopped

Salt and pepper

1. Brown onion and garlic in oil. Add rice.
2. When nicely browned, add tomato, and then other ingredients.
3. Cook until rice is tender, adding more broth if needed.

Arroz con Pollo y Pimiento
(Chicken and Rice with Pimiento)

1 boiled chicken
1 cup rice

Pinch of saffron or curry powder
3 pimientos

1. Cut up fowl and cover with boiling water. Simmer one hour.
2. Cook rice in two cups of boiling, salted water for fifteen minutes. Add saffron.
3. Add rice and chopped pimiento to chicken, and boil until water has been absorbed.

Arroz à la Valencia (Rice à la Valencia)

2 or 3 slices ham, cubed
1 onion, chopped
Few sprigs parsley, minced
1 clove garlic, minced
1 tablespoon lard or oil
1 tomato, cut in pieces
1 cup rice
2 sweet peppers, cut in pieces
Salt and pepper

1. Brown ham, onion, parsley, and garlic in fat. Add tomato.
2. Cook rice separately, and before all water is absorbed, add peppers.
3. Combine two mixtures, season, and heat thoroughly.

Pollo Asado (Baked Chicken)

1 cup cracked corn or hominy
1 chicken
1 onion
Sage
Salt and pepper
1 tablespoon olive oil
1 cup hot water

1. Soak corn or hominy overnight, and then stuff the chicken with it.
2. Rub the chicken with cut onion and sage. Season.
3. Place in a roasting pan, pour oil and water over top.
4. Roast until tender. Twenty-five minutes per pound. (450°.)

Pepitoria de Gallina (Spanish Stewed Chicken)

5-pound chicken, cut in pieces
¼ cup butter or fat
2 medium onions, chopped
2 cups tomatoes (No. 2 can)
1 teaspoon sugar
2 teaspoons salt
1 green pepper, chopped
1 cup cooked peas (No. 2 can)
1 can mushrooms
Cold water to cover
2 tablespoons green olives (stoned and minced)
Flour to thicken

1. Prepare chicken as for fricassee. Sprinkle with salt and pepper and dredge with flour. Brown lightly in fat, and then remove chicken.
2. Brown onions. Add tomatoes, sugar, salt, and green pepper. Simmer ten minutes.
3. Add liquor from the can of peas and the can of mushrooms. Add the chicken and enough water to cover. Cover and let simmer one and a half hours, or until tender.
4. Add peas, mushrooms, olives, and a tablespoon of flour mixed with a little cold water for each cup of liquid. Stir until it boils. Let it simmer fifteen minutes longer.
5. Pour into a deep dish. Garnish with toast points.

Note: This may be cooked in a casserole for two hours at 250°. One cup of ripe olives may be added.

Guisado Español (Spanish Stew) No. 1

¼ cup olive oil
3 small onions, chopped
1 clove garlic, minced
2 tablespoons minced
    parsley
2 pounds bottom round of
    beef, cut in one-inch
    cubes

2 teaspoons salt
⅛ teaspoon pepper
3 green peppers, cut in
    strips
4 cups water
6 potatoes
Flour to thicken

1. Cook onions, garlic, and parsley in oil until brown.
2. Add meat and brown. Add salt, pepper, green peppers, and water. Cover and cook slowly for two hours. Add potatoes and cook another hour, or until both meat and potatoes are tender.
3. For each cup of liquid, stir in a tablespoon of flour mixed with a little water. Cook fifteen minutes more.

Guisado Español (Spanish Stew) No. 2

1 pound pork sausage
2 large slices bacon
¼ cup diced carrots
¼ cup diced turnips
½ cup chestnuts

1 cup brown sauce
½ cup button mushrooms
¼ cup truffles if available
Salt and paprika
Boiled rice

1. Form sausage into small balls and fry.
2. Fry bacon crisp and break into small pieces.
3. Cook carrots, turnips, and chestnuts separately until tender.
4. Make a rich brown sauce and season with mushrooms, truffles, salt, and paprika
5. Mix all the above together.
6. Serve on a bed of rice.

Guisado Español (Spanish Stew) No. 3

4 slices bacon, diced
3 onions, sliced

1½ pounds ground beef
1 quart tomatoes

Salt and pepper

1. Brown bacon and add onions.
2. When onions are half cooked, add beef, and then tomatoes. Season.
3. Simmer one hour or longer.

Asado Español (Spanish Roast)

Round steak two inches thick   6 large onions, sliced
Flour, salt, pepper   1 can tomatoes

1. Place meat in a roaster. Sprinkle with flour, salt, and pepper.
2. Cover with onions and tomatoes. Roast until tender, about two hours. (350°.)
3. Thicken the gravy and serve with the meat.

Jellied Meat

2 pounds beef or veal without bones
2 thin slices salt pork or bacon
Salt and pepper
2 cups minced onion
1 tablespoon olive oil
1 clove garlic
1 bay leaf
1 pound veal
2 pig's feet
½ cup minced celery
½ cup diced pimientos
2 tablespoons stoned olives
Capers if desired
1 tablespoon minced parsley
2 pods minced chili or cayenne

1. Cut gashes in beef or veal and insert pieces of bacon or salt pork, well mixed with salt and pepper.
2. Brown half the onions in oil, and then the meat. Add garlic, bay leaf, and enough water or stock to cover. Simmer about three hours, or until tender. Keep pot covered.
3. In another pot, cook the veal and pig's feet, one cup of onions, celery, salt, and pepper. Boil until meat is very tender. Remove the veal and pig's feet, mince them very fine, and return to liquid.
4. Put the meat from the first pot in a mold. Add the liquid to the second pot and allow it to simmer until it thickens. Remove from the fire, and add pimientos, olives, capers, parsley, and chili. Pour it over the meat in the mold.
5. Serve cold in slices.

Albondigon (Meat Loaf)

3 pounds finely ground pork
½ pound green string beans
12 cloves
12 peppercorns
2 pimientos
½ cup green peas
2 carrots
2 green peppers
1 eucalyptus or bay leaf
1 large onion, sliced
Salt and pepper

1. Divide the meat into three parts. Roll out each one-fourth inch thick.
2. On the first, spread the string beans, four cloves, and four pepper-corns. Cut the pimientos in strips and spread between beans.
3. On the second square of meat spread the peas, four cloves, and four peppercorns.
4. Cut the carrots and peppers in strings and alternate on the third layer of the meat. Put on the last cloves and peppercorns.
5. Carefully pile the three layers together, and roll to form a round loaf. Tie a string around the loaf to hold it firm.
6. Place in a kettle, cover with boiling water, and add eucalyptus leaf, onions, salt, and pepper. Simmer one and a half hours.
7. Serve hot or cold with any meat sauce.

Michel Español

½ package macaroni
1 green pepper, chopped
1 onion, chopped
4 tablespoons fat

3 tablespoons malt extract
1 can tomatoes or soup
1½ pounds leftover meat
Salt and pepper

1. Cook macaroni in well-salted, boiling water until tender.
2. Fry pepper and onion in fat and mix with the macaroni.
3. Dissolve the malt in tomatoes and mix with meat. Add to macaroni. Mix well and season with salt and pepper.
4. Put in a greased bread pan. Bake in a slow oven thirty minutes. (375°.)
5. Serve with tomato sauce.

Frico

3 cups raw sliced potatoes
1 onion, minced
Salt and chili powder

Cracker crumbs
2 pounds beef, or any meat
cut in pieces

1 pint cream or milk

1. Line the bottom of a casserole with potatoes. Sprinkle with onion and seasonings. Add a layer of cracker crumbs, and then a layer of meat. Repeat until all ingredients are used, having crumbs on top.
2. Pour cream or milk over all. It should come just to the top layer.
3. Cover closely and bake two or three hours. (350°.)
4. Serve with Spanish or tomato sauce.

Guisados Riñones (Kidney Stew)

2 beef kidneys
1 onion, minced
2 or 4 slices bacon, diced

Salt and pepper
3 or 4 carrots, cubed
3 or 4 potatoes, cubed

2 tablespoons flour

1. Wash kidneys and cut in cubes. Cover with boiling water and parboil fifteen minutes. Drain.
2. Add onion, bacon, salt, and pepper. Cover with boiling water and simmer for three hours.
3. Add carrots and potatoes. Cook fifteen minutes.
4. Mix flour with a little cold water and add to mixture. Stir until thick. Cook slowly ten minutes longer, or until vegetables are tender.

Spanish Baked Veal

3 pounds veal
1 onion, sliced
1 carrot, sliced
1 stalk celery, sliced
Few cloves

2 cups soft bread crumbs
¾ cup minced bacon
½ cup grated Gruyère
cheese
Salt and pepper

1. Cook veal in water with onion, carrot, celery, and cloves.
2. When tender, place in a baking dish.
3. Mix bread, bacon, cheese, salt, and pepper.
4. Add broth to moisten slightly. Place on top of veal and bake in oven until browned. (450°.)

Riñones de Carnero de Madrid (Lamb Kidneys)

5 or 6 lamb kidneys, cut in
thin slices
2 tablespoons butter
Salt and pepper
1 small onion, minced
1 tablespoon minced parsley

5 tablespoons white wine
1 quart Spanish sauce
2 cups shelled peas, cooked
2 truffles
12 mushrooms
3 slices lean ham

1 hard-cooked egg, sliced

1. Melt butter in frying pan and put in kidneys. Season with salt and pepper.
2. Add onion, parsley, and white wine. Cook about three minutes.
3. Add Spanish sauce, peas, truffles, and mushrooms. Cook until kidneys are tender.
4. Garnish with ham, fried, and hard-cooked eggs.

Salteados Riñones (Sautéd Kidneys)

3 lamb kidneys, cut in small
    pieces
2 tablespoons lard
Salt and pepper

½ cup sherry
3 tablespoons Spanish sauce
1 tablespoon chopped
    parsley

Triangles of toast

1. Melt lard and fry kidneys. Add salt and pepper. Cook about three minutes. Remove from pan.
2. Put sherry in pan and add Spanish sauce. Add kidneys and cook a few minutes.
3. Put on a dish and garnish with parsley and toast.

Albondigas (Meat Balls) No. 1

2 cups ground cooked meat
½ cup mashed potatoes or
    rice

Salt and pepper
1 teaspoon chili powder
1 egg

1. Mix the above and make into little cakes.
2. Brown in hot fat. Serve with the following sauce.

3 tablespoons butter
2 tablespoons flour
1 cup tomatoes

2 tablespoons minced onion
1 teaspoon salt
1 teaspoon chili powder

1. Melt butter, add flour, blend well, and add other ingredients. Cook five minutes over direct heat. Cook five minutes longer over hot water.

Albondigas (Meat Balls) No. 2

1 slice bread, fried
2 hard-cooked eggs
1 pound ground beef
½ pound ground pork

Salt and pepper
2 cups tomato sauce
3 cups stock or water
2 tablespoons grated cheese

1. Mash bread and egg yolks and mix with meat. Add salt and pepper, and mix well.
2. Form into balls. Cook in tomatoes and stock for thirty minutes.
3. Mince the egg whites and add to sauce.
4. Place all in a casserole, sprinkle with cheese, and heat in oven until the cheese melts.

Albondigas (Meat Balls) No. 3

1 pound ground beef
¼ pound ground pork
2 tablespoons raw rice

Salt and pepper
2 cups tomato sauce
3 cups water

1. Mix meat, rice, salt, and pepper. Form into small balls.
2. Mix tomato sauce and water and add meat balls. Simmer for forty-five minutes, or until both rice and meat are tender .

Chanfaina (Liver Ragout)

½ pound lamb liver, cubed
1 cup stale bread cubes
1 onion, chopped
Parsley and mint, chopped

Pinch cloves, cinnamon,
saffron, and salt
Tabasco sauce
1 tablespoon olive oil

1 cup broth

1. Scald liver for three minutes. Drain.
2. Soak bread in water and squeeze dry. Mix with onion, parsley, mint, salt, and pepper. Add oil and broth. Heat.
3. Add liver and bring to the boil.

Lentejas Guisadas con Chorizo
(Lentils and Sausage)

½ pound lentils
2 tablespoons oil
3 chipolata sausages, cut in
   pieces
1 onion, chopped

2 tomatoes, cut in pieces
2 pimientos, cut in pieces
1 clove garlic, minced
1 tablespoon minced parsley
Salt and pepper

1. Cook lentils in boiling, salted water until tender. Drain.
2. Place oil in a pan and add lentils; then add other ingredients. Cook until tender. Moisten if necessary.

Callos à la Catalana (Catalonian Tripe)

1 pound tripe, cut in pieces
1 onion, chopped
Fat
3 or 4 tomatoes, cut in
   pieces

Mixed herbs
1 clove garlic, minced
1 tablespoon minced parsley
Salt, pepper, nutmeg
½ cup white wine

1. Boil tripe several hours until tender.
2. Fry onion in fat and add tomatoes, herbs, garlic, parsley, salt, pepper, and nutmeg.
3. Add wine and cook fifteen minutes in a covered pan.
4. Serve with fried potatoes.

Menestra Catalan (Spanish Pot Pie)

2 tablespoons lard or oil
½ pound sausage, sliced
2 cloves garlic, minced
1 tomato, chopped
½ teaspoon cinnamon
½ teaspoon pepper
½ teaspoon saffron
1 cup leftover meat, minced
1 hard-cooked egg, sliced
1 cup green lima beans

2 cups green peas
2 artichoke bottoms
½ teaspoon salt

Crust—
2 cups sifted flour
2 teaspoons baking powder
1 teaspoon salt
½ cup shortening
⅓ cup milk
1 egg, well beaten

1. Heat oil in a saucepan, add sausage, and cook a few minutes. Remove sausage and add garlic, tomato, and seasonings. Cook until well blended.

2. Add meat, sausage, egg, beans, peas, artichoke bottoms, salt, and boiling water to cover. Simmer until thick and well blended. Pour into a baking dish.

3. Sift flour, baking powder, and salt. Cut in shortening.

4. Mix milk and egg and add to flour to make a soft dough.

5. Roll one inch thick. Cut to fit baking dish and place on top of meat mixture.

6. Bake until nicely browned. (400°.)

Ropa Vieja (Leftover Meat)

Cold boiled meat, cut in
    pieces
2 or 3 onions, chopped
1 clove garlic, minced
1 bell or chili pepper,
    chopped
2 tablespoons fat

Chili powder or paprika
½ can tomatoes
2 sprigs parsley, minced
2 slices bread, fried until
    brown, and diced
2 potatoes, sliced
Salt

1. Fry meat, onion, garlic, and pepper with fat and chili powder or paprika.

2. Add tomatoes, parsley, bread, and potatoes. Season with salt. Cover and simmer until tender.

Lengua con Salsa de Nueces
(Tongue with Walnut Sauce)

1 fresh tongue
Broth or stock
1 cup diced vegetables
1 green pepper, chopped
4 slices bread, soaked in
    water

1 tablespoon fat
Salt, pepper, and paprika
A kitchen bouquet (mixed
    herbs)
½ cup walnuts, chopped

1. Boil tongue one hour in water that just covers it. Skin and trim carefully. Boil again in soup stock until tender.
2. Add diced vegetables.
3. Squeeze bread and mash with fat and seasonings. Add enough strained broth to make a smooth, creamy sauce. Add nuts. Bring to a boil.
4. Serve tongue with sauce and sliced tomatoes.

Tortas de Carne (Meat Cakes)

1 cup finely chopped meat
1 cup cooked vegetables
1 teaspoon onion juice

Salt and pepper or paprika
Batter or beaten egg
Fat for frying

Tomato sauce

1. Mix meat and vegetables. Season with onion juice, salt, and paprika.
2. Form into round cakes. Dip in batter and fry in deep fat.
3. Serve with tomato sauce.

Fritura Mixta (Fried Meat Mixture)

Pieces of cooked fowl, lamb,
    brains, kidney, ham, or
    bacon

Fritter batter
Fat for frying
Tomato sauce

1. Dip each piece of meat into batter and fry in deep fat. Drain.
2. Serve on a platter with tomato sauce.

Note: Pieces of cooked fish, crabs, clams, and oysters can be substituted for meat. More than one kind can be used. This is good for leftovers.

Fritura Mixta (Vegetables)

Any mixed vegetables
Thick cream sauce

Batter
Fat for frying

1. Parboil vegetables until nearly done. Drain.
2. Mix with thick cream sauce to hold together. Pour into a rectangular pan. Chill. Cut into cubes.
3. Dip in batter and fry in deep fat.
4. Drain and pile on a platter.

Puchero (Stew)

½ pound garbanzos (chick-peas)
1 pound beef
1 onion, chopped
Bacon fat

½ head cabbage or greens, shredded
A few carrots, diced
2 potatoes, cut in cubes
Salt and pepper

1. Soak the garbanzos overnight. In the morning, drain, cover with boiling, salted water, and simmer for one hour.
2. Add beef and onion and cook another hour .
3. Add bacon fat, cabbage, carrots, potatoes, salt, and pepper, and cook slowly an hour or more until tender.

Note: This is served as a luncheon dish almost every day in Spain.

Pimientos Rellenos (Stuffed Peppers) No. 1

6 green or red bell peppers
1 cup ground boiled ham
1 egg, well beaten

2 cups boiled rice which has been cooked with chili powder

½ teaspoon salt

1. Cut small ends from peppers. Remove seeds and white membrane.
2. Mix the above ingredients and fill the cavities of the peppers.
3. Place peppers in a baking dish, add one cup of water, and bake until tender, about thirty minutes. (400°.)

Note: Peppers may be parboiled first to remove the strong flavor or hurry the cooking.

Pimientos Rellenos (Stuffed Peppers) No. 2

6 bell peppers
1 small can red salmon
2 tablespoons cracker meal
2 tablespoons minced onion
2 tablespoons olive oil

2 tablespoons minced peppers (from tops)
½ teaspoon chili powder or cayenne
Salt

1. Cut small ends from peppers. Remove seeds and white membrane.
2. Mix the above ingredients and fill cavities of peppers.
3. Place in a casserole, and add one cup of water. Bake in a moderate oven thirty minutes, or until tender. (400°.) Baste occasionally during cooking.
4. Serve with tomato or chili sauce.

Pimientos Rellenos (Stuffed Peppers) No. 3

2 cups cooked macaroni	1 egg, slightly beaten
1 cup canned tomato soup	6 green peppers
¾ cup grated cheese	Buttered crumbs

1. Add macaroni to undiluted soup with cheese and egg.
2. Cut a slice from the stem end of the pepper and remove the seeds and white membrane. Parboil for five minutes in salted water. Drain.
3. Fill the peppers and cover with buttered crumbs.
4. Bake in a hot oven until the peppers are tender. Twenty-five to thirty minutes. (450°.)

Pimientos Rellenos (Stuffed Peppers) No. 4

½ onion, chopped	1 can corn
½ green pepper, chopped (use pieces cut from ends)	1 can tomato sauce
	½ cup corn meal
	2 cups milk
1 tablespoon oil	Seasoning
1 pound hamburger or left-over meat	1 egg, well beaten
	Olives

8 peppers

1. Cook onion, pepper tops, and meat in oil until brown. (If cooked meat is used, don't add until onions are brown.)
2. Add corn and tomatoes, then corn meal, milk, salt, and pepper. Add eggs and olives.
3. Cut tops from peppers, remove seeds and white membrane, and fill. Bake in a slow oven about one hour, or until the filling is solid and the peppers are tender. (350°-400°.)

Note: This mixture may be cooked in a casserole without peppers.

Spanish Cheese

5 tablespoons sugar	2 cups milk
1 cup flour	10 oz. grated cheese (Gruyère)

12 eggs, beaten

1. Mix sugar and flour. Add milk. Heat until thick. Cool.
2. Mix grated cheese and eggs and add to cold mixture .
3. Bake in a greased pan for one hour. (300°-325°.)

Legumbres Españolas (Spanish Vegetables)

Colache (Spanish Style)

2 cups shredded string beans
1 to 4 tablespoons minced onion
1 cup tomato pulp

2 tablespoons drippings, bacon fat or oil
1 bell pepper, chopped
1 cup boiling water
Salt and pepper

1. Cook beans and onions in fat for five minutes.
2. Add other ingredients and cook until tender. Season to taste.

Note: Summer squash and corn may be added.

Espinacas Español (Spinach with Brown Sauce)

Spinach (1½ pounds or 2 cups cooked)

1 cup brown sauce
Salt and pepper

Cooked ham garnish

1. Cook and chop spinach.
2. Make a brown sauce, then add spinach and seasonings, and heat until well blended.
3. Serve hot, garnished with thick slices of ham which have been fried. boiled, or baked.

Maiz Español (Spanish Corn)

2 cups canned corn
2 tablespoons flour
Salt, pepper, cayenne
1 teaspoon chili powder

1 cup grated cheese
1 onion, minced
1 dozen olives
1 clove garlic, minced

1 small can tomatoes

1. Stir flour into corn and add salt, pepper, cayenne, and chili powder. Cook fifteen minutes.
2. Add cheese, onion, olives, and garlic, and pour into a baking dish.
3. Bake slowly until the cheese is melted, about thirty minutes. (350°.)
4. Heat tomatoes and serve as a sauce over the top.

Note: Cheese, onion, olives, or garlic may be omitted if desired.

Chilies Fritos (Green Peppers in Batter)

Green peppers	1 teaspoon baking powder
1 egg	¼ teaspoon salt
¾ cup flour	⅓ cup milk

1. Split the peppers and take out seeds and membrane.
2. Make a batter of the other ingredients and dip peppers into it.
3. Fry in deep fat and serve with sliced lemon.

Note: Cheese may be put into the peppers before frying.

Cebollas (Onion Blades)

4 slices bacon	⅛ teaspoon cayenne
2 cups minced onion blades	Salt and pepper
(tops)	2 tablespoons vinegar

2 hard-cooked eggs, minced

1. Dice bacon and fry. Add onion blades, salt, and pepper. Cook five minutes.
2. Add vinegar and simmer until tender.
3. Serve hot in a casserole. Cover the top with minced eggs.

Ejotes Guisados (String Beans)

4 cups string beans	2 tablespoons tomato
1 tablespoon lard or oil	2 cups water
½ onion, minced	Salt and pepper

1. Wash and string beans.
2. Put them into a frying pan with the fat, and brown. Add onion.
3. Add tomato and then the water, salt, and pepper.
4. Cook until tender, one and one-half to two hours.

La Col Español (Spanish Cabbage)

1 tablespoon butter	1 quart shredded cabbage
1 onion, diced	Water
1 green pepper, diced	Salt and pepper

1. Melt butter, and add onion and pepper. Cook five minutes.
2. Add cabbage and mix well. Partly cover with water. Add salt and pepper and simmer twenty to thirty minutes.

Tomates Rellenos (Stuffed Tomatoes)

6 tomatoes
1 cup cracker crumbs
2 eggs, beaten
½ cup melted butter or oil
1 tablespoon minced parsley

1 tablespoon minced onion
1 tablespoon paprika
Salt and pepper
½ cup hot water
Butter

1. Scoop out tomatoes. Place shells in a casserole.
2. Mix tomato pulp with crackers, eggs, butter, parsley, onion, salt, and pepper. Add hot water and stir well.
3. Place equal portions in each tomato and dot with butter.
4. Bake in a moderate oven one-half hour. (375°.)

Tomates Rellenos con Maiz
(Tomatoes Stuffed with Corn)

6 tomatoes
1 cup corn
Salt and pepper

⅛ teaspoon cayenne
1 tablespoon butter
1 egg, beaten

1 tablespoon grated cheese

1. Scoop out tomatoes. Place shells in a casserole.
2. Heat tomato pulp, corn, salt, and pepper. When hot, add butter and egg.
3. Fill the tomatoes and sprinkle them with cheese.
4. Bake in a medium oven until light brown. About one-half hour. (375°.)

Espinaca y Tomates (Spinach and Tomato)

2 cloves garlic, minced
½ cup minced onion
½ cup lard or oil
2 cups tomato purée

2 tablespoons chili powder
2 tablespoons vinegar
Salt and pepper
3 cups cooked spinach

2 tablespoons grated cheese

1. Fry garlic and onion in fat until light brown. Add tomato, chili powder, vinegar, salt, and pepper. Cook five minutes.
2. Add the cooked spinach and mix well.
3. Pour into a casserole and cover with cheese.
4. Bake until the cheese melts. About one-half hour. (375°.)

Arroz Español (Spanish Rice) No. 1

1 small Spanish onion,
   minced
1 bell pepper, minced
Olive oil
1 cup rice

1 pimiento, chopped
1 teaspoon salt
Any other seasoning, such
   as garlic, paprika, or
   chili powder

1 quart tomatoes

1. Fry onion and pepper in oil. Then add rice and fry until brown.
2. Add tomatoes, pimiento, and seasonings. Cover and cook until rice is soft. Add a little boiling water if tomato juice is absorbed before the rice is tender.

Note: One cup of fresh peas may be added with the tomatoes.

Arroz Español (Spanish Rice) No. 2

1 cup rice
3 cloves garlic, minced
½ cup minced onion
Olive oil

1 quart stock or water
1 tablespoon minced parsley
Salt and pepper
2 sprigs mint

1. Fry rice, garlic, and onions in oil for about two minutes, or until brown. Add stock or water, parsley, salt, and pepper.
2. Stir well and place mint leaves on top. Do not stir again.
3. Cover and cook over a slow fire or in the oven until nearly dry.

Note: Serve with chicken or poached eggs and chili sauce.

Arroz Español (Spanish Rice) No. 3

1½ cups rice
½ cup oil
½ cup minced green onion
2 cloves garlic, minced
1 cup tomato purée

1 cup sliced bell peppers
1 cup green peas
1 teaspoon each of paprika,
   green chili, and chili
   powder

Salt and cayenne to taste

1. Fry rice in oil. When it separates and colors, add onion and garlic. Cook two minutes.
2. Add tomato, pepper, peas, and seasonings. Mix well, but do not stir again. Cover and simmer over a slow fire until nearly dry.

Note: Summer squash, artichokes, or clams may be used in place of peas.

Chilies Reinas

6 large bell peppers	Lard
Grated cheese	2 tomatoes
6 eggs	1 small white onion
Flour	Salt

1. Roast peppers until the skins blacken. Wash in cold water and rub off blackened skin. Cut around the stem and remove seeds and coarse veins. Fill the peppers with cheese.
2. Beat egg yolks, add stiffly beaten whites, then enough flour to make a thin batter. Dip peppers into batter.
3. Have a pan of boiling lard and dip the peppers into it. Remove quickly and dip again into batter. Return to lard and fry to a light golden brown, keeping peppers entirely covered.
4. Take the tomatoes, onion, and pepper seeds, and grind to a pulp. Add salt and cook for ten minutes.
5. Turn the remainder of the batter into the tomato mixture and cook twenty minutes.
6. Serve the sauce over the peppers.

Note: Ground meat may be used instead of cheese.

Coliflor al Ajo Arriero
(Cauliflower with Garlic)

1 cauliflower	3 tablespoons oil
2 or 3 cloves garlic, minced	1 tablespoon vinegar
Salt, pepper, cayenne	

1. Boil cauliflower in salted water until tender. Drain.
2. Return to pan and add other ingredients. Simmer ten minutes.
3. Serve hot or cold.

Berengenas Rellenas (Stuffed Eggplant)

1 eggplant	½ cup cooked chicken or
2 tomatoes, chopped	ham, chopped
1 onion, chopped	Salt and pepper
1 tablespoon oil	1 tablespoon minced parsley

1. Cut eggplant in half lengthwise.
2. Cook ten minutes in hot water.
3. Remove pulp but do not break skins.
4. Mix eggplant pulp, tomatoes, onion, oil, chicken or ham, salt, and pepper. Fill eggplant shells.
5. Place in a baking dish in a hot oven and bake fifteen minutes. (475°.)
6. Garnish with minced parsley.

Fondas de Alcachofas à la Catalan
(Artichokes and Eggplant)

3 eggplants, peeled and
    sliced
1 cup chopped ham
2 tablespoons oil
½ cup white wine

Salt and pepper
6 or 8 cooked artichoke
    bottoms
¼ cup crumbs
¼ cup grated cheese

Stock or tomato

1. Place eggplant in a casserole. Sprinkle with ham, oil, wine, salt, and pepper.
2. Put in a moderate oven and bake until almost done. (400°.)
3. Add artichoke bottoms. Sprinkle with crumbs and cheese. Moisten with stock or tomato and bake one-half hour longer.

Seta Sobre Las Parrillas
(Grilled Mushrooms)

1 pound mushrooms
¼ cup oil
Salt and pepper

1 clove garlic, minced
1 tablespoon minced chives
1 tablespoon minced parsley

1 tablespoon vinegar

1. Mix mushrooms, oil, salt, and pepper. Let stand for a few hours.
2. Grill mushrooms.
3. Place garlic, chives, and parsley in frying pan and add the oil from mushrooms. Cook a few minutes, then add the vinegar. Pour over mushrooms and serve.

Ensaladas (Salads)

Spanish Dressing No. 1

¾ cup powdered sugar
½ teaspoon salt
¼ teaspoon mustard
½ teaspoon paprika

¼ teaspoon pepper
1 teaspoon vinegar
¼ cup olive oil
Juice of one lemon

1. Mix sugar, salt, mustard, paprika, and pepper.
2. Add vinegar slowly. Then beat in oil and add lemon juice. Beat briskly with a fork or beater.

Spanish Dressing No. 2

6 tablespoons Roquefort
cheese
2 tablespoons cream
1 tablespoon minced onion

1 tablespoon minced pi-
miento
1 tablespoon chili sauce
1 teaspoon malt extract

½ cup French dressing

1. Mash cheese, add cream, and then other ingredients. Blend well.

Note: This is very good with vegetable combinations.

Spanish Fruit Salad Dressing

1 egg white
½ cup cream
½ cup vinegar

1 cup mayonnaise
1 teaspoon minced mint
leaves

½ cup honey

1. Beat the egg white stiff. Add cream, vinegar, honey, mayonnaise, and mint. Beat until well mixed.

Red Dressing

1 cup mayonnaise
1 tablespoon lemon juice

1 tablespoon tomato pulp
Cayenne or paprika to taste

1. Mix well.

Note: Serve on fish or salads.

Ensalada de Melocaton (Peach Salad)

Peach halves
Lettuce

Strips of canned pimiento
Shredded pineapple

1. Lay three halves of medium-sized peaches on lettuce leaves.
2. Garnish with strips of pimiento and grated pineapple.
3. Serve with Spanish dressing.

Ensalada de Pescado (Shrimp Salad)

1 head lettuce
Sliced tomatoes
2 egg yolks
½ teaspoon mustard
Lemon juice

¾ cup olive oil
Salt and pepper
1 cup shrimps
Pickles, minced
1 can peas

Sliced green pepper

1. Slice lettuce and place on plate. Slice tomato and arrange on lettuce.
2. Beat the egg yolks with mustard and a little lemon juice. Add oil slowly. Mix well until thick. Add salt and pepper.
3. Add shrimps, a little pickle, sliced pepper, and peas to the mayonnaise mixture.
4. Pour the dressing over lettuce.

Note: Mayonnaise may be used for oil, mustard, egg, and lemon juice.

Esqueixada (Mixed Salad)

½ pound dry salt cod	2 red bell peppers, minced
6 boned anchovies	Lettuce
6 stoned olives	French dressing
½ onion, sliced	2 hard-cooked eggs

1. Soak fish several hours or overnight. Drain. Cover with fresh water, boil fifteen minutes. Drain, cool, and flake.
2. Mix cod, anchovies, olives, onion, and peppers.
3. Place lettuce in a salad bowl, add French dressing, and toss lightly.
4. Garnish with the fish mixture and top with hard-cooked eggs.

Ensalada de Verano (Summer Salad)

2 eggplants, cooked and diced	1 small chili pepper, chopped
2 pimientos, chopped	1 spring onion, chopped
2 tomatoes, peeled and sliced	1 teaspoon chopped chervil
	French dressing

Lettuce

1. Mix the above and serve on lettuce.

Ensalada de Queso y Pimiento
(Pimiento Cheese Salad)

1 teaspoon gelatin	5 tablespoons cream
1 tablespoon cold water	Salt and pepper
¼ pound pimiento cheese	Green peppers

Lettuce

1. Soften gelatin in cold water and dissolve over hot water.
2. Mash cheese and mix with cream. Season with salt and pepper. Add dissolved gelatin.
3. Cut tops from peppers, remove the seeds and membrane, and fill with cheese mixture. Place on ice.
4. When cold, slice across and arrange on lettuce.
5. Serve with French or Spanish dressing.

Note: Chopped olives may be added to the cheese. Plain cheese may be used, and chopped pimiento added.

Ensalada de Naranja (Orange Salad)

Oranges
Water cress
Maraschino cherries, if
desired

French dressing
Few grains mustard
Paprika
Pimiento cheese

1. Peel oranges very deep in spiral fashion. Remove sections by cutting between white membrane.
2. Arrange orange sections in rows or around a center on water cress. Garnish with cherries.
3. Add mustard and paprika to French dressing and pour on salad.
4. Make small balls of cheese and serve as a garnish.

Ensalada de Fruta (Fruit Salad)

1 cup seedless grapes
1 cup minced orange
1 cup minced apple
2 cups minced walnuts
2 cups minced celery
½ cup sherry

2 tablespoons Madeira
4 tablespoons sugar
Lettuce
6 tablespoons whipped
cream
6 maraschino cherries

1. Mix fruits, nuts, and celery in a bowl and pour sherry, Madeira, and sugar over them. Let stand a few minutes.
2. Arrange on crisp lettuce on individual plates. Top with whipped cream and a cherry.

Ensalada de Langousta (Lobster Salad)

3 cups lobster meat
1 cup minced onion
1 cup minced celery
Salt and pepper
⅔ cup mayonnaise

⅓ cup cream, whipped
Water cress or lettuce
1 sliced pimiento
1 dozen stuffed olives
Sliced lemon

1. Mix lobster, onion, celery, salt, and pepper. Add mayonnaise and cream.
2. Serve on lettuce or water cress or both.
3. Garnish with pimiento, olives, and sliced lemon.

Olla Podrida Fria (Cold Olla Podrida)

½ Spanish onion, shredded
Bits of leftover vegetables
(string beans, beets, cauliflower, or asparagus)

2 cups shrimps
French dressing
Toast
1 cup ice water

1. Mix onion, vegetables, and shrimps with French dressing. Marinate about an hour.
2. Just before serving, put as many pieces of toast in a bowl as there are guests. Spread salad over them and add ice water.

Ensalada de Cebollas Españolas (Spanish Onion Salad)
(Individual Salad)

3 slices of onion
Sugar (about 1 tablespoon)
Lettuce

3 slices tomato
French dressing
Dash of cayenne

1. Sprinkle sugar over onion and let stand for one hour.
2. Arrange lettuce on a plate. Alternate slices of onion and tomato.
3. Pour French dressing over this, then a dash of cayenne.

Gazpacho (Vegetable Salad)

1 clove garlic
4 or 5 tomatoes, cut in
pieces
1 onion, minced

1 or 2 cucumbers, sliced
2 chopped green chilies
Lettuce, if desired
French dressing

Salt and pepper

1. Rub a salad bowl with garlic and put in other ingredients.
2. Serve with bread.

Ensalada de Pescado y Lechuga
(Fish and Lettuce Salad)

2 heads lettuce, sliced
2 hard-cooked eggs, sliced
½ pound ripe olives

½ pound pickled fish, broken in pieces
French dressing

Small green onions

1. Mix above ingredients and garnish with small onions.

Ensalada de Lechuga (Lettuce Salad Bowl)

Lettuce   Tomatoes
French or Spanish   Olives
    dressing   Radishes

1. Tear lettuce in pieces with the fingers.
2. Put French or Spanish dressing in a bowl.
3. Add lettuce and toss with forks or salad set.
4. Cut tomatoes in bits and garnish top with tomato, olives, and radishes.

La Coliflor Fria (Cold Cauliflower)

1 cauliflower   French or Spanish dressing

1. Break cauliflower in pieces and cook in boiling, salted water until tender. While still warm, marinate in the dressing. Chill.

Escalibada (Eggplant)

1 eggplant, diced   3 tablespoons oil
2 pimientos or red bell pep-   1½ tablespoons vinegar
    pers, cut in half   French dressing

1. Mix eggplant, oil, and vinegar. Place halves of pimientos or peppers in a baking dish and fill with eggplant. Cover and bake until eggplant is tender. About half an hour. (350°.)
2. Serve cold with French dressing.

Ensalada Andaluza (Andalusian Salad)

1 sweet red pepper, sliced   1 cup cooked rice
1 teaspoon chopped chives   4 or 5 tomatoes, sliced
1 clove garlic, minced   1 teaspoon minced parsley
            French dressing

1. Mix pepper, chives, garlic, rice, and tomatoes.
2. Sprinkle with chopped parsley.
3. Serve with French dressing.

Dulces (Desserts)

Puddings

Crema Española (Spanish Cream)

1½ tablespoons gelatin
3 cups milk
½ cup sugar

3 eggs
½ teaspoon salt
1 teaspoon vanilla

1. Soak gelatin in milk for five minutes. Place over hot water. When gelatin is dissolved, add sugar. Pour onto slightly beaten egg yolks and return to double boiler until thickened, stirring constantly.
2. Remove from heat and add salt and flavoring.
3. Beat egg whites stiff and fold custard into them.
4. Turn into one large mold or into individual molds, first dipped in cold water.
5. Set in the refrigerator until stiff.
6. Unmold and serve with whipped cream or sliced fruit or thickened fruit juice.

Variations:

1. Add two squares of melted chocolate to milk and sugar.
2. Add macaroons, dried and rolled, nut meats, and candied cherries.
3. Use two cups of strong coffee and three-fourths cup milk instead of three cups of milk. Add one-third more sugar.
4. Add one cup orange juice for one cup of milk. Serve with sliced oranges.
5. Use one-third cup of lemon juice and two cups of water instead of milk. Add one-half cup more sugar.
6. For butterscotch, use three-fourths cup brown sugar in place of white sugar. Add two tablespoons butter with sugar. Garnish with nut meats.
7. Serve with plain cream and sprinkle sweetened chipped chocolate on top.
8. Serve with plain cream and crushed, sweetened berries.

Flan Española (Baked Custard)

2 eggs
½ teaspoon salt

½ cup sugar
2 cups milk, scalded

½ teaspoon vanilla, or spices

1. Mix slightly beaten eggs, salt, and sugar. Then add scalded milk slowly. Add flavoring.
2. Pour into buttered mold and sprinkle with nutmeg.
3. Bake in a very slow oven in a pan of warm water for one hour at 250°.

Variations:

1. Add one-third cup ground chocolate or two squares melted.
2. Caramel: melt the sugar in an iron pan before adding milk.
3. Butterscotch: use brown sugar for white, but use two tablespoons more.
4. Add one-third cup coconut, dates, macaroons dried and rolled, or fruit pulp. Add another egg if fruit pulp is used.
5. With caramel sauce: mix one-fourth cup water and one cup sugar in a frying pan. When slightly brown, put into buttered custard cups. Pour custard over this mixture. Unmold when cold and use caramel for sauce.

Higos y Arroz Conde (Fig and Rice Conde)

¼ cup rice	2 cups milk
¼ cup sugar	1 egg
½ teaspoon salt	6 dried figs

Flavoring: vanilla or lemon

1. Cook rice, sugar, salt, and milk in double boiler until rice is tender.
2. Add beaten egg and chopped figs. When egg is set, remove from heat and add flavoring.
3. Turn into small molds which have been buttered and dredged with sugar. Set away in a warm place until firm. Chill.
4. Unmold and serve with apricot sauce.
5. Garnish with whipped cream and top with a fig.

Arroz con Leche (Rice Pudding)

¾ cup rice	½ teaspoon salt
3 cups milk	4 tablespoons butter
¾ cup sugar	Vanilla or nutmeg

1. Boil rice for five minutes. Place it in a sieve and run water through it.
2. Heat milk and add sugar, salt, butter, and flavoring. Add rice. Cook a few minutes over fire.
3. Pour into buttered baking dish and bake about one hour, or until rice is cooked and milk thickened. (325°.)

Cookies and Cakes

Tortas Viejas Españolas (Old Spanish Cookies)

½ cup butter
1⅓ cups brown sugar
1 egg, beaten
½ cup molasses
1½ teaspoons soda
½ cup water

4 cups flour
1⅓ cups currants
½ cup chopped lemon peel
1½ tablespoons mixed spices
1 teaspoon salt

1. Cream butter and sugar and add egg.
2. Add molasses, in which soda has been dissolved. Add water and fruits mixed with one fourth of the flour. Beat well, and then add the rest of flour mixed with spices and salt.
3. Roll out a small portion at a time. Cut with a cooky cutter.
4. Brush each with milk and roll in sugar. Place a dot of jam in the center of each.
5. Bake at 500°. Do not allow cookies to brown, for it spoils the flavor.

Roscas (Corn-meal Cookies)

Yolks of 6 eggs
1 egg white
1¾ cups powdered sugar

3 cups fine corn-meal flour
½ cup melted butter
Grated rind and juice of 1 lemon

1. Beat egg yolks and egg white. Add powdered sugar and blend well.
2. Add corn-meal flour, then melted butter and lemon juice and rind.
3. When it forms a smooth paste, spread out on a board and sprinkle with corn meal.
4. Break off pieces, form into little round cakes with the hands, and put on a buttered tin. Bake in a moderately hot oven about fifteen minutes. (400°-450°.)

Piedras Españolas (Spanish Rocks)

½ cup milk
2 cups flour, or more
1 teaspoon cinnamon
1 teaspoon soda
1 teaspoon salt

1 cup shortening (scant)
1½ cups brown sugar
2 eggs
1 cup nut meats
1 cup raisins

1. Cream shortening, add sugar, and mix thoroughly.
2. Beat eggs with a rotary beater, and add.
3. Add nuts and raisins, and mix well.
4. Sift flour, salt, cinnamon, and soda together.
5. Add milk and dry ingredients alternately.
6. Drop from a teaspoon onto a well-greased and floured pan. Bake about fifteen minutes. (400°-450°.)

Choux Paste (Spanish Pastries)

1 cup water	1 tablespoon sugar
Rind of 1 lemon	Flour (about 1 cup)
½ cup butter	4 eggs

1. Put water, lemon rind, butter, and sugar into a pan. Boil five minutes. Remove lemon rind.
2. Stir in enough flour to make a thick paste, stirring continually over fire. Stir until mixture leaves sides of pan (about five minutes). *Never stop stirring.*
3. Take pan from fire, and break in an egg. Beat until it is thoroughly mixed into paste. Add other eggs, one at a time.
4. Cool and drop by spoonfuls, about two inches apart, on a greased sheet. A variety of shapes can be made with the spoon or a pastry tube.
5. Put in a hot oven, 450°, for ten minutes; then reduce the heat to 375° and complete the cooking. (About thirty to forty-five minutes, depending on the size of the puffs.)
6. Split and fill with cream or fruit filling.

Sponge Cake

5 eggs	Grated rind of 1 lemon
1 tablespoon lemon juice	⅛ teaspoon salt
1 cup sugar	1 cup flour

1. Beat egg yolks until thick. Add lemon juice, rind, sugar, and salt.
2. Beat egg whites stiff and *fold* into yolk mixture.
3. Lastly *fold* in the flour. *Do not stir.*
4. Bake in a tube pan for one hour in a slow oven (350°) or in small muffin tins for thirty minutes.

Naranja Rellena (Orange Filling)

Grated rind of 1 orange	2 tablespoons butter
½ cup sugar	1 egg
2 tablespoons cornstarch	⅓ cup orange juice
⅔ cup boiling water	1 teaspoon lemon juice

1. Put grated orange rind, sugar, and cornstarch in a pan, mix well, and pour on boiling water. Cook ten minutes and add butter.
2. Pour mixture over well-beaten egg, return to the saucepan, and cook one minute, stirring constantly.
3. Add orange and lemon juice. Beat well.

Note: When cool, use as a filling for sponge cake or pastries.

Torta Sevilla (Seville Cake)

Sponge cake cut 1½ Orange marmalade
inches thick Coconut

1. Bake above cake one-and-a-half inches thick. Split into two layers.
2. Spread orange marmalade between layers.
3. Cover cake with a thin coating of marmalade and a thick layer of coconut.

Sospiros (Sighs) No. 1

5 egg yolks 1 cup blanched almonds,
1 cup powdered sugar toasted and pounded

1. Beat egg yolks until light, and add sugar; then beat in almonds.
2. When very thick and light, pour into small paper cups. Bake in a slow oven fifteen to twenty minutes. (350°-375°.)

Sospiros (Spanish Kisses) No. 2

1 pound powdered sugar Grated rind of 1 lemon
5 eggs, beaten light

1. Add sugar and lemon slowly to eggs.
2. Drop by the teaspoonful on a buttered cooky sheet.
3. Bake slowly for twenty to thirty minutes. (350°.)

Tortas de Polvoron (Dusted Cookies)

1 pound lard 1 tablespoon each cinnamon
1 pound sugar and cloves
2 eggs, beaten 1 teaspoon salt
2 cups flour 2 tablespoons sesame seed
Powdered sugar and cinnamon

1. Cream lard and sugar. Add eggs, and then flour and spices.
2. Knead thoroughly. Roll out one-fourth inch thick and cut with a small cutter.
3. Place on a baking tin two inches apart. Sprinkle with sesame seeds and bake in a moderate oven. (400°.)
4. Dust with powdered sugar and cinnamon while warm.

Pasteles Españoles (Spanish Buns) No. 1

½ cup butter
1½ cups sugar
2 eggs
½ cup currants

3 cups flour
2 teaspoons baking powder
¼ teaspoon nutmeg
½ teaspoon salt

¾ cups milk

1. Cream butter, add sugar, and cream well. Add well-beaten egg yolks, then currants.
2. Sift flour, baking powder, nutmeg, and salt together. Add alternately with milk.
3. Fold in stiffly beaten egg whites.
4. Bake in a shallow tin twenty to twenty-five minutes. (400°.)
5. Ice with boiled icing.

Pasteles Españoles (Spanish Buns) No. 2

½ cup butter
1 cup brown sugar
2 egg yolks, beaten
1½ cups cake flour
½ teaspoon cloves

2½ teaspoons baking powder
½ teaspoon allspice
½ teaspoon cinnamon
½ cup sweet milk

½ teaspoon vanilla

ICING

¾ cup brown sugar
2 egg whites

¾ cup chopped nuts
Salt

1. Cream butter and sugar. Beat in egg yolks. Sift dry ingredients together and add alternately with milk. Add vanilla.
2. Line an eight-by-eleven-inch pan with oiled paper, and pour in batter.
3. Prepare icing by beating sugar gradually into stiffly beaten egg whites. Add half of the nuts and salt.
4. Spread icing on batter. Sprinkle with remaining nuts.
5. Bake thirty to thirty-five minutes. (350°.)

Pasteles Españoles (Spanish Buns) No. 3

½ cup butter
1½ cups sugar
1 whole egg and 2 yolks
　(or 3 whole eggs)

½ cup ground chocolate
2 cups flour
4 teaspoons baking powder
¾ cup milk

1 teaspoon vanilla

1. Cream butter, add sugar, and cream well together.
2. Add chocolate and mix well.
3. Mix flour and baking powder and add alternately with milk. Add vanilla.
4. Bake in muffin tins twenty to twenty-five minutes. (400°.)

Fried Breads

Ojaldas (Fried Cakes)

2 eggs, beaten light	Fat for frying
Pinch of salt	Hot sirup flavored with
Flour	lemon, cinnamon, or honey

1. Add salt to eggs, and enough flour to make a stiff dough. Knead for ten minutes. Roll dough out and let stand a few minutes. Divide it and roll out as thin as possible.
2. Cut into diamond pieces and fry it in deep fat to a golden brown. Drain and serve with sirup.

Tortillas Españolas (Spanish Pancakes)

2 eggs	½ teaspoon salt
1½ cups milk	1 tablespoon butter, melted
2 tablespoons flour	Guava jelly
Powdered sugar	

1. Beat eggs very light. Add milk and flour alternately and then salt and melted butter.
2. Bake on a griddle like ordinary pancakes. Make several small cakes or one large one.
3. While cakes are hot, spread them with jelly and roll them.
4. Sprinkle them with powdered sugar and serve hot.

Fritters

2 small French loaves, sliced	1 cup sugar
	½ cup white wine
2 cups milk	½ cup oil
2 or 3 eggs, beaten	1 stick cinnamon
3 cups water	

1. Soak bread in milk, dip in egg, and fry in oil.
2. Make a sirup of sugar, wine, oil, cinnamon, and water. Cook until well blended.
3. Pour sirup on fritters. Sprinkle with sugar and grated cinnamon.

Torrija (French Toast)

6 slices bread, ½ inch thick

½ cup milk or more
2 eggs, beaten

1. Dip bread in milk, but do not soak. Then dip in egg.
2. Drop into boiling fat. Fry brown.
3. Serve with sirup.

Miscellaneous

Frozen Fruit

1 watermelon
1 pound grapes
1 pound apricots

1 pound prunes
1 pound peaches
1 bottle sherry or camomile wine

1. Cut fruit in pieces. Lay in alternate layers in a freezer.
2. Pour sherry or camomile wine over fruit.
3. Leave in freezer to set.

Turron de Gandia (Almond Brittle)

1 pound almonds, blanched and roasted

1½ cups sugar

1. Chop almonds with half the sugar. Add remaining sugar gradually.
2. Place in an iron saucepan or skillet.
3. Let it bubble, stirring constantly.
4. When thick pour it on greased plates or pans.

Note: One-half cup of honey may be added when nut mixture is placed in pan.

Membrillo (Quince Dessert)

Quinces

Sugar

Powdered sugar

1. Peel and core quinces. *Immediately* place peeling and cores in a bowl of cold water to prevent discoloring; in another bowl of cold water, place the flesh, cut in pieces.
2. Place cores and peeling in an *enameled* pan, cover with cold water, and cook until soft.

3. Strain, extracting all juice and pulp. Weigh liquid, return to enameled pan, and add an equal amount of sugar. Then add quince flesh and cook until soft, mashing and beating frequently.

4. Spread one inch thick on glass or china plates. Cover thickly with powdered sugar. Cover and let stand six or seven days. Place in sun under glass.

5. When solid, cut in squares, roll in powdered sugar, and pack in tin boxes lined with oiled paper.

Mexican Foods

Delicious Mexican dishes,
That satisfy our wishes.

Mexico

Pungent odors and vivid colors are generally associated with Mexico. Here we find old Aztec food with a Spanish flavor.

The true Mexican cuisine has long been noted for a peculiar piquancy—an elusive flavor that is different, delicate, and hard to produce. Tradition plays a large part in Mexican cooking and is responsible for the awesomely prolonged processes.

Patient, unhurried preparation is all-important in Mexican cookery. Long, slow blending and cooking is quite necessary to their delectable dishes. The best Mexican cook prefers to grind her own peppers and mix other seasonings according to tradition, but many prepared seasonings can be purchased in the market. The chili powder is a blend of Mexican chili ancho peppers with other Mexican spices. No onions, hot peppers, or color adulterants are used in the best products. Contrary to the general opinion, this chili pepper is not hot, but has a mild flavor like paprika. The flavor of garlic is essential to Mexican dishes, but should be used sparingly.

There are three foods that form the basis of Mexican cookery—corn meal, chilies, and beans. The tortilla is not appreciably different from that the Aztecs were eating when Cortez conquered Mexico. Today, most of the tortillas are made of corn meal ground in great modern machines, while in the older method the corn was ground by women on stone metates. The taste has not changed much. The beans used today are the same variety as those the Indians were raising four hundred years ago.

A variety of vegetables and fruits can be found, such as beans, maize, squash, tomatoes, peppers, peas, string beans, chayotes, nuts, limes, avocados, and bananas. Meat is tough and is used sparingly or minced. Chicken and turkey are better and are used more frequently.

Sopas (Soups)

Cordero (Mexican Olla Podrida)

1 pound young lamb	1 cup green peas
1 slice onion	1 cup corn cut from cob
Lard	½ cup rice
3 tomatoes, peeled and sliced	Salt and chili powder or pepper
3 green peppers, chopped	1 egg
2 quarts water	1 teaspoon vinegar

1 teaspoon olive oil.

1. Cut lamb in pieces and fry with onion in lard. When brown add tomatoes, peppers, and water. Simmer slowly for one hour.
2. Add peas, corn, rice, salt, and chili powder. Simmer for one hour longer.
3. Beat egg, add vinegar and oil, and pour into soup tureen. Add soup, stir, and serve.

Sopa con Albondigas (Soup with Meat Balls)

1½ pounds lean beef, chopped	Salt and pepper
3 green onions, chopped	4 eggs
Several sprigs mint, parsley, and sage, minced	1 tablespoon lard, melted
	Flour
	2 quarts boiling water

2 cups tomatoes

1. Mix meat, onions, and seasonings. Add two well-beaten eggs and lard.
2. Roll into balls the size of a walnut. Dust with flour and drop into the boiling water. Simmer for one hour.
3. Add tomatoes and boil another hour. Then stir in the other eggs, well beaten. Season.

Chili Bisque

8 large sweet chilies	1 egg
½ cup boiled rice	½ cup cream
Salt	1 quart hot milk
Tobasco sauce	Toasted bread

1. Remove seeds and veins from chilies. Boil and press through sieve.
2. Mix rice and pulp. Mash smooth, and add salt and tabasco.
3. Beat egg with cream and add to hot milk. Add pepper mixture and let it boil up once.
4. Serve at once over squares of toasted bread.

Monterey Sopa de Arroz (Monterey Rice Soup)

3 tablespoons oil or fat
1 medium onion, minced
2 cups raw rice
¾ teaspoon salt
¼ teaspoon pepper
Water or chicken broth
½ teaspoon saffron
2 teaspoons cold water

1. Heat oil in saucepan. Add onion, rice, salt, and pepper, and cook until brown.
2. Add enough broth or water to cook rice.
3. When done, add saffron mixed with cold water.
4. Serve with Mushroom and Giblet Sauce (p. 92).

Caldo Colado (Clear Soup)

1½ pounds lamb (meat and bone)
2 quarts water
1½ teaspoons salt
1 chili pepper
3 tablespoons lard
1 onion, minced
¼ clove garlic, minced
1 cup dry sifted bread crumbs

1. Place meat and bones in a kettle, and add water and salt. Bring to a boil and simmer for four hours. Skim several times.
2. Soak chili pepper several hours in warm water. Remove seeds and scrape pulp from skin.
3. Melt lard in a frying pan. Add onion and garlic. Brown, and add bread crumbs. Fry until delicately browned. Add chili pulp.
4. Strain soup. Reheat, and just before serving, add bread-crumb mixture.

Salsas (Sauces)

Salsa de Chili (Chili Sauce)

1 pound dry red chilies
1 onion
1 clove garlic
Sprig of parsley
¼ cup oil
1 tablespoon flour
1 teaspoon vinegar
½ teaspoon oregano (marjoram)
½ teaspoon salt
1 teaspoon sugar

1. Remove stems, seeds, and veins from peppers. Wash, cover them with hot water, and bring to a boil. Mash and cool.
2. Press them through a sieve to remove the skins.
3. Chop onion, garlic, and parsley, and fry them in oil. When they are brown, add flour, then seasonings and pepper pulp.

Pasta de Chili (Pepper Pot)

1 pound dry red chili peppers

Remove the seeds and inside veins from the peppers. Wash them well, cover with hot water, and soak in a warm place overnight. Grind through a food chopper several times. This paste mixes easily with other foods, and the very best flavor is obtained.

Salsa Mexicana de Chili (Mexican Chili Sauce)

2 tablespoons minced onion	2 cups tomato purée
1 green pepper, chopped	¼ cup chopped celery
2 tablespoons butter	½ teaspoon salt
1 tablespoon flour	2 teaspoons chili powder

1. Cook onion and green pepper in butter until brown. Add flour, tomato, celery, salt, and chili powder.
2. Simmer until celery is tender, adding water from time to time, if necessary.

Salsa de Chili Colorado (Red Chili Sauce)

3 red chili peppers	3 tablespoons olive oil
4 ripe tomatoes	1 tablespoon minced parsley
3 cloves garlic	Salt and pepper

1. Remove stems, seeds, and veins from peppers. Wash, cover with hot water, and bring to a boil.
2. Peel the tomatoes and press through a sieve with peppers and garlic.
3. Heat oil and add tomato mixture, parsley, salt, and pepper.
Note: This sauce is used with meats, beans, and tamales.

Salsa de Chili Verde (Green Chili Sauce)

4 large green tomatoes	1 tablespoon minced onion
4 green chilies (fresh or canned)	1 tablespoon minced parsley
	Salt and pepper

½ cup oil or lard

1. Boil tomatoes, chilies, onion, and parsley together in enough water or stock to cover well. Cook until quite soft.
2. Press through a sieve and add salt and pepper.
3. Heat oil and add chili mixture. Cook for fifteen minutes.

Note: This sauce is served on eggs, meats, or tamales.

Salsa Mexicana de Pescado (Mexican Fish Sauce)

2 link pork sausages
¼ cup minced onion
¼ cup minced parsley
1 clove garlic, minced
6 olives, minced

2 cups tomato purée
¼ cup olive oil
¼ cup vinegar
Pinch cinnamon and cloves
Salt and pepper

1. Heat sausages, onion, parsley, garlic, and olives. Mash to a pulp.
2. Mix with tomato purée and heat the whole in hot oil.
3. Add vinegar and seasonings.
4. Serve on boiled or baked fish.

Salsa de Tomates (Tomato Sauce)

2 pounds tomatoes
½ pound raisins
¼ pound blanched almonds
1 ounce garlic

1 ounce green ginger
½ ounce dried chilies
½ pound sugar
1 pint vinegar

Salt

1. Cut tomatoes in pieces, add a very little water, and boil for about thirty minutes. Put through a sieve.
2. Put raisins, nuts, garlic, ginger, and dried chili through a grinder and add to tomato.
3. Add sugar, vinegar, and salt, and boil until thick. Stir occasionally.

Salsa Nuez (Walnut Sauce)

2 tomatoes peeled
1 onion, minced
Few pepper seeds

Salt
2 green peppers, chopped
½ cup walnut meats

1. Stew tomatoes, onion, pepper seeds, and salt until thick. Strain.
2. Add green peppers and walnuts.
3. Reheat and serve hot.

Mushroom and Giblet Sauce

1 tablespoon butter   Salt and pepper
1 onion, minced   ½ pound chicken giblets,
¼ pound mushrooms, sliced   chopped
¼ to ½ cup grated cheese

1. Brown butter and onion in a saucepan.
2. Add other ingredients, except cheese.
3. Use cheese to sprinkle on top of sauce after it has been poured over food.

Salsa Mexicana (Mexican Sauce)

2 tablespoons butter   2 tablespoons flour
1 small onion, chopped   ½ teaspoon salt
1 green pepper, chopped   ½ teaspoon chili powder
1 clove garlic, minced   ½ cup meat stock
1 cup strained tomatoes

1. Melt butter in a saucepan, add onion, pepper, and garlic, and cook until soft.
2. Add flour, salt, and chili powder, and blend well.
3. Slowly add stock and tomato. Simmer until smooth and well blended, stirring constantly.
4. Serve hot.

Salsa Dulce (Sweet Sauce)

2 tablespoons lard   2½ tablespoons sugar
1 onion, minced   ½ teaspoon salt
2 tomatoes, sliced   3 tablespoons vinegar

1. Heat lard in a frying pan, add onion, and cook until light brown.
2. Add other ingredients and cook until thickened. Stir constantly.
3. Serve hot.

Salsa Picante (Piquant Sauce)

2 chili peppers   ½ teaspoon salt
½ onion, minced   3 tablespoons vinegar
2 tomatoes, minced   1 tablespoon olive oil

1. Soak chili peppers in warm water for several hours. Remove seeds and scrape pulp from skins.
2. Place all ingredients in a bowl and beat until smooth and well blended.

Anchovy Sauce Mazatlan

1½ tablespoons anchovy
    paste or essence

1 cup butter
1½ teaspoons lemon juice

1. Place butter and anchovy paste in a saucepan and cook slowly, stirring constantly, until melted and beginning to bubble.

2. Remove from fire and stir in lemon juice.

3. Serve hot.

Huevos (Eggs)

Emvueltos de Huevos (Stuffed Omelet)

6 eggs
Salt
2 tablespoons lard

½ cup grated cheese
Onions, chopped
3 or 4 tomatoes

2 green peppers, chopped

1. Beat the eggs, and add salt. Heat fat in a frying pan, pour in eggs and cook slowly until set. When cooked, sprinkle with grated cheese. Roll and cut in strips.

2. Cover with a sauce made from onion, tomatoes, and peppers cooked together for about one hour. Season to taste.

Chili y Huevos con Queso (Peppers and Eggs with Cheese)

2 or 3 peppers
½ cup chopped onion
Lard for frying

½ cup tomatoes
Salt
Eggs

½ cup grated cheese

1. Toast peppers in fire, remove seeds, and cut into slices.

2. Brown onion in lard and add tomatoes and salt. Add a little water.

3. Break in as many eggs as desired. Poach until whites are set. Add sliced peppers.

4. Remove to a platter and sprinkle with grated cheese.

Tortas de Chili Serrano (Flat Cakes)

6 eggs   Salt
1 onion, chopped   ½ pound of cheese, cut in
½ cup flour   cubes
1 teaspoon baking powder   Hot lard
              Hot chili sauce

1. Beat eggs and add onion, flour, baking powder, salt, and cheese.
2. Heat fat in a frying pan.
3. Take up a piece of cheese and as much egg as a large spoon will hold, and fry until brown.
4. Serve with hot chili sauce.

Blanquillos

2 large onions, chopped   1 teaspoon dry chili
Olive oil   ½ dozen hard-cooked eggs,
2 tomatoes, peeled   quartered
                Toast

1. Chop onions and fry in oil. Add tomatoes and dry chili. Cook for twenty minutes.
2. Just before serving, add eggs. Heat through and serve on toast.

Buey Ahumado y Huevos

1 cup chipped beef   1 tablespoon grated cheese
1 cup strained tomatoes   1 onion, grated
2 hard-cooked eggs,   1 chili pepper, chopped
   chopped fine   1 tablespoon butter, melted
              2 eggs

1. Soak beef in hot water, drain, and chop fine.
2. Add tomatoes, chopped eggs, cheese, onion, pepper, and butter, and mix well.
3. Beat eggs and add to meat mixture.
4. Scramble in a frying pan.

Mexican Eggs

1 small onion, chopped   ¼ teaspoon pepper
1 tablespoon fat   ¼ teaspoon paprika
1 quart tomatoes, cut in   ⅛ teaspoon soda
   pieces   1 tablespoon flour, mixed
1 teaspoon salt   with a little cold water
           3 eggs, slightly beaten

1. Fry onion in fat for five minutes.
2. Add tomato and seasonings. When hot, add soda.
3. Five minutes before serving, stir in the eggs and flour.
4. Serve on crackers, toast, or tortillas.

Huevos Revueltos Estilo Mexicano
(Mexican Scrambled Eggs)

12 green peppers	6 or 8 eggs
1 tablespoon butter	2 tablespoons fat

Salt

1. Roast peppers a few minutes. Peel and remove seeds.
2. Chop peppers, place in a saucepan with a little water, and simmer until tender. Add butter and salt.
3. Beat eggs, and add peppers.
4. Heat fat in a frying pan, add pepper-and-egg mixture, and cook as scrambled eggs.

Pescado (Fish)

Pescado à la Mexicano (Mexican Fish)

3 pounds any firm fish	1 quart tomatoes, peeled and cut in pieces
1 tablespoon each, salt and flour	1 pint corn cut from cob
½ teaspoon nutmeg or pepper	2 green peppers, chopped
2 cups diced potatoes, white or sweet	1 red pepper, chopped
6 apples, chopped	1 quart onions, chopped
	1 pound bacon, cubed
	Salt and pepper

1. Remove skin from fish and wipe fish dry. Rub fish inside and out with a mixture of salt, flour, and nutmeg. Put in a well-greased baking pan.
2. Prepare vegetables and mix thoroughly with bacon in a chopping bowl. Season.
3. Put one half of mixture over fish and bake one hour in a hot oven (450°) to brown vegetables. Put on rest of vegetables and cook for one hour longer. If vegetables get too dry, baste them with salad oil.

Pescado à la Veracruzana (Vera Cruz Fish)

3 onions, chopped
1 can tomatoes
2 cloves garlic, minced
Minced parsley

1 cup olive oil
Salt and pepper
6 slices halibut
Few stuffed olives

1. Cook onions, tomatoes, garlic, and parsley thoroughly in oil. Add salt and pepper.
2. Add halibut and olives, and cook until fish is tender.

Bacalao (Codfish) No. 1

1 pound salt codfish
1 clove garlic
¼ cup olive oil
¼ pound potatoes, sliced

1 can tomatoes
Pulp of 6 chili peppers
Oregano
1 cup sour wine or vinegar

Ripe olives

1. Soak fish overnight in water to cover. Drain and flake.
2. Fry garlic in oil, remove, and add potatoes. When brown, add fish.
3. Mix well and add other ingredients, except olives.
4. Cook slowly for one-half hour or more. Strew with olives before serving.

Bacalao (Codfish) No. 2

2 pounds salt codfish
2 cups garbanzos (chick-
   peas)
3 large potatoes
1 cup tomatoes

Onion juice
Seasonings if needed
1 large can sweet peppers
2 dozen green olives, pitted
1 pint olive oil

1. Soak codfish overnight in water to cover. Drain, add fresh boiling water, and parboil fifteen or twenty minutes.
2. Soak garbanzos overnight in water to cover. Drain and remove skins.
3. Parboil potatoes in their jackets, skin them, and slice.
4. Make a sauce of tomatoes, onion juice, and seasonings.
5. Place alternate layers of potatoes, fish, peas, and peppers in a casserole. Stick olives in here and there. Pour sauce over this and oil over all.
6. Bake in a slow oven for one and one-half hours. (350°.)

Brandad de Bacalao (Creamed Codfish)

2 pounds salt codfish
1 slice of onion
1 clove garlic
½ cup thick cream

2 egg yolks, beaten
Juice of ½ lemon
Pinch cayenne
½ cup olive oil

1. Soak codfish overnight. Drain, break into pieces, cover with boiling water, add onion, and boil twenty-five minutes. Drain.
2. Mince garlic and add cream, egg yolks, lemon juice, and cayenne. Stir in a double boiler until it thickens. Add oil little by little.
3. Add fish and heat thoroughly.

Gitano (Beans and Codfish)

1 pound salt codfish
1 cup Mexican beans
3 quarts stock (beef)
⅛ pound salt pork

1 onion, chopped
4 cloves garlic, minced
Seasoning if needed
Chorizo (Mexican sausage)

Potatoes, diced

1. Soak codfish and beans overnight in separate dishes. Drain.
2. Heat stock, add fish, beans, pork, onion, and garlic. Cook slowly for one hour.
3. Season. Add sausages and potatoes. Cook until potatoes are done.

Huachinango (Red Snapper)

1 onion, chopped
Few sprigs parsley,
    chopped
Oil

Salt and pepper
1½ cups tomato
Olives and capers if de-
    sired

Red snapper fish

1. Fry onion and parsley in oil. Add salt, pepper, and tomatoes, and cook thirty minutes.
2. Add fish, and cook thirty minutes longer.
3. Garnish with olives and capers.

Huachinango Asado (Baked Red Snapper)

5-pound red snapper
1½ teaspoons salt
½ teaspoon white pepper
2 cloves garlic
½ cup olive oil
½ cup minced onions
½ cup minced celery
1 cup hot stock
1 tablespoon minced parsley
⅛ teaspoon cayenne
1 teaspoon salt

½ cup minced olives
½ cup capers
½ teaspoon dry mustard, mixed to a paste with a little cold water
1 tablespoon Worcestershire
1 tablespoon paprika
3 cups strained tomato pulp
2 bay leaves
1 cup white wine

1. Wash and wipe fish. Rub inside and out with salt and pepper. Cut garlic in several pieces, placing half inside fish and the other half on top.
2. Heat oil in a saucepan, add onions and celery, cook three minutes, and then add stock, parsley, cayenne, salt, olives, capers, mustard, Worcestershire sauce, and paprika. Simmer until vegetables are tender. Add tomato pulp and bay leaves. Bring all slowly to boiling point.
3. Place fish in a baking pan. Pour sauce over it and bake forty minutes, basting frequently. (400°.)
4. Add wine and cook five minutes longer.

Note: Any firm white fish may be substituted for red snapper.

Baked Mackerel

1½ cups bread crumbs
½ cup melted butter
2 tablespoons chopped parsley
½ teaspoon oregano
½ teaspoon summer savory

2 tablespoons capers
4 tablespoons sherry wine
6 young mackerel
1 cup sifted bread crumbs
2 to 4 tablespoons melted butter

1 teaspoon salt

1. Mix well the bread crumbs, butter, parsley, oregano, savory, salt, capers, and wine. If not stiff enough, add more crumbs.
2. Clean mackerel and stuff with mixture. Place in an oiled baking pan.
3. Cover with sifted crumbs and brush with melted butter.
4. Bake twenty-five minutes at 375°.
5. Serve with Anchovy Sauce Mazatlan (p. 93).

Note: Grape juice may be substituted for wine, if desired.

Caldo de Pescado (Boiled Fish)

4 onions, chopped
2 tablespoons oil, or more
4 tablespoons flour
6 tomatoes, peeled and cut in pieces
1 chili pepper, chopped

1 bouquet herbs
1 sprig parsley
½ cup white wine
6 cups water
6 slices fish
Seasonings, if needed

1. Fry onions in oil, add flour, and blend. Add tomatoes, chili pepper, herbs, parsley, and wine. Boil for one-half hour.

2. Add water and fish. Boil one-half hour longer.

3. Remove herbs and add seasonings.

4. Pour over crusts of bread.

Arroz con Pescado (Fish and Rice)

1 cup rice
2 tablespoons butter
1 tablespoon chopped onion

1 cup finely shredded cooked fish
Salt and paprika

1. Boil rice for twenty minutes in salted water. Drain. Set aside to dry.

2. When cold, fry in butter. Keep warm.

3. Fry onion in butter and add fish. When warm, mix with rice. Season and serve.

Pescados Mexicano (Mexican Fish)

½ cup butter
2 onions, chopped
1 pound fish
1 tablespoon flour
12 small mushrooms

½ cup hot water
¼ cup white wine
1 teaspoon grated chocolate
Salt and pepper

1. Melt butter in a baking dish, add onions, and cook until soft. Add fish and flour.

2. Mix water, wine, chocolate, salt, and pepper, and pour over fish. Cook it slowly until tender. (375°.)

3. Ten minutes before serving, add mushrooms.

Atún Fresco (Fresh Tuna)

1½ pounds tuna fish, cut in six pieces
1 cup tomato sauce
1 teaspoon lemon juice
3 cloves garlic
½ cup bread crumbs
¼ cup chopped parsley
4 tablespoons oil
3 potatoes, pared and cut in half
1 bay leaf
Salt and pepper

1. Place fish in a baking dish, and cover with tomato sauce and lemon juice.
2. Chop one clove of garlic, mix with bread crumbs, and sprinkle over fish, using some of the parsley and two tablespoons of oil.
3. Bake fifteen minutes. (400°.)
4. Heat the remaining parsley, oil, and garlic, minced. Add potatoes, bay leaf, salt, and pepper. Add enough water to cover, and cook until tender.
5. Serve potatoes with fish.

Pescado Guisado (Stewed Fish)

2 tablespoons olive oil
1 clove garlic, minced
2 tomatoes, chopped
1 pound fish, sliced (any kind desired)
1 cup boiling water
½ cup ground almonds
¼ teaspoon pepper
¼ teaspoon cloves
¼ teaspoon cinnamon
½ teaspoon minced parsley
¼ teaspoon saffron
Few sprigs parsley

1. Heat oil in a saucepan, and add garlic and tomatoes. When boiling, add fish. Simmer a few minutes.
2. In another saucepan combine the boiling water, almonds, seasonings, and parsley. When it boils, add saffron, mixed with a little cold water. Boil until blended.
3. Add sauce to fish mixture and simmer until the fish is tender.
4. Remove fish to a hot platter. Pour sauce over fish. Garnish with parsley.

Almejas con Arroz (Clams and Rice)

½ cup rice
1 pint small clams
Salt and chili powder

1. Boil rice until dry in salted water. Add clams, which have been cooked in their own juice. Season.
2. Mix rice and clams. Heat, and press into a greased mold. Dry them in the oven for a few minutes.
3. Turn onto a hot dish.

Cangrejuelos No. 1

1 teaspoon lard
1 pound ham, chopped fine
1 onion, chopped
Salt and chili powder

Bay leaf, thyme, parsley
1 pint shrimps
2 cups rice
Water

1. Heat lard in a saucepan, and add ham, onion, and seasonings.
2. When brown, add shrimps. Stir until hot, and add rice.
3. Cover with water and cook until each rice grain stands alone. Remove herbs.

Cangrejuelos No. 2

1 large onion, chopped
1 tablespoon fat
½ teaspoon paprika or cayenne or chili powder
2 tomatoes, cut fine

1 teaspoon grated chocolate
½ teaspoon salt
½ teaspoon vinegar
½ teaspoon sugar
1 cup boiled rice

1 cup cooked shrimps

1. Fry onion in fat and add cayenne, paprika, or chili powder. Add tomatoes, sugar, chocolate, salt, and vinegar. Simmer for fifteen minutes.
2. Add rice and shrimps. Simmer for fifteen minutes and serve.

Bollos de Abalone (Abalone Meat Balls)

1 pound abalone meat, ground
1 cup cooked rice
1 onion, chopped
1 or 2 eggs, beaten

Salt and pepper (nutmeg or cinnamon, if desired)
1 sprig coriander, parsley, or other herbs, minced
Fat for frying

1. Mix the meat, rice, onion, eggs, and seasonings.
2. Roll into balls and press flat.
3. Fry in fat in a frying pan.

Note: These may be covered with any sauce desired.

Tortillas

Tortilla No. 1

1 cup corn meal   1 cup boiling water
1 teaspoon salt

1. Pour the boiling water over the corn meal and salt, stirring constantly until very thick. Cool enough to handle.
2. Pat into very thin cakes, six inches in diameter.
3. Brown slightly on an ungreased griddle.

Tortilla No. 2

Use y   ı avorite recipe for hot cakes, substituting corn meal for half the flour. ɪhese are not the true tortillas but are often more popular.

Leche Tortilla (Milk Tortilla) No. 3

2 cups flour   ½ teaspoon salt
½ cup lard or butter   ¾ cup milk

1. Rub flour and lard together until well mixed.
2. Add salt and milk.
3. Form into eighteen round balls and roll each thin on a floured board.
4. Toast on a hot griddle on both sides until they begin to color.

Tortilla No. 4

2 cups flour   2 teaspoons lard
½ teaspoon salt   Water

1. Sift flour and salt together and work in lard.
2. Add enough water to make a stiff pastry.
3. Roll out very thin.
4. Bake on an ungreased griddle until it begins to blister.

Potato Tortilla No. 5

1 large, cold boiled potato   1 teaspoon salt
1 teaspoon lard   2 cups flour
Water

1. Mix the potato, lard, and salt with the flour. Add water until about the consistency of bread dough. Knead thoroughly.
2. Divide into pieces the size of an egg. Roll very thin.
3. Brown very quickly on a smooth, hot stove, turning often, or use griddle.

Frijole or Bean Tortilla No. 6

2 cups Mexican beans | Chili sauce
Salt | Lard for frying

1. Soak beans overnight. Drain, cover with boiling salted water, and simmer until tender. Drain again.
2. Season with chili sauce. Mold into flat cakes. Fry in lard.

Cocoles Tortillas No. 7

Make the same as No. 1, but add two tablespoons shortening to the hot water. Make them two and one-half inches thick and two inches in diameter.

Chavacanes Tortillas No. 8

Make the same as No. 1, but add two eggs and two tablespoons of shortening. These are often made square.

Entradas de Mexicana (Mexican Entrees)

Chile con Carne No. 1

1 pound round steak | 1 sprig parsley, minced
¼ pound pork steak | 3 tablespoons chili powder
¼ cup lard or oil | and 1 quart water or
1 onion, chopped | 1 quart chili sauce or
1 clove garlic, minced | catsup

Salt

1. Cut meat in one-half-inch cubes. Brown in fat.
2. Add onion, garlic, parsley, salt, and chili powder, or chili sauce, or catsup. Add water.
3. Bring to a boil and simmer two hours over a slow fire, adding water if needed. .

Note: Canned beans or thoroughly cooked Mexican pink beans may be added to this sauce before serving.

Chile con Carne No. 2

Leftover meat	Water
1 onion, chopped	Cooked rice, macaroni, or
Salt	beans
2 tablespoons fat	1 tablespoon chili powder

1. Chop the meat very fine, and add onion and salt. Brown them in fat for ten minutes. Add water enough to cover meat, and then rice. Heat.
2. Add chili powder and cook fifteen minutes longer.

Chile con Carne No. 3

1 pound Mexican beans	2 tablespoons wild marjo-
2 pounds beef	ram (oregano)
½ pound suet	⅛ teaspoon cayenne
3 cloves garlic, minced	5 tablespoons chili powder
1 tablespoon paprika	Salt and pepper to taste

1. Wash beans and soak overnight. Drain.
2. Add fresh hot water and simmer over a slow fire until they are half done.
3. Dice meat and suet and fry to a golden brown. Mix with the beans.
4. When both meat and beans are nearly done, add other ingredients.
5. Simmer until well blended.

Note: Serve with crackers or tortillas. French bread also goes very nicely with chile con carne.

Chile con Carne No. 4

1 pound Mexican beans	5 tablespoons chili powder
2 pounds beef, diced	1 tablespoon paprika
½ cup lard or oil	½ teaspoon cayenne
2 cups minced onion	2 tablespoons wild marjo-
3 cloves garlic, minced	ram (oregano)
2 cups tomato purée	Salt and pepper

1. Wash beans and soak overnight. Drain.
2. Add fresh hot water and simmer until beans are almost tender.
3. Add meat and continue cooking until both meat and beans are almost done.
4. Put lard, onions, and garlic in a pan. Brown slightly and add tomato and remaining seasonings. Add to meat and beans.
5. Cover and let simmer until well blended, and beans are tender.

Chile con Queso (Chili with Cheese)

1 onion, chopped fine
1 tablespoon bacon fat
1 small can tomato pulp
½ cup milk

¼ cup chilipepines or 3 tea-
  spoons chili powder
1 cup grated cheese
2 eggs

Salt

1. Brown onion in fat. **Add** tomato and milk. Crush chilipepines and add. Cook the mixture well—thirty to forty minutes.
2. Add cheese and simmer until thick.
3. Add eggs, well beaten, and salt. Stir for a few seconds.
4. Serve on toast.

Guisado à la Mexicana (Mexican Stew)

¼ cup garbanzo peas or
  white beans
1 pound boiling beef
2 cups tomato purée

2 bay leaves
Salt and cayenne to taste
3 medium-sized potatoes
2 bell peppers, sliced thin

1. Wash peas and soak a few hours or overnight. Drain.
2. Cut meat in three-inch squares. Simmer peas, meat, tomato, bay leaves, salt, and cayenne until peas are nearly tender. Then add peppers and stock, or water, if necessary. Cook until thoroughly done.
3. Split potatoes in half, and fry in deep fat. Place in stew and cook five minutes longer.

Note: Serve with tortillas and avocados.

Cocido Mexicano (Mexican Pork Stew)

1 pound pork, cubed
2 pounds beef, cubed
3 slices bacon, diced
2 ears corn cut in 3 or 4
  pieces
1 turnip, cubed
1 cup garbanzos
6 carrots, diced
2 onions, sliced

1 stalk celery, chopped
2 white potatoes, cubed
2 sweet potatoes, cubed
½ head cabbage, cut in
  several pieces
2 summer squash, quar-
  tered
1 apple, quartered
1 pear, quartered

1. Place in a large kettle, pork, beef, bacon, corn, potatoes, cabbage, and turnip. Cover with cold water and bring to a boil. Then add garbanzos, which have been soaked overnight. Simmer an hour and a half.
2. Add carrots, onions, celery, squash, apple, and pear. Simmer another

hour or two. If squash and fruits become soft before stew is done, take out and keep warm until ready to serve.

3. Strain and serve liquor as soup for first course. Follow this with the meat-and-vegetable mixture as a second course.

4. Serve both Salsa Dulce (Sweet Sauce) and Salsa Picante (Piquant Sauce) with the meat course. (p. 92.)

Note: The second day, Mexicans cut corn from cob, put meat and vegetables through a meat grinder and sauté all in one large cake until nicely browned. The same sauces are repeated.

Carne de Marrano y Chili (Pork with Chili)

12 red chili peppers	1 clove garlic, minced
⅛ teaspoon coriander	½ teaspoon salt
⅛ teaspoon sage	1 leg of pork

1. Toast chilies over fire until skins are blistered. Remove skins and seeds.

2. Mash pulp in a bowl, add coriander, sage, garlic, and salt. Mix to a paste.

3. Cut five or six deep gashes in meat. Fill with paste. Place in a roasting pan and roast in a slow oven (300°), allowing thirty minutes to the pound.

4. Half an hour before roast is done, cover with remaining paste.

5. Serve hot or cold.

La Olla Podrida

4 cups flour	½ pound lean veal, diced
4 teaspoons baking powder	½ pound lean beef, diced
2 teaspoons salt	1½ teaspoons salt
2 cups shortening	⅛ teaspoon cinnamon
1 cup boiling water	⅛ teaspoon allspice
4 teaspoons lemon juice	⅛ teaspoon nutmeg
1 egg yolk, well beaten	⅛ teaspoon cloves
½ pound lean pork, diced	½ teaspoon pepper
½ pound lean, chicken, diced	2 tablespoons flour
	1 wineglass sherry

1. Sift together, flour, baking powder, and salt. Cut in one cup of shortening.

2. Place second cup of shortening in a bowl. Add boiling water, and lemon juice, and mix. Add egg yolk. Add this liquid to flour and mix well. Knead the paste a few minutes, and roll about three eighths of an inch thick.

3. Line a baking dish with this paste.
4. Season diced meat with salt, pepper, and spices. Place in pastry-lined dish. Sprinkle with two tablespoons of flour and add cold water to come just to top of mixture. Cover with pastry, cutting two or three vents in center.
5. Bake for twelve minutes at 450°-500°. Then reduce temperature to 325°-350° and bake two hours.
6. Carefully remove top crust and pour wine evenly over the meat. Replace crust.
7. Serve hot or cold.

Ternera con Almendras (Veal Cutlets with Almonds)

4 cups cold water
1 teaspoon thyme
1 bay leaf
¼ teaspoon oregano
¼ teaspoon pepper
¼ teaspoon nutmeg
1 tablespoon butter
4 veal cutlets

1 cup finely ground blanched almonds
1 teaspoon minced onion
2 tablespoons meat stock
1 egg
1 teaspoon flour
½ cup fine dry bread
   crumbs

3 tablespoons butter

1. Pour water in a saucepan. Add thyme, bay leaf, oregano, pepper, nutmeg, and butter. Bring to a boil and simmer five minutes.
2. Add cutlets and cook until tender. Drain.
3. Place almonds, onion, and stock in a saucepan and cook a few minutes until blended.
4. Beat white of egg until stiff. Add yolk of egg, also well-beaten, and the flour.
5. Dip the cutlets first in the egg mixture and then in the ground almonds. Then roll them in bread crumbs.
6. Melt butter in a frying pan, add cutlets, and brown on both sides.

Aguacates Rellenos (Stuffed Avocados)

1 tablespoon butter
¼ pound lean pork, ground
1 cup tomato pulp
1 tablespoon minced olives
1 teaspoon capers
1 teaspoon minced green
   pepper
1 clove garlic, minced

4 whole cloves
1 tablespoon finely ground
   blanched almonds
⅛ teaspoon cinnamon
1 teaspoon minced parsley
Salt and pepper
3 firm avocados (not too
   ripe)

3 egg whites

1. Melt butter in a saucepan, add pork, and fry until lightly browned.
2. Add tomato, olives, capers, green pepper, garlic, and cloves. Simmer one hour. Remove cloves.
3. Take the tomato mixture from the fire and add almonds, cinnamon, parsley, salt, and pepper.
4. Peel avocados, cut in half lengthwise, and remove stone. Fill cavity with meat mixture and place avocados in a buttered baking dish.
5. Beat whites of eggs until stiff. Spread evenly over avocados.
6. Place in a slow oven (250°-300°). Bake until meringue is nicely browned.
7. Serve with Mexican Chili Sauce or Tomato Sauce. (Pp. 90, 91.)

Albondigon Mexicano or Niño (Mexican Meat Loaf)

1½ pounds ground round steak
¼ pound ground veal
¼ pound ground salt pork
1 tablespoon minced parsley
2 pimientos, minced
2 eggs, beaten
¼ teaspoon paprika
1¼ teaspoons salt
2 onions, minced
1 green pepper, minced
Small onions, parboiled

1. Mix together the above ingredients, except parboiled onions.
2. Shape into a loaf in a casserole, brush with butter, and sprinkle with crumbs. Place parboiled onions around meat.
3. Bake in a hot oven for one hour or longer. (450°.)

Albondigon de Chile (Chile Meat Loaf)

2 pounds ground beef
1 pound ground pork
½ pound ground ham
1 cup cracker crumbs
2 eggs, beaten
½ cup milk
2 tablespoons minced onion
1 teaspoon salt
½ clove garlic, minced
6 drops tabasco sauce
1 tablespoon chili powder

1. Mix above ingredients in a large bowl.
2. Mold into a loaf pan. Pour one-half cup of water over it.
3. Bake in a hot oven from forty to fifty minutes. If pan is uncovered, baste several times during cooking.

Albondigas (Mexican Meat Balls)

½ pound ground pork
½ pound ground beef
4 hard-cooked eggs
1 slice bread, fried brown
½ onion, minced

1 sprig coriander, minced
1 teaspoon cinnamon, if desired
Salt and pepper
4 cups tomato sauce

1. Crumble bread and mix with meat. Cut up two eggs and add along with seasonings.
2. Divide the other two eggs and meat into eighteen parts. Form the meat into round balls, placing a piece of egg in center of each.
3. Put tomato sauce in a double boiler and add balls.
4. Cook for about one hour.
5. Serve with rice and tortillas.

Note: If tomatoes are used for sauce, add onion, peppers, and chili powder, and cook thirty minutes before adding meat balls.

Arroz à la Mexicano (Mexican Rice)

1 small onion, sliced
Fat
1 bell pepper, minced

1 cup rice
1 quart stewed or canned tomatoes
1 teaspoon salt

1. Mix onion, fat, and pepper, and fry slightly.
2. Wash rice and fry until brown.
3. Add strained tomatoes and salt, cover closely, and cook until rice is soft. Add a little boiling water, if tomato juice is absorbed before rice is tender.

Note: Tomato soup or tomato sauce may be used, but dilute with water to make one pint. One cup of peas may be added if desired. Meat stock or a bouillon cube adds materially to flavor.

Frijoles No. 1

½ cup olive oil
2 cloves garlic, minced
½ cup minced onion
3 cups tomato purée
Salt and pepper

4 bay leaves
1 tablespoon paprika
⅛ teaspoon cayenne
3 cups boiled Mexican beans
1 tablespoon grated cheese

1. Heat oil, garlic, and onion, and when browned add tomato, salt, pepper, bay leaves, paprika, and cayenne.
2. Add beans and let boil a minute. Put in a casserole.
3. Cover with grated cheese and bake in a slow oven until cheese is brown. (350°.)

Note: One cup of Mexican sausages may be added with onion.

Frijoles No. 2

1 pint red beans	1 tablespoon bacon fat
2 medium-sized onions	1½ cloves garlic, minced
3 green peppers	2 teaspoons salt

½ teaspoon black pepper

1. Wash beans and soak several hours or overnight. Boil for two hours. Drain and rinse.
2. Chop onion and pepper, and brown in fat. Add garlic, salt, and pepper. Cook these about five minutes and add to beans.
3. Add enough water to cover, and let boil slowly until soft. Add hot water when necessary during cooking.

Note: Serve with corn bread, a green salad, and a fruit dessert.

Enchiladas No. 1

2 pounds hamburger	2 tablespoons fat
2 cups ground onions	2 cups tomato pulp
3 teaspoons chili powder	½ pound cheese
1 teaspoon salt	Tortillas

1. Mix hamburger, onions, chili powder, and salt, and brown in fat.
2. Add tomatoes and cheese and let simmer while preparing tortillas and sauce.
3. Soften tortillas with a damp cloth, or in a covered pan in the oven.
4. Dip tortillas in the sauce and put a spoonful of filling on each. Roll like a jelly roll and place in an oblong pan.
5. Put a slice of cheese on each enchilada and cover with sauce.
6. Cook in a moderate oven for twenty to thirty minutes. (375°.)

SAUCE

2 tablespoons red chili powder	2 cups tomato juice
½ cup flour	2 onions, ground fine
	1½ tablespoons shortening

Salt

1. Mix chili powder and flour with a little water.
2. Add other ingredients and simmer until thick.

Enchiladas No. 2

½ dozen hard-cooked eggs, chopped fine
1 small bottle stuffed olives
1 pound cheese, cut fine

½ dozen onions, chopped fine
Salt
Tortillas No. 4

1. Mix above and use for filling the tortillas.
2. Make following sauce:

½ cup flour
2 tablespoon melted fat

4 tablespoons chili powder or chili peppers

Water, or tomato juice, if desired

1. Mix flour and fat. Add chili powder and water, or tomato juice. Simmer until thick.
2. Dip tortilla in the sauce, add filling, and roll. Place in a pan. Cover with remaining sauce.
3. Cook in a hot oven about half an hour. (450°.)

Enchiladas No. 3

2 cups cold, cooked chicken
3 hard-cooked eggs, chopped
1 pound hard cheese, grated

Minced parsley
3 dozen olives, chopped
1 cup raisins
Juice of 1 lemon

Tortillas No. 1 or 2

1. Mix above as filling for tortillas.
2. Dip tortilla in any chili sauce and place the filling on half of cake. Put a spoonful of chili sauce on this. Fold over other half of tortilla and roll lightly.
3. Sprinkle with more grated cheese and more chili sauce.
4. Heat in a pan until thoroughly hot.

Enchiladas No. 4

7 corn-meal pancakes (6-inch)
Hot chili sauce

Chopped onion
Grated cheese
Stoned olives, chopped

1. Dip pancakes or tortillas in hot chili sauce. Cover with onion, cheese, and olives. Repeat with other pancakes.
2. Pile on top of each other in a pan. Pour remaining sauce over top. Set in a hot oven for a few minutes.
3. Serve hot, cutting like a layer cake.

Enchiladas No. 5

6 chili peppers
1 small onion, minced
1 clove garlic, minced
Salt
3 heads lettuce

French dressing
6 hard-cooked eggs,
   chopped
1 cup chopped olives
1 dozen tortillas

Cheese

1. Remove veins and seeds of peppers and boil with onion, garlic, and salt until soft. Press through a sieve. Return sauce to stove.
2. Shred lettuce and mix with French dressing, eggs, and olives.
3. Warm tortillas. Dip in lard for a minute, then in sauce.
4. Place tortillas on a platter with a spoonful of salad in the center of each. Sprinkle with cheese and roll.
5. Pour on remaining sauce and serve hot.

Mole de Guajolote (Hot Turkey)

1 young turkey
Shallots
Salt
½ pound red peppers, or
   red and green chilies

1 teaspoon each of black
   pepper, celery seed,
   mustard, and allspice
Turkey broth
1 pound lard

1. Cut turkey into pieces and boil with shallots and salt.
2. Scald and seed red peppers. Grind, mix with a little turkey broth, and add black pepper, celery seed, mustard, and allspice.
3. Heat lard until it boils, and then put in turkey and pepper mixture. Cook ten minutes and serve hot.

Mexicana Mole Verde (Mexican Green Mole)

Turkey
1 cup minced lettuce
2 cloves garlic
2 tablespoons minced green
   chili
½ cup minced onion
4 cups green tomato purée

½ cup almond or corn meal
1½ cups oil or lard
1 teaspoon cloves
Salt and pepper
2 tablespoons minced coriander or chili powder
   to taste

1. Cut turkey into joints and simmer in salted water until it is tender.
2. Steam lettuce, garlic, chilies, and onion in tomato purée until tender, and then press through a sieve.
3. Fry meal in oil until it colors, and add to tomato mixture, stirring continuously until it thickens. Add a little turkey broth and remainder of seasonings. Add turkey and simmer fifteen minutes.
4. Serve hot with tortillas.

Pollo con Jerez (Chicken with Sherry)

1 chicken
2 onions, chopped
3 cloves garlic, minced
2 bay leaves
½ tablespoon salt
1 teaspoon oregano
Pulp of one red or green
  chili or ½ tablespoon
  chili powder
2 cups ripe olives, stoned
  and chopped

2 cups sherry
3 or 4 tablespoons flour
¾ cup olive oil
1½ cups rice
2 cloves garlic, minced
½ cup minced onions
1 cup tomato pulp
½ tablespoon paprika
1 tablespoon minced parsley
1 teaspoon salt
¼ teaspoon pepper

Stock

1. Disjoint chicken, place in a saucepan, and cover with boiling water. Boil fifteen minutes.
2. Add onions, garlic, bay leaves, salt, and oregano, and simmer one hour.
3. Add chili pulp, olives, and sherry. Simmer until chicken is tender.
4. Thicken gravy with flour that has been blended with a little cold water.
5. Heat oil in a frying pan. Add rice after it has been well washed, and cook, stirring constantly, until slightly browned.
6. Add remaining ingredients, cover with stock, and stir until well blended. Cover and cook slowly until rice is soft and nearly dry.
7. Place chicken on a hot platter and surround with rice. Serve gravy in a separate dish.

Note: Rabbit may be cooked in this same manner.

Pollo en Salsa Mezcla (Chicken in Mixed Sauce)

1 chicken (3-5 pounds)
3 cups strained tomato pulp
2 tablespoons olive oil
1 cup sliced onions
½ cup chorizo
½ cup minced citron
½ cup seedless raisins
½ cup minced, blanched
  almonds
½ cup capers
½ cup ripe olives, pitted

1 teaspoon salt
⅛ teaspoon cayenne
⅛ teaspoon cloves
⅛ teaspoon cinnamon
2 cups boiling water
1 large firm peach, sliced
1 banana, sliced
1 yam, sliced thin
1 peeled and cored apple,
  sliced
1 pear, sliced

1 cup sherry or grape juice

1. Disjoint chicken and place in a saucepan. Add tomato, bring to a boil, and simmer five minutes.
2. Heat oil in a saucepan, add onion, and sauté until soft. Add sausage and cook until done. Then add to chicken.
3. Add citron, raisins, almonds, capers, olives, salt, cayenne, cloves, and cinnamon. Mix well until mixture boils. Then add water and bring again to a boil.
4. Mix together peach, banana, yam, apple, and pear, and place on top of stew. Cover and simmer until fruits and yam are done.
5. Add sherry, heat to boiling point and serve.

Note: If chorizo cannot be obtained, a satisfactory substitute for this dish can be made by grinding together several times one-half cup of ordinary pork sausages and two cloves of garlic.

Pollo Guisado (Chicken Stew)

2 spring chickens	1 sprig parsley, minced
1 can tomatoes	Salt, paprika, celery, salt,
1 can corn	cayenne
1 green pepper, chopped	Cracker crumbs
Butter	

1. Steam chickens twenty minutes and cut into fricassee pieces.
2. Strain tomatoes and mix with corn, chopped pepper, and parsley.
3. Season and add chicken and crumbs enough to thicken.
4. Turn into a baking dish. Dot with butter. Bake one-half hour. (400°.)

Gallina con Garbanzos (Hen with Chick-Peas)

Chicken for frying	½ cup garbanzos or chick-
Lard	peas, soaked overnight
2 cloves garlic, minced	Few small red peppers,
1 large onion, minced	minced
½ cup tomato	Salt

1. Brown chicken in lard. Add garlic and onion.
2. When brown, add tomatoes, peas, minced red peppers, and salt. Cook until peas are tender.

Chicken and Corn Mince

Tomatoes	Chopped cooked chicken or
Chopped onion	other cooked meat
Minced garlic	Corn cut from cob, or
Salt and pepper	canned corn
Cooked potatoes	

1. Stew gently together tomatoes, onion, garlic, salt, pepper, and chicken.
2. Ten minutes before serving, add potatoes and corn.

Note: This is made from leftovers, and ingredients may be proportioned to suit.

Carnero Mexicana (Mexican Lamb Stew)

1 pound neck of lamb, cut in small pieces	½ tablespoon salt
	¼ teaspoon pepper
2 tablespoons flour	1 cup green peas
1 tablespoon fat	1 cup corn
1 onion, chopped	½ cup rice
3 green peppers, chopped	1 egg
3 tomatoes, chopped	1 teaspoon oil
2 quarts hot water	½ teaspoon vinegar

1. Roll lamb in flour and brown in fat with onions. Add peppers and tomatoes. Add water, pepper, and salt, and simmer for one hour.
2. Add peas, corn, and rice. Cook until rice is soft.
3. Mix egg, oil, and vinegar, and put in a serving dish. Pour stew over this.

Jamón con Pimientos (Ham with Peppers)

1 pound ham, cut in pieces	1 pint boiling water
1 pound sausage meat	Few comino seeds
Butter or drippings	Dried chili peppers or chili powder
2 tomatoes, sliced	
2 onions, sliced	Salt
1 sprig parsley, minced	1 pound rice

1. Fry ham and sausage in drippings with tomatoes, onions, and parsley. Add boiling water and season with parsley, comino seeds, chili, and salt.
2. Add the rice. Cover and cook slowly, without stirring, until rice is soft.

Puerco en Estofado (Pork Stew)

1 pound young pork	1 tablespoon wine vinegar
2 chicken livers	1 tablespoon Worcester-shire sauce
2 chicken gizzards	
3 stalks celery, minced	Dash cloves, salt, pepper
1 ounce ginger root, minced	½ cup boiling water
2 tablespoons olive oil	1 cup bean sprouts
1 cup mushrooms	

1. Cut meat in small pieces and brown in hot fat with livers, gizzards, celery, and ginger.
2. Add oil and vinegar, a little at a time. Season. Add water.
3. Cook until nearly done, and add bean sprouts and mushrooms.

Guisado (Stew)

1 small round steak	2 cups boiling water
1 tablespoon drippings	4 Mexican peppers
4 tablespoons boiled rice	Salt
1 onion, sliced	Flour to thicken

1. Wipe meat and cut into small pieces. Brown in pan with drippings, rice, onion, and half of the water. Cover and cook slowly until tender.
2. Pour other cup of water over the peppers. Let stand until cool. Squeeze out water and all pulp. Add salt and thickening.
3. Pour over cooked meat. Boil five minutes and serve.

Chorizo

1 pound fresh pork	$\frac{1}{3}$ teaspoon cloves
1 pound beef	$\frac{1}{2}$ teaspoon pepper
2 teaspoons olive oil	1 teaspoon oregano
2 cloves garlic, minced	Salt
1 teaspoon ground chili	$\frac{1}{4}$ cup port wine
2 eggs, beaten	

1. Cut meat in small pieces and fry with oil and seasonings. Add wine and cook until tender.
2. When ready to serve, add eggs and scramble together.

Lomo de Ternera (Rump Roast)

$\frac{1}{4}$ pound suet	2 whole cloves
1 onion, sliced	1 teaspoon vinegar
4-pound beef roast	1 teaspoon sugar
1 tomato	1 teaspoon salt
1 chili pepper	Dash of pepper

1. Fry suet until melted; then brown onion.
2. Brown meat. Add juice of tomato, pulp of pepper, and cloves, vinegar, sugar, salt, and black pepper.
3. Add a little water. Cover mixture and cook slowly until tender for about three hours.

Puchero (Mexican Stew)

2 or 3 mutton shanks
3 carrots, cut lengthwise
3 ears of green corn, broken in half
½ cabbage, shredded
6 small summer squash, cut in pieces

3 sweet and 3 Irish potatoes, pared and split lengthwise
6 small onions
6 apples, quartered
6 pears, quartered
Thyme, pepper, and salt

1. Boil mutton shanks in water for two hours without skimming.
2. Add vegetables and seasonings, and cook until tender. Let water boil away, or use very little.

Sopa de Arroz (Mexican Thick Rice Soup)

½ pound lard
1 onion, chopped fine
1 clove garlic, minced
1 to 2 pounds rice
1 pound tomatoes, chopped

1 to 2 pounds carrots, chopped
Few green peppers, chopped
Salt

Water enough to cover rice

1. Allow lard to come to a boil. Add onions and garlic. When brown, add rice.
2. Add tomatoes, carrots, peppers, and salt. Add sufficient boiling water to cover, and cook two or three hours without stirring. The soup is done when mixture cooks dry.

Tamal de Cazuela (Pot Pie)

1 quart cooked corn meal
Flour (about ½ cup)
2 eggs, beaten
Broth
2 or 3 green peppers, chopped

5 or 6 tomatoes
4 tablespoons lard
1½ pounds meat (boiled chicken or pork, chopped)
Salt

1. Stir flour into corn meal, add eggs, and enough broth to make a thin batter. Spread on sides and bottom of a large bread pan, reserving enough to cover top.
2. Mix chopped peppers with plenty of tomatoes, and cook in lard about twenty minutes. Add meat and salt. Pour into a corn-meal-lined pan, and cover with remaining corn meal.
3. Bake very slowly for one hour or longer. When almost done, grease top with lard and continue cooking until nicely browned.

Chalupas (Corn Pie)

1 cup tamale meal or
  kornlet
1 tablespoon lard or butter,
  melted
½ teaspoon salt
½ teaspoon chili powder
Hot water
1 slice onion

Pieces of chorizo (sausage)
  or pork sausage fried in
  oil and garlic
Few stoned olives
½ cup butter
1 hard-cooked egg, chopped
Salt, pepper, vinegar
Water or broth

1 dozen blanched almonds

1. Mix meal, lard, salt, and chili powder. Add hot water to make a thick mush. Fill a small well-greased pan with it. Make hollow cups in mixture, using back of spoon. Brush with melted lard. Bake slowly for one hour.
2. Chop sausage, onion, and olives. Add butter, egg, salt, pepper, and vinegar. Simmer a few minutes in water or broth. Season to taste.
3. Thicken sauce with blanched almonds, chopped and pounded.
4. Pour into little cups and serve.

Jamón de Tostada (Ham Pancake)

1 cup chopped boiled ham
1 tablespoon butter
3 eggs
1 tablespoon cream

1 teaspoon flour
Salt
¼ to ½ teaspoon chili
  powder

1. Heat ham in butter.
2. Beat eggs and add cream, flour, and seasonings. Pour over ham.
3. Stir for a moment, then brown on one side. Fold over carefully.
4. Serve on a hot platter.

Tostada Seca (Dry Tostada)

1 tablespoon fat
1 tablespoon chopped onion
3 tortillas, rolled thin
Salt

Pinch oregano (sweet marjoram) or mint
Cayenne pepper
½ cup broth

1. Heat fat and fry onion with seasonings. Then fry tortillas until brown. Add broth.
2. Cover and steam until all liquid is gone.
3. Serve a spoonful on a plate before soup course.

Note: Rice or vermicelli can be cooked in same way.

Tamales No. 1

6 chili peppers
1 chicken
Broth
3 quarts corn or hominy

3 tablespoons marjoram or
chili powder
1 tablespoon olive oil
Salt

1. Remove seeds and veins from peppers. Cover with water, boil until soft, and rub through a sieve.
2. Boil chicken until tender. Set aside half of broth.
3. Mix rest of broth with part of corn which has been ground. Add pepper pulp and marjoram.
4. Mix rest of corn and broth with oil and salt. Make a dough thick enough to spread.
5. Place alternate layers of dough and chicken-and-corn mixture in a casserole, and bake thirty to forty minutes; or spread dough on cornhusks, fill center with chicken mixture, roll, tie, and steam until hot through.

Tamales No. 2

1 pound pork, boiled
1 clove garlic
Seeded raisins
Almonds

2½ dozen chilies
Stock from meat
1 cup corn meal
4 cups boiling water

½ cup lard

1. Grind meat. Add raisins and almonds and simmer twenty minutes.
2. Wash chilies well, and soak in hot water. Remove seeds and veins, and grind fine.
3. Add enough stock to make a sauce. Strain. Add meat mixture, and simmer twenty minutes.
4. Gradually stir corn meal into boiling water, add lard, and salt to taste, and cook slowly about two hours.
5. Heat corn-meal dough and sauce in layers in a casserole or spread dough on cornhusks. Fill center with sauce, roll, tie, and steam until hot through.

Tamales No. 3

4-pound chicken
1 cup corn meal
4 cups boiling water
1 teaspoon salt
2 pounds raisins or olives
1 dozen ears corn

½ teaspoon cayenne
3 red chilies
4 onions, chopped
1 clove garlic, minced
1 stick cinnamon
10 whole allspice

10 cloves

1. Boil chicken until tender. Cut in pieces.
2. Make a mush of corn meal and water, and season with salt.
3. Add raisins, corn cut from cob, and cayenne.
4. Wash chilies, and soak in hot water. Remove seeds and veins, and grind fine.
5. To chicken broth add chilies, onions, garlic, cinnamon, allspice, cloves, and salt to taste. Simmer until thick.
6. Place alternate layers of mush, chicken, and sauce in a casserole, and bake until well heated through, about one hour. (400°.) Or spread mush on cornhusks, add a piece of chicken and a little sauce, roll, tie, and steam until hot through.

Tamales à la Mexicana No. 4

1 chicken
½ cup minced onion
1 bay leaf
1 tablespoon chili powder or
 ½ tablespoon oregano and 1 tablespoon coriander

4 cups tortilla dough
½ cup olive oil or bacon fat
1 yeast cake
24 cornhusks
12 olives
1 cup red chili sauce
12 pickled red chilies

Salt and pepper

1. Disjoint chicken, place in a kettle, and cover with boiling water. Add onion, bay leaf, and other seasonings. Simmer until tender.
2. Mix dough and fat well. Mix yeast in lukewarm broth and slowly beat it into dough. Add sufficient warm broth to moisten dough. Add salt and pepper, and set in a warm place for two hours.
3. Wash and soften cornhusks in warm water.
4. Place one-third of a cup of dough on a cornhusk. On this place a piece of chicken, one olive, one tablespoon of chili sauce, and one pickled chili. Roll the husk carefully, enclosing a second husk, and tying the ends.
5. Place in a steamer or wire basket and steam for two hours or more.

Tamales Calientes (Hot Tamales) No. 5

1 pound chicken, beef, veal, or pork
2 cups Indian meal or corn meal
Water or broth from meat
½ pound seeded raisins

½ cup stoned olives
1 young red pepper, chopped
1 teaspoon sugar
Onion juice
Salt and pepper

6 hard-cooked eggs

1. Boil the fowl or meat in salted water until tender. Strip meat from bones and chop fine.
2. Make a mush of corn meal and chicken broth or water.
3. Mince raisins, olives, and red pepper very fine. Add chicken and corn meal.
4. Add onion juice and pepper, and cook twenty minutes. Add more water if necessary.
5. Mince hard-cooked eggs and add to sauce.
6. Take some inner husks of green corn. On two of these husks, place as much filling as they will hold. Wrap husk over and around filling, and tie with a piece of stripped husk and string.
7. Steam or boil in salted water for one to two hours.

Note: Raisins may be omitted.

Umitas (Corn Tamales) No. 6

1 cup grated corn or hominy	2 tablespoons thick cream or butter
2 eggs	1 teaspoon flour
Salt and pepper	Husks from six ears of corn

1. Mix corn, slightly beaten eggs, melted butter, flour, salt, and pepper.
2. Remove the husks from corn, cut edges neatly, and scald until pliable. Drain leaves and dry.
3. Place a spoonful in each cornhusk. Fold lengthwise and place in a steamer, with the folded end at bottom.
4. Cover and steam for twenty minutes.

Tamale Loaf

1 cup corn meal	1 clove garlic, minced
3 to 4 cups water or stock	1 to 2 tablespoons fat
1 pound ground meat	1 can tomatoes
1 onion, chopped fine	1 pint olives
1 green pepper, chopped	1 tablespoon chili powder
Parsley, minced	Salt and pepper

1. Make a mush of corn meal, water, and salt.
2. Brown meat, onion, pepper, parsley, and garlic in fat. Add tomato, olives, salt, pepper, and chili powder.
3. Combine mush and meat mixture and put in a casserole.
4. Bake one-half hour. (400°.)

Pastel de Puerco (Pork Pie)

1 pound loin of pork	Salt and pepper
Butter	2 cups corn meal
3 cups water	4 cups boiling water
1 teaspoon chili powder	2 eggs, well beaten
2 tablespoons flour	1 dozen chopped olives

1. Cut pork in small pieces and brown in butter. Add water and stew until tender.
2. Add chili powder, salt, and pepper. Thicken gravy with flour.
3. Make mush with corn meal and boiling water. Add two eggs .
4. Put a layer of mush in a baking dish. Add olives, meat, and gravy. Cover with remainder of mush.
5. Bake twenty to thirty minutes. (400°.)

Pastel de Tamal (Tamale Pie)

1 can corn	2 cups ground, cooked meat
1 can tomatoes	1 cup yellow corn meal
1 large onion, minced	1 tablespoon chili powder
4 tablespoons oil	Salt
2 cups stock	1 cup ripe olives
2 cups milk	4 eggs, well beaten

1. Cook corn, tomatoes, and onion in oil. Add stock, milk, and meat.
2. Add corn meal, chili powder, salt, and olives. Simmer fifteen minutes. Stir to keep from sticking. Add eggs, and put all in a well-greased casserole or baking pan.
3. Bake for forty-five to fifty minutes. (400°.)
4. Serve with Mexican Chili Sauce No. 2. (P. 90.)

Frijoles Refritos (Fried Beans)

1 pint pink beans	Salt and pepper
1 clove garlic, minced	1/4 cup olive oil

1. Soak beans overnight. Drain, cover with fresh water, add garlic, salt, and pepper, and cook until soft.
2. Drain off about one inch of juice.
3. Mash some of the beans for thickening.
4. Pour rest of the beans into hot oil and fry. Add mashed beans.
5. Mash all together and fry until partly dry and crisp.

Garbanzos (Mexican Peas)

2 cups garbanzos
½ pound pork
3 cups tomato purée

2 or 3 chili peppers
1 to 2 tablespoons chili
powder and paprika

Salt

1. Soak peas overnight in slightly salted water.
2. Add pork and tomato, and cook until almost soft.
3. Pour hot water over chili peppers, and boil until soft. Rub through a sieve.
4. Add chili powder, paprika, and salt, and simmer until peas are tender.

Fideos (Mexican Noodles)

¾ cup olive oil
½ onion, minced
4 stalks celery, diced
1 small can mushrooms
2 cups tomato purée

Salt, pepper, cayenne
1 can tuna fish
½ pint fresh oysters or 1
cup canned oysters
1 package noodles

1. Heat oil and brown onions slightly. Add celery and barely heat through.
2. Drain mushrooms, add, and· heat mixture through again.
3. Add salt, pepper, and cayenne to tomato purée, and cook for fifteen minutes. Add to first mixture, together with fish and oysters. Simmer an hour and a half.
4. Place in a casserole with noodles, which have been previously boiled in salted water. Cook thirty minutes. (400°.)

Note: This sauce is often served with plain boiled noodles.

Fideos (Mexican Spaghetti)

¼ pound dried mushrooms
1¼ pounds lean boiling
beef
1 cup chicken fat or olive oil
3 cans tomatoes (No. 2½)
1 can green chilies

2 onions, minced
2 cloves garlic, minced
1 sprig parsley, minced
Salt and pepper
Cayenne, if desired
1 package spaghetti

Parmesan cheese, grated

1. Wash mushrooms, cover with warm water, and soak overnight.
2. Brown meat on all sides in fat or oil. Place in a large kettle.
3. Add mushrooms and water in which they were soaked, tomatoes,

chilies, onions, garlic, parsley, salt, and pepper. Simmer three or four hours.

4. Remove meat, grind, and return to sauce.
5. Cook spaghetti in boiling salted water until tender.
6. Serve spaghetti on individual plates. Pour some sauce over spaghetti and sprinkle with cheese.

Tehuantepec (Cheese Soufflé)

3 cups grated bread crumbs
1¼ cups grated cheese
2 tablespoons minced pimiento
¼ teaspoon salt
½ teaspoon mustard

1 tablespoon Worcestershire sauce
1½ cups thin cream, or rich milk
2 egg yolks, well beaten
2 egg whites, stiffly beaten

1. Mix thoroughly all ingredients except egg whites.
2. Fold in egg whites and pour mixture into a buttered baking dish. Set in a pan of hot water and bake until firm—thirty-five to forty minutes in a slow oven. (300°-325°.)
3. Serve with Salsa Mexicana (Mexican Sauce). (P. 92.)

Legumbres (Vegetables)

Colache

1 onion, chopped
1 tablespoon butter
1 bell pepper
1 cup tomatoes
Salt and pepper

6 summer squash, cut in pieces
1 cup shredded string beans
Corn cut from 3 ears or ½ cup

1. Fry onion in butter until brown. Add chopped pepper.
2. Then add tomatoes and squash and string beans. Cover and let simmer until beans are tender.
3. Add corn, salt, and pepper. Let simmer a few minutes.

Ejotes con Vino (String Beans with Wine)

2 pounds string beans
2 small onions, minced
2 green peppers, minced

4 tablespoons olive oil
2 tablespoons wine or cider
Salt and pepper

1. String, slice, and cook beans in salted water until tender.
2. Fry onion and pepper in oil and add to beans with wine, salt, and pepper. Simmer a few minutes.

Chilies Rellenos No. 1

2 cups browned bread
  crumbs
1 cup diced cheese
2 teaspoons minced parsley
1 cup chopped nuts
2 tomatoes, chopped
2 small onions, chopped
Salt and pepper
8 green peppers

1. Combine crumbs, cheese, parsley, nuts, tomato, onion, salt, and pepper. Add tomato juice, water, or stock, if not moist enough.
2. Cut tops from peppers and remove seeds. Place in a baking dish close enough together to stand erect. Fill with mixture.
3. Add about a half cup of water or stock to dish, and cook about one-half hour in a moderate oven. (400°.)
4. Dip tops of peppers into beaten egg, and fry. Place on top of stuffed peppers before serving.

Chilies Rellenos de Queso No. 2

6 fresh or canned chilies or
  pimientos
2 eggs, beaten
½ cup flour
½ pound cheese, cut in
  thick pieces
½ cup fat
Salt

1. Parboil or roast chilies, or use canned chilies or pimientos.
2. Make a batter of eggs and flour and salt.
3. Stuff chilies with cheese and dip them in batter. Fasten with a toothpick if necessary.
4. Fry in boiling fat until golden brown. Turn when necessary.
5. Drain and serve.

Note: Bell peppers will fry in this same way, and are very nice.

Chilies Rellenos No. 3

6 peppers or chilies
1 onion, chopped fine
2 tablespoons butter
⅓ cup brown sauce
3 tablespoon bread crumbs
4 tablespoons chopped raw
  ham
4 tablespoons chopped
  mushrooms
Salt and pepper

1. Cut slices from stem end of each pepper, remove seeds, and parboil for fifteen minutes.
2. Cook onion in butter. Then add brown sauce, crumbs, ham and mushrooms, salt, and pepper. Cool and put into peppers.
3. Cover with additional bread crumbs.
4. Bake chilies ten minutes. Peppers thirty to forty minutes.
5. Serve with toast and brown sauce.

Note: Brown sauce is made like white sauce, except that flour and butter are allowed to brown *but not burn.*

Chilies Rellenos No. 4

6 large long chili peppers	Salt, pepper, cayenne, and flour
½ cup raisins	
1 pound cream cheese, diced	6 cups cooking sauce or tomato sauce
3 eggs	

Olive oil or lard

1. Broil peppers over a fire until skins blister. Wrap in cloth for ten minutes to sweat skins loose. Remove skins and open peppers on one side. Remove veins and seeds. Do not break stem.
2. Fill centers with raisins and cheese. Fasten with a toothpick.
3. Beat egg whites to a froth. Add egg yolks and beat again.
4. Dust peppers with salt, pepper, cayenne, and flour. Handle by stem. Dip in egg batter.
5. Fry in hot fat or olive oil to an amber brown. Drain.
6. Heat sauce and place peppers in it. Simmer for twenty minutes.
7. Serve on a hot platter, garnished with avocados.

Flan de Maiz (Mexican Sweet Corn Custard)

4 eggs	1 teaspoon salt
1½ cups corn	1 teaspoon paprika
2 tablespoons chopped green pepper	1 clove garlic, minced
	1½ cups milk

1. Beat eggs and add other ingredients.
2. Bake in a casserole or in custard cups in a slow oven (300°) until set, or place dish in a pan of water as you would for a custard.

Pasteles de Legumbres Mexicano (Mexican Vegetable Tarts)

1 small cabbage	½ cup string beans
2 large carrots	4 eggs
2 large turnips	Salt and pepper
1 cup peas	2 cups lard or oil for frying

1. Boil vegetables in salted water until tender. Chop very fine and press out all water. Add pepper and form chopped vegetables into cakes.
2. Beat egg whites to a froth and add yolks. Beat both again.
3. Dip each cake in egg and fry in fat until brown. Drain.
4. Serve on a platter with water cress.

Note: Any leftover vegetables can be used.

Chayote (Squash)

2 cups diced chayote or summer squash
½ teaspoon minced onion

1 tablespoon lard
Salt and pepper
½ cup corn to each 2 cups squash

1. Dice squash and put it in a saucepan with onion and lard. Salt and pepper. Fry ten minutes.
2. Add corn cut from cob. Cook to a mush.

Calabacito (Very Young Pumpkin)

2 very young pumpkins
½ pound veal or pork, cut in pieces
1 tablespoon fat

1 small onion, minced
2 cups tomatoes
1 teaspoon salt
Red and black pepper

1. Peel and slice pumpkin. Remove seeds.
2. Brown meat in fat. Add onion. Cook a few minutes and add pumpkin, tomatoes, salt, and pepper.
3. Cover with water. Put a lid on and cook until tender.

Suculento (Succotash)

½ pound salt pork
1 onion, sliced
6 green peppers, cut small

1 can corn
4 summer squash, sliced
Milk

1. Fry pork, onion, and peppers. When brown, add corn and squash.
2. Cover with milk and cook slowly for two hours, without stirring.

Flor de Calabaza (Squash Blossoms)

6 fresh blossoms of squash
Thin batter

Deep fat
Cream sauce

1. Dip blossoms into cold salted water. Shake well.
2. Dip each into a thin batter and fry in deep fat. Drain on paper.
3. Serve with cream sauce.

Mollete (Squash Pancakes)

1 cup milk	1 cup corn meal
2 eggs, beaten	1 cup flour
1 cold boiled squash	2 teaspoons baking powder

½ teaspoon salt

1. Mix milk, eggs, and squash. Beat well. Sift dry ingredients together and add, mixing thoroughly.
2. Bake on both sides on a hot griddle. Sprinkle with sugar and serve.

Patatas Colorada Caliente (Red-hot Potatoes)

1 long dry red chili pepper	½ can tomatoes (No. 2½)
1 tablespoon lard, melted	1 tablespoon flour
1 onion, chopped	2 cups diced boiled potatoes

Salt and pepper

1. Soak pepper in hot water several hours. Drain, add fresh hot water, and soak several hours longer.
2. Scrape pulp from pepper, and add lard, onion, and tomatoes. Cook forty-five minutes. Strain.
3. Thicken with flour and add salt and pepper. Simmer until well blended.
4. Pour over potatoes and serve.

Note: This sauce is also nice over meat.

Nopales (Cactus)

Young nopales or cactus	Butter
1 teaspoon grated orange	2 eggs, beaten
peel	¼ cup tomato juice

1. Wash nopales in soda water.
2. Fry in butter until brown. Add eggs, and when half cooked, add tomato juice and orange peel.

Note: Nopales are the small, young leaves of branched cactus, dethorned, boiled, stewed, or fried, or made into omelets.

Cebollas en Casserole (Onions in Casserole)

12 medium-sized onions	2 stalks celery, minced
4 cups tomato purée	2 bell peppers, minced

Salt and pepper

1. Peel onions and place in a casserole.
2. Combine tomato purée, celery, peppers, salt, and pepper. Pour over onions.
3. Bake in a slow oven for two and one-half hours. (250°-300°.)

Ensaladas Mexicanas (Mexican Salads)

Avocado

2 avocados
1 tablespoon onion juice
½ cup chopped pimiento
Sliced tomatoes

Juice of 1 lemon or lime
Salt and pepper
Lettuce

1. Peel and mash avocados. Add onion juice, pimiento, lemon juice, salt, and pepper. Blend well.

2. Serve on lettuce or tomato or both.

Guacamole

2 avocados
½ can green chilies
Salt and pepper
Vinegar or lemon juice

1 pound seedless grapes or pomegranates
Lettuce
Paprika

1. Peel avocados and mash.

2. Wash chilies, and mash avocados.

3. Add salt and pepper, and vinegar or lemon juice. Add grapes.

4. Serve on lettuce and sprinkle with paprika.

Ensalada de Avocado (Avocado Salad)

3 or 4 avocados
3 or 4 small tomatoes
1 tablespoon minced green onion

1 tablespoon minced chili
1 tablespoon minced parsley
Salt to taste
Lettuce

French dressing

1. Peel avocados and cut in half lengthwise.

2. Slice tomatoes in half and place in cavity of avocado.

3. Sprinkle with onion, chili, and parsley. Season with salt.

4. Serve on lettuce with French dressing, thick with paprika.

Ensalada Mexicana de Legumbres (Mexican Vegetable Salad)

1½ cups diced cooked meat
½ cup kidney beans
½ cup cooked peas
½ cup chopped celery
1½ tablespoons chopped pepper

1 tablespoon chopped onion
French dressing
Salt
½ cup mayonnaise
½ teaspoon chili powder
5 tomatoes

Lettuce

1. Marinate meat and vegetables, except tomatoes, in French dressing for half an hour. Drain. Add salt.
2. Combine lightly with mayonnaise to which chili powder has been added.
3. Serve in tomato cups on a bed of greens.

Ensalada de Frijoles (Bean Salad)

1 bell pepper
1 small onion
1 ripe sweet pepper
1 sprig parsley
2 cucumbers

2 cups cooked pink beans
1 clove garlic
1 pint cider vinegar
2 tablespoons tarragon vinegar

French dressing

1. Chop bell pepper, onion, sweet pepper, parsley, and one cucumber.
2. Mix with beans.
3. Mix garlic, the other cucumber sliced, a sprig of parsley, a piece of onion, and the vinegars. Let stand to blend. Strain and pour over the vegetables. Let stand an hour or longer.
4. Drain off vinegar. Serve in a bowl or on lettuce with French dressing.

Ensalada de Chili Verde (Green Pepper Salad)

Small red or yellow tomatoes
½ cup minced green chili or canned green chili

½ cup minced stuffed olives
½ cup minced onion
Salt, pepper, paprika
French dressing

Lettuce

1. Split tomatoes, or dice and mix with other ingredients.
2. Serve with French dressing on crisp lettuce leaves.

Ensalada de Noche Buena (Christmas Night Salad)

Lettuce
French dressing
3 cooked beets, sliced
2 bananas, sliced

2 oranges, sliced
1 tablespoon lemon juice
½ cup finely chopped
  peanuts

1. Wash and dry lettuce, then chop fine.
2. Put French dressing in a bowl and add lettuce. Then add other ingredients. Toss lightly together.

Ensalada Mexicano No. 1

2 Spanish onions, sliced
2 fresh chilies, cut in rings
2 ripe tomatoes, sliced

Parsley, minced
Bread crumbs
French dressing

1. Put onions, chilies, and tomatoes in alternate layers in a shallow bowl. Sprinkle with parsley and bread crumbs.
2. Cover with French dressing. Serve ice cold.

Ensalada Mexicano No. 2

3 large tomatoes, cut in
  pieces
1 medium onion, cut fine
3 large green peppers

4 slices bacon
¼ cup vinegar
¼ teaspoon chili powder
Lettuce

1. Mix tomatoes, onion, and peppers, which have been cut in pieces.
2. Fry bacon and remove from the pan. Add vinegar and chili powder to the fat. Boil and pour over vegetables.
3. When cool, add bacon, and serve on lettuce.

Ensalada de Garbanzos (Pinto Bean Salad)

1½ cups cooked beans
½ cup diced celery
½ cup diced cheese

½ cup cooked carrot cubes
1 teaspoon minced onion
¼ cup French dressing
Lettuce

1. Mix ingredients with French dressing. Chill and serve on lettuce.

Note: The beans should be boiled until tender, and then washed in cold water so that they will not become mushy.

Dulces (Desserts)

Mantecado (Ice Cream)

½ cup sugar
½ cup chopped nuts
1 cup boiled custard
½ cup crumbled macaroons
1 cup whipped cream
½ teaspoon almond flavoring

1. Melt sugar in a heavy iron pan until brown. Stir constantly.
2. Add nuts and turn into a buttered pan. When cold, crush with a rolling pin.
3. Fold cold custard into flavored cream and half freeze it. Then add macaroons and crushed-nut mixture and complete freezing.

Note: Peanut brittle may be substituted for sugar and nuts.

Banana Gelatin

2½ tablespoons gelatin
2 cups boiling water
1 cup sugar
Grated rind of one lemon
2 tablespoons lemon juice
4 medium-sized bananas

1. Soak gelatin in a little cold water. Add boiling water and stir until gelatin is dissolved. Add sugar, lemon rind, and juice.
2. Mash bananas, and add to gelatin mixture. Pour into a mold and chill.
3. Serve with chocolate sauce.

SAUCE

4 tablespoons sugar
1 tablespoon flour
1 square chocolate or 4 tablespoons ground chocolate
Pinch of salt
1 cup boiling water
1 tablespoon butter
1 teaspoon vanilla

1. Combine sugar, flour, chocolate, and salt.
2. Add water slowly, stirring well.
3. Cook until smooth and thick.
4. Add butter and vanilla.

Leche de Piña (Pineapple Custard)

¼ pound blanched almonds
4 egg yolks, beaten
1 pint grated pineapple
½ cup sugar
1 quart milk

1. Chop almonds and pulverize. Add egg yolks. Drain pineapple and add juice.
2. Add sugar to milk and scald. Cool and add pineapple pulp.
3. Combine mixtures and cook in a double boiler until they thicken, stirring constantly.
4. Pour into sherbet glasses, chill, and serve.

Ranfanote

1 cup corn sirup
1 tablespoon grated orange
   peel
3 sticks cinnamon
Bread crumbs

Nut meats
Cloves
Shredded coconut
2 tablespoons butter
Ground cinnamon

1. Boil sirup, orange peel, and stick cinnamon.
2. Add bits of dry bread, nuts, cloves, and coconut.
3. Cook to soft ball when tried in cold water. Remove cinnamon, cloves, and orange peel, and add butter. Cool on plates.
4. Sprinkle with cinnamon. Break, and serve.

Pudín de Mexicano (Mexican Soufflé)

1 cup clear black coffee
½ cup sugar
3 tablespoons butter
3 tablespoons cornstarch

2 tablespoons grated chocolate
3 eggs
⅓ cup butter, melted

1. Scald coffee, sugar, and three tablespoons butter, which has been creamed, with cornstarch and chocolate.
2. Remove from fire and stir it slowly into well-beaten egg yolks, to which one third of a cup of melted butter has been added.
3. Fold in stiffly beaten egg whites.
4. Pour into a pudding dish, set in a pan of warm water and bake for twenty-five minutes in a slow oven. (350°.)

Cajeta de Leche (Molded Custard)

4 cups brown sugar
1½ cups water

1 egg white
2 tablespoons flour

2 quarts milk

1. Make a sirup of brown sugar and one cup of water. Boil a few minutes.
2. Beat egg white with other half cup of water. Add to sirup to clarify. Skim clear, and reduce to a thick sirup.

3. Mix flour with one quart of milk and add. Boil again, stirring constantly until it thickens. Little by little, add other quart of milk. Stir it to consistency of a custard.
4. Remove from fire and beat until lukewarm. Spread one third of an inch thick on a platter.
5. When cold, cut it in diamonds. Dust with sugar.

Bien me Sabe (Coconut Trifle or You-Know-Me-Well)

1 large coconut, grated	4 tablespoons sugar
1 cup milk	Sponge cake
4 eggs	Vanilla to flavor

1. Mix grated coconut with milk or coconut milk. Heat slowly.
2. Squeeze through cheesecloth until all milk is extracted.
3. Beat egg yolks, and add sugar and milk. Place in a double boiler and cook until it thickens, stirring constantly.
4. Spread over squares of sponge cake.
5. Make a meringue with egg whites. Add a little sugar and vanilla.
6. Spread over top of cake. Sprinkle with coconut.

Buñuelos (Little Fritters) No. 1

3 tablespoons butter	1 teaspoon baking powder
1 cup water	3 eggs
1 cup flour	½ cup fat

1. Place butter and water in a saucepan and bring to a boil.
2. Sift flour and baking powder into this.
3. Remove from fire and add eggs, well beaten. Beat hard until cool. Knead until smooth.
4. Drop by spoonfuls into boiling fat. Cook until brown.
5. Serve with powdered sugar and sirup, flavored with cinnamon.

Buñuelos (Little Fritters) No. 2

1 cup water	1 teaspoon baking powder
2 tablespoons butter	3 eggs, well beaten
1 cup flour	Fat

Honey and cinnamon

1. Boil water and butter, and sift in flour and baking powder. Stir until smooth.
2. Remove batter from fire and add eggs. Beat until cool.
3. Knead to a smooth dough and drop by tablespoonfuls into hot fat, a few at a time. When golden brown, remove and drain on paper.
4. Serve with honey, flavored with cinnamon.

Capirotada (Mexican Bread Pudding) No. 1

2½ cups bread cubes
1 egg
Deep hot fat
¼ cup sugar
1 teaspoon cinnamon

½ cup minced citron
¾ cup pine nuts
2 cups sugar
⅛ teaspoon cream of tartar
1 cup water

½ teaspoon cinnamon

1. Brown bread cubes in oven.
2. Beat egg white until stiff; add yolk and beat until blended.
3. Dip bread cubes in egg and fry them in deep fat until brown. Drain and pile on a serving dish.
4. Mix sugar and cinnamon and sprinkle over bread cubes.
5. Combine citron and nuts and sprinkle over cubes.
6. Place other ingredients in a saucepan and boil to thread stage.
7. Pour over bread cubes and serve at once.

Capirotada (Mexican Bread Pudding) No. 2

4 cups water
2 cups crushed Mexican sugar or brown sugar
1 medium onion, sliced
2 tomatoes, sliced
1 cup raisins

1 loaf dry bread, broken in small pieces
1 cup butter or lard
½ teaspoon cinnamon
1 cup grated Mexican goat's cheese

1. Put water and sugar in a saucepan and boil until consistency of maple sirup.
2. When half done, add onion and tomatoes. Discard when sirup is cooked.
3. Place in a buttered baking dish a layer of bread. Add a little sirup, then a layer of raisins, dot with butter, and sprinkle with cinnamon. Repeat until all ingredients are used.
4. Sprinkle cheese on top and bake forty-five minutes. (350°.) Serve hot.

Mexican Honey Ginger Cake

1 tablespoon melted butter
1 cup honey
1 egg yolk, slightly beaten
½ cup buttermilk
¼ teaspoon soda
2 cups sifted flour
½ teaspoon cinnamon
1 teaspoon ginger
½ teaspoon mace

1 egg white, stiffly beaten
2 cream or Neufchâtel cheeses
Medium cream or evaporated milk
2 cups finely chopped dates
1 cup chopped almonds or walnuts
½ teaspoon salt

1. Beat butter and honey until well blended.
2. Mix egg yolk, buttermilk, and soda, and beat well.
3. Combine two mixtures and blend.
4. Sift flour and spices together and beat into honey mixture.
5. Fold in egg white.
6. Pour into a shallow buttered pan. Bake twenty-five minutes. (350°.)
7. Split cake while hot and spread with following filling.

DATE-CREAM CHEESE FILLING

1. Mash cheese and add cream to make a soft filling. Then add dates, nuts, and salt. Mix well.
2. Spread between layers of split cake, and serve while cake is warm.

Cajeta de Camote y Piña (Sweet Potato and Pineapple Jelly)

2 pounds sweet potatoes	1 cup water
¼ large fresh pineapple	1 egg white
3 cups sugar	1 cup cold water

1. Boil potatoes until soft. Mash and rub through a sieve.
2. Grate pineapple and force through a sieve.
3. Put sugar and water in a saucepan.
4. Beat egg white and water, and add to sugar mixture. Heat until a scum appears. Remove from fire and skim. Repeat until no scum appears.
5. Remove from heat and add potatoes. Return to fire and cook until so clear you can see bottom of pan.
6. Add pineapple and cook again until it is so clear you can see pan.
7. Serve cold.

Note: Stewed apples forced through a sieve may replace pineapple.

Dulce de Naranja (Mexican Orange Candy)

1 cup sugar	Grated rind of 2 oranges
¾ cup evaporated milk	Pinch salt
¾ cup water	1 cup black walnuts or
2 cups sugar	pecans

½ cup butter

1. Caramelize first cup of sugar by sifting it slowly into a hot iron skillet.
2. Scald milk and water and add to caramelized sugar.
3. Add rest of sugar, and cook to soft-ball stage.
4. Just before it is done, add orange rind, salt, nuts, and butter.
5. Cool and beat until creamy. Pour onto a buttered platter.

Dulces Mexicano (Mexican Sweets)

Raisins
Red wine
Fig leaves

Infusion: Cognac
Marsala wine
Sliced lemon

1. Pick stems from raisins and wash raisins in red wine. Soak in infusion for three days.
2. Heap in bunches and wrap each bunch in a fig leaf. Bake one-half hour. (400°.)
3. Serve hot on leaves.

Planquetas (Pralines)

1 cup white sugar
1 cup dark brown sugar

1 cup water
¼ cup butter

1 pound pecans or walnuts

1. Cook sugar, water, and butter until it forms a soft ball when tested in cold water.
2. Drop by tablespoonfuls onto an oiled slab or dish. Quickly press nuts around each one before it gets cold.
3. Patties should be about three inches in diameter and rather thin.

Dulce de Pecan (Mexican Pecan Candy)

3 cups dark brown sugar
½ cup water

¼ cup cider vinegar
1 tablespoon butter

1½ cups heated pecans

1. Mix sugar, water, vinegar, and butter, and cook until it spins a thread when dropped from a spoon.
2. Cool slightly and stir in heated nuts. Cool enough to hold its shape.
3. Drop in small cakes on a well-greased platter or into greased-paper candy cups.

Panocha

1 cup dark brown sugar
1 cup white sugar
½ cup milk or cream
Pinch salt

1 tablespoon corn sirup
1 teaspoon vanilla
1 cup nut meats
1 tablespoon butter

1. Mix sugar, milk, salt, and corn sirup. Stir until dissolved.
2. Place lid on kettle until it boils. Cook without stirring until mixture forms a soft ball in cold water.
3. Let stand until slightly cool. Add vanilla, nuts, and butter.
4. Beat until it can be handled, just before it sets.
5. Pour into a pan and cut into squares.

Candied Fruits

1½ cups fruit   2 cups water
1 cup light corn sirup   Sugar

1. Place fruit in a bowl.
2. Mix sirup and water. Bring to a boil and pour over fruit. The liquid must cover fruit. Let stand twenty-four hours.
3. Pour off sirup. Measure. For every four cups of liquid, allow one-half cup sugar.
4. Bring to a boil. Pour over fruit, and let stand for twenty-four hours.
5. Repeat this process, adding sugar each time, over a period of six to nine days.
6. Drain on wire racks for seven days. When fruit is no longer sticky it is ready to use or store in an uncovered jar or box.

Note: This is good for apricots, figs, dried prunes, pineapple, orange slices, cherries, cactus, coconut, melons, and pickling pears.

Latin-American Foods

Across the sea from Portugal and Spain,
Comes Latin America's culinary fame.

Latin America

The present-day foods of Latin America have been greatly influenced by Spain and Portugal.

These countries to the south of Mexico do not share the tasty and unique traditions of the Aztec Indians. Whereas the Aztecs would spend hours in the preparation of a single dish, the Indians to the south of them have always been satisfied with much simpler fare.

This Indian, or peon, gets the greatest satisfaction when he slays a steer or calf and cooks it, gridiron-fashion, over the open fire. The meat is roasted in the skin, a few hours after killing, and is therefore very unsightly and tough. The old peon was satisfied to consume large amounts of this meat as he sipped his maté.

Today, the average peon eats a better-balanced dinner. He has a meat allowance which he eats either boiled, as *puchero*, with *sapallo* (sort of squash) and sweet potatoes, or as *guisado* (stew) with rice, or as *asado* (plain roast) In addition to the meat, he has his ration of biscuits, *torta frita* or *fideos* (spaghetti), and a cereal substance called farina. With this, he must always have his gourd of maté.

Yerba maté is the sociable bowl of Paraguay and the surrounding country. It is a cured dried leaf, infused like tea in a gourd. The gourd is refilled for each one present, and passed from one to the other in turn. Occasionally the maté is sucked up through a tube or straw.

Our Central American neighbors always show hospitality to their guests by offering them a delicious cup of coffee instead. The Brazilian often uses half an hour sipping his coffee in the café in the middle of the morning or afternoon.

In addition to the Yerba maté and the coffee, we find another universal beverage. Long before the use of tea or coffee was known in Europe, the Aztecs of Mexico and the natives of Ecuador and Guatemala were accustomed to serve their afternoon "chocolath."

Aristocratic foods have been introduced from time to time by the English, Spanish, Portuguese, and Germans. They planted partridges, rabbits, pheasants, pigeons, and other game. Here is a sportsman's paradise, but he finds few consumers for his game. The peon is ever faithful to his mutton and beef.

Native foods also have an influence on the menu. South America supplies the tropical worlds, both old and new, with the tapioca from the cassava roots. The juice of this cassava is boiled to a thick soup under the name of "cassareep," and forms the basis for the best Indian dishes: the pepper pot, and the well-known Worcestershire sauce. Cassava meal is made into cakes and cooked as a staple food, and is highly palatable and nutritious. Like hardtack, it will keep in any climate.

Avocados, also, are abundant and available almost the year around. They are not raised for the market in these Latin-American countries, but the natives depend upon them for food. Indians consider an avocado, four or five tortillas, and a cup of coffee a good meal. Avocados are valuable as a fruit and for their oil. The natives have various methods of eating them. Sometimes they break the avocado in half and sprinkle with salt; sometimes they scoop the pieces out with their fingers on a tortilla; or add it to their meat or soup at the time of serving; or mash the pulp with chopped onions and seasonings.

Other foods made use of by the natives are: arrowroot, sago, coconuts, plantains (bananas), sweet potatoes, oranges, tunas (prickly pears), figs, mangoes, grapes, squashes, melons, chayote, maize, potatoes, coffee, and chocolate; also turkeys, ducks, hens, and other meat.

In the recipes to follow, let us consider just what can be developed, when the traditional Spanish and Portuguese dishes are blended with the natural resources and native customs of a wonderful country.

Sopas (Soups)

Amazon Cream

3 avocados	1½ teaspoons salt
2 quarts milk	4 tablespoons flour
2 sprigs parsley	2 tablespoons butter
2 stalks celery	1 egg yolk
Cayenne and nutmeg	½ cup cream

1. Peel and cut avocados and cook with milk, parsley, and diced celery for twenty minutes.
2. Add parsley, cayenne, nutmeg, and salt, and cook slowly for thirty-five minutes.
3. Put through a sieve, add flour and butter, and return to saucepan. Add egg yolk diluted with a tablespoon of milk and the cream. Cook three minutes more.
4. Serve with croutons.

Argentine Potage

1 beef marrowbone	2 carrots, diced
1 veal knuckle	2 leeks, diced
1 teaspoon salt	2 onions, chopped
½ teaspoon pepper	1 turnip, diced
Sprig of thyme	½ cup tapioca
1 bay leaf and 1 clove	Grated meat and milk of 1 coconut

1. Put bone and knuckle in one gallon of water. Add seasonings and let come to a boil. Skim and add vegetables.
2. Cover and simmer two and a half hours. Skim fat from surface and strain.
3. Add tapioca and cook fifteen minutes. Then add coconut and cook ten minutes longer.

Bolivienne Potage

½ pound raw veal	2 quarts water
½ cup diced raw ham	Leeks, celery, parsley, chevril
2 tablespoons butter	
2 onions, chopped	Salt and pepper
1 quart broth	2 tomatoes
⅓ cup tapioca	

1. Cut meat into small pieces and brown in butter with onion. Add a quart of broth and two quarts of water, herbs tied together, and other seasonings Cook forty-five minutes.
2. Peel tomatoes and add to soup. Cook twenty-five minutes longer.
3. Remove herbs and add tapioca. Boil twenty minutes.

Sopa Sudra
(Brazil)

Bacon drippings	3 or 4 onions, chopped
Saffron or curry powder	Salt and pepper
1 tablespoon vinegar	6 eggs
Chopped mint or herbs	Bread or crackers

1. Mix bacon drippings, saffron, vinegar, and mint with three or four cups of water. Add onions, salt, pepper, and herbs, and boil until onions are well cooked.
2. When done, poach eggs in this liquid and place on pieces of bread in a soup plate. Pour soup over all.

Ajiaco (Pigeon Pea Soup)
(West Indies)

1½ cups pigeon peas	Salt and pepper
1 onion	2 sweet potatoes or yams
2 or 3 slices bacon or ham bones	2 tanias or white potatoes
Thyme, parsley	4 or 5 tomatoes
	½ pound pork

1. Boil peas until soft. Season with salt and pepper.
2. Make a soup of other ingredients, properly sliced or diced.
3. Combine mixtures and cook until well blended. Remove bones.

Sopa de Crema de Gandules (Cream of Pigeon Pea Soup)
(Puerto Rico)

½ cup pigeon peas	Herbs as desired
1 quart water slightly salted	¼ teaspoon garlic juice
1 tablespoon onion juice	3 cups thin, seasoned white sauce
¼ teaspoon celery salt	

1. Boil peas in salted water until soft.
2. Mash peas and press through a sieve, saving water.
3. Mix other ingredients, add to peas, and heat.

Sopa de Avocado (Avocado Soup)
(Guatemala)

Consommé or beef tea	Salt and pepper
Sprig of mint	Lemon juice
1 avocado	

1. Make a beef tea and add mint. Season. Add lemon just before serving.
2. Cube avocado, place in a soup dish, and add soup. Allow one cube for each spoonful of soup.

Note: Mushrooms may also be added.

Sopa de Queso (Cheese Soup)
(Cuba)

1 quart consommé or stock	2 tablespoons butter
Squares of toast	1 tablespoon cheese for each
4 onions, sliced	serving

1. Boil consommé and add onions, which have been sautéd in butter.
2. Arrange toast in soup plates. Pour on soup and sprinkle with cheese.

Mondongo (Pepper Pot)
(Venezuela)

1 cup garbanzos	2 or 3 cloves of garlic, fried
1 pound tripe	in lard
1 calf's foot	6 tomatoes, cut in pieces
6 quarts water	1 onion, chopped
Lemon	2 yams, diced
Bouquet of herbs	1 pumpkin, cubed
Salt, vinegar, Worcester-	4 carrots, sliced
shire	36 small masa balls (dried
½ pound ham, cubed	corn)
1 cabbage, shredded	

1. Soak garbanzos overnight in salted water. Drain.
2. Cook tripe, calf's foot, and garbanzos in lemon water. Cook all day. The longer they cook the better.
3. Add bouquet of herbs and seasonings on second day, and cook again.
4. About two hours before serving, add other ingredients.

Colór

1 cup beef suet
½ onion, chopped

3 red peppers, chopped
⅓ teaspoon cayenne

1. Heat suet in a frying pan and add onion, peppers, and cayenne.
2. Simmer a few minutes. Strain.

Cazuela (A Little Pot)
(Chile)

6 loin pork chops or fowl
2 quarts water
1 summer squash, diced
Pieces of pumpkin, diced
Dozen string beans, cut
2 ears green corn, cut from
   cob or in inch lengths
2 onions, diced
1 bell pepper, cut in pieces
½ cup peas
1 tablespoon colór

1 teaspoon comino (cumin-
   seed)
Salt and pepper
1 egg white, slightly beaten
2 tablespoons rice
Sprig of mint
2 tablespoons minced
   parsley
2 potatoes
1 egg yolk, slightly beaten
1 tablespoon vinegar

1. Simmer meat in water until tender.
2. Add vegetables, except potatoes, colór, seasonings, rice, and herbs, and cook until tender. Add egg white and cook five minutes. Skim.
3. Boil potatoes and make a paste of potatoes, egg yolk, and vinegar. Put in a tureen and pour soup over it.

Sopitas (Little Soup)
(Chile)

4 slices stale bread
Colór
1 or 2 sprigs mint
1 teaspoon vinegar

1 egg
Salt and cayenne
Beef or mutton broth
Grated cheese

1. Cut slices of bread in half and fry in colór until crisp. Place in tureen with mint and vinegar.
2. Beat egg, add seasoning, and pour it on the toast.
3. Cover all with broth and sprinkle with cheese.

Cream of Yautia Soup (Cream of Sweet Potato Soup)

(Puerto Rico)

1 cup yautia	1 teaspoon salt
2 cups water	Herbs as desired
1 teaspoon onion juice	4 tablespoons butter
¼ teaspoon garlic juice	2 tablespoons flour
¼ teaspoon celery salt	2 cups milk
⅛ teaspoon pepper	Chopped parsley

1. Cut yautia in cubes and boil in water with seasonings.
2. Remove herbs and force yautia through a sieve.
3. Cream butter and flour, and add milk. Then add this sauce to yautia.
4. Reheat for ten minutes and serve hot. Garnish with chopped parsley.

Salsas (Sauces)

Criolla Sauce

(Puerto Rico)

¼ cup chopped ham	1 tablespoon herbs (marjo-
¼ cup chopped salt pork	ram, coriander, parsley)
2 teaspoons salt	½ cup chopped onion
1 teaspoon vegetable	½ cup chopped tomato
coloring	¼ clove garlic
1 tablespoon capers	½ cup chopped peppers

1. Sauté ham and salt pork well.
2. Add all other ingredients and cook for five minutes.
3. Add to soup or stews as desired.

Salsa Herida (Boiled Dressing)

(Puerto Rico)

1 teaspoon mustard	2 egg yolks, beaten
2 teaspoons flour	2 tablespoons butter, melted
Cayenne	¾ cup milk
2 teaspoons salt	¼ cup vinegar

1. Combine dry ingredients with egg yolks, and add butter and milk.
2. Add vinegar slowly.
3. Place in upper part of a double boiler and cook over hot water until it thickens. Stir constantly.

Peruvian Sauce

4 tablespoons butter
1 medium onion, sliced thin
1 small red chili pepper, minced (or ¼ teaspoon cayenne)

1 clove garlic, minced
1 pimiento, minced
½ cup grated American cheese
Salt and pepper

1 teaspoon vinegar

1. Melt butter in a saucepan, and add onion, garlic, chili pepper, and pimiento. Sauté until onion is yellow.
2. Add cheese, salt, and pepper, and cook until the cheese is melted and well blended.
3. Add vinegar just before serving.

Note: Serve with boiled potatoes, summer squash, cucumbers, or cauliflower.

Huevos (Eggs)

Huevos (Spanish Eggs) No. 1

2 onions
3 tomatoes
2 chili peppers

Parsley, minced
1 tablespoon melted butter
⅓ teaspoon salt

6 eggs

1. Chop onions, tomatoes, and chili peppers. Brown with parsley in the butter, add salt, and cook five minutes.
2. Fry eggs on both sides and pour sauce over them.

Huevos (Spanish Eggs) No. 2

1 can tomatoes
Bread
1 onion, sliced

2 or 3 green peppers, sliced
Salt
Butter

Eggs

1. Empty a can of tomatoes in a frying pan and thicken with bread. Add onions, peppers, and seasoning.
2. Simmer gently and add butter. Break eggs on top and simmer until eggs are cooked. Dip some of the mixture over eggs as they are cooking.

Havana Eggs

1 cup oil or lard
1 cup tomatoes
3 hard-cooked eggs, minced
½ cup cracker crumbs
Salt and pepper

2 Spanish peppers
6 raw eggs
2 tablespoons minced parsley

1. Heat oil in a frying pan, and add tomatoes, minced eggs, and cracker crumbs. Cook a few minutes to blend.
2. Chop peppers and add to tomato mixture.
3. Break in raw eggs, season, and add parsley.
4. Cook in oven eight to ten minutes. (350°.)

Huevos Rellenos (Stuffed Eggs)
(Valparaiso)

4 hard-cooked eggs
Cream
Bread crumbs
Salt and pepper
1 cup warm milk

1 egg, well beaten
Flour
1 teaspoon olive oil
Fat for frying
Cream sauce

1. Cut eggs lengthwise. Mash yolks with a little cream and bread crumbs. Season and fill whites.
2. Make a batter of milk, egg, flour, salt, and olive oil. Let stand one hour.
3. Pour a large spoonful of batter into a pan of smoking fat. Place half an egg on the batter, face down. Fry it until brown. Drain.
4. Serve with cream sauce, to which the rest of egg mixture has been added.

Note: The batter can be seasoned with anchovy paste, sardines, grated cheese, or chopped ham.

Plátanos Soufflé (Banana Soufflé)

3 ripe plantains or more (5 bananas)
4 tablespoons butter
4 tablespoons flour

1 teaspoon salt
1 tablespoon sugar
Dash of pepper
⅔ cup milk

3 eggs

1. Wash, peel, and steam plantains. Press through a sieve.
2. Melt butter, and add flour, salt, and pepper. Add milk gradually. Cook until slightly thickened.
3. Remove from heat, and add plantains and beaten egg yolks. Fold in stiffly beaten egg whites.
4. Bake in a buttered pan or pyrex dish in a slow oven for fifteen minutes. (350°.)

Tortilla de Amarillo (Yellow Omelet)

2 or 3 bananas	6 tablespoons milk
1 teaspoon salt	6 eggs
Dash of pepper	Chopped parsley

1. Wash and peel bananas and cook in boiling, salted water for five minutes.
2. Cut into crosswise slices and sauté.
3. Add salt, pepper, and milk to the beaten egg yolks. Fold in stiffly beaten egg whites.
4. Put into a buttered baking dish and add bananas. Cook until set. Finish in the oven.
5. Fold over, remove to a hot platter, and garnish with parsley.

Tortilla de Arroz (Rice Omelet)
(Puerto Rico)

2 cups cooked rice	Pepper
1 teaspoon salt	6 eggs

1. Add rice, salt, and pepper to well-beaten egg yolks.
2. Fold in stiffly beaten egg whites. Cook in a buttered pan.
3. Fold over and serve with legumes (peas or beans).

Soufflá de Arroz (Rice Soufflé)
(Puerto Rico)

1 cup milk	Salt and pepper
2 tablespoons fat	1 cup cooked rice
2 tablespoons flour	3 eggs

1. Make a white sauce of milk, fat, flour, salt, and pepper.
2. Mix rice and well-beaten egg yolks, and add to white sauce. Fold in stiffly beaten egg whites.
3. Pour into a greased mold. Cook in a slow oven until mixture is set and lower surface brown. (350°.)
4. Serve with legumes.

Huevos de Guatemala (Guatemala Eggs) No. 1

3 green peppers	6 slices ham
Hot butter	6 slices toast
	6 eggs

1. Split peppers lengthwise and fry in hot butter for two minutes.
2. Fry ham and place each slice on a piece of toast along with peppers.
3. Poach eggs and place on top of ham.

Huevos de Guatemala (Guatemala Eggs) No. 2

2 Spanish onions
2 bell peppers
3 tablespoons olive oil

½ cup corn
6 large tomatoes, sliced
½ teaspoon salt

6 eggs

1. Slice onions and peppers and fry in oil. Add tomatoes and salt. Simmer a half hour and put in a baking dish. Cover with corn.
2. Cover with a little oil. Break six eggs at equal distances. Cover and cook until eggs are set.

Queso (Cheese)

Empanaditas (Fried Cheese Cakes)
(Bolivia)

1¼ cups flour
2 tablespoons melted lard
Tepid, salted water

1 cup thin white sauce
½ pound cheese, cubed
Deep fat or plenty of hot lard

1. Mix flour, melted lard, and enough tepid water to make a soft dough. Divide into bits and roll very thin.
2. Make a white sauce and add cheese. Cook until blended. Cool before putting it onto the thinly rolled paste.
3. Put a spoonful of cheese mixture at intervals on paste. Fold over, pressing the part between the mixture. Cut out with a cutter.
4. Fry in hot lard.

Ajoqueso (Cheese and Garlic Rarebit)

3 Spanish peppers
1 onion
1 clove garlic
2 tablespoons oil, or more
1 cup grated cheese

1 tablespoon butter
Salt
Dash of cayenne or tabasco
Cream to make it pour nicely

Toasted biscuits or tortillas

1. Boil peppers and rub pulp through a sieve.
2. Chop onion and garlic and fry in oil. Add other ingredients, except cream. Add cream as it heats.
3. Serve immediately on toasted biscuits or tortillas.

Migas (Crumbs) No. 1

4 slices stale bread	Crumbled cheese
1 onion, chopped fine	Stoned olives
1 chili, ground	2 hard-cooked eggs,
Pinch of sweet marjoram	chopped fine

Lard

1. Soak slices of bread in water and squeeze dry.
2. Fry onion, chili, and marjoram in lard. Add bread and cook ten minutes, stirring to cook on all sides.
3. Remove to a hot platter and cover with freshly grated cheese, stoned olives, and hard-cooked eggs.

Migas de Queso (Cheese Crumbs) No. 2
(Paraguay)

1 small loaf stale bread	1 red pepper, minced
2 tablespoons butter or bacon fat	¾ pound cream cheese cut in pieces (or ¾ pound cottage cheese)
1 large onion, thinly sliced	
2 small tomatoes, thinly sliced	½ teaspoon salt
	¼ teaspoon pepper

Paprika

1. Cover bread with hot water and soak fifteen minutes.
2. Press all water possible from bread and break into small pieces.
3. Heat butter in a saucepan, and add onion and cook until soft, and then add the pepper and tomatoes. Cook ten minutes.
4. Add bread, cheese, salt, pepper, and a dash of paprika. Cook until smooth and well blended, stirring constantly.
5. Serve either plain, or poured over poached eggs.

Pudín de Queso (Cheese Pudding)
(Brazil)

2 cups sugar	1 cup grated cheese
8 egg yolks	1 cup milk
4 egg whites	1 tablespoon butter

Salt and pepper

1. Melt sugar to a sirup and line an angel food cake pan.
2. Add well-beaten egg yolks and cheese to milk, which has been thickened with butter and flour. Season. Fold in stiffly beaten egg whites.
3. Pour mixture into pan and steam for one hour.

Ballos con Queso (Cheese Rolls)
. (Costa Rica)

2 pounds Edam or Ameri-   1 cup milk
    can cheese   Tabasco sauce
    2 loaves fresh bread

1. Grate cheese and mix with milk and tabasco sauce. Spread it on bread sliced very thin, and make a roll of each slice.
2. Bake rolls in the oven until brown.

Note: These may also be made with some of the prepared cheeses on the market.

Empanadas de Queso (Cheese Turnovers)
(Ecuador)

3 tablespoons butter   A little water
2 cups flour   ¼ to ½ cup white cheese
Salt   2 hard-cooked eggs,
1 egg, beaten   chopped
    ¼ cup raisins

1. Cut butter into flour and salt. Add egg and water to make a dough. Roll out thin. Spread the following paste over it.
2. Mash cheese and mix well with raisins and hard-cooked eggs.
3. Cut into squares of four or five inches. Fold corner to form a triangle. Flute edges.
4. Cook as a fritter in boiling lard. Sprinkle with sugar.

Patatas y Queso (Potatoes and Cheese)

2 egg yolks   Cheese, grated or chopped
2 cups mashed potatoes   1 egg, beaten
Salt and chili powder   Bread crumbs
Thick cream   Deep fat

1. Beat egg yolks and add potatoes, salt, and chili powder. Roll into balls the size of a peach.
2. Make a paste of cream and cheese. Insert a spoonful in middle of each ball. Close.
3. Roll in beaten egg and bread crumbs. Fry in deep fat.

Note: Soft cream cheese may be used for cream and cheese.

Emparedado (Fried Potato Cakes)

1 cup cold mashed potatoes
1 cup thick sour cream or milk
2 eggs, beaten
1 cup flour
½ teaspoon soda

½ teaspoon salt
Minced ham or grated cheese
Chopped olives
Chopped parsley
Chili sauce

1. Beat potato, milk, and eggs. Sift flour, soda, and salt into it.
2. Drop by spoonfuls on a hot griddle. Cook on both sides.
3. Put ham or cheese, chopped olives, and parsley on one cake. Place another cake on top to form a sandwich.
4. Serve hot with chili sauce.

Spanish Rarebit No. 1
(Panama)

1 small onion, chopped
1 tablespoon butter
1 can tomato soup
½ pound cheese, cut fine

2 eggs, beaten
1 tablespoon Worcestershire
½ teaspoon dry mustard

Dash cayenne

1. Cook onion in butter until soft, but not colored. Add tomato soup.
2. When well blended and hot, add cheese.
3. When cheese is melted, add eggs and condiments.
4. Stir a few minutes until thick and smooth. Do not boil.
5. Serve on crackers.

Spanish Rarebit No. 2
(Panama)

1 Bermuda onion, grated
1 tablespoon butter
½ can tomato soup
1 pound cheese, grated
4 eggs, beaten

1 tablespoon Worcestershire
1 teaspoon dry mustard
¼ to ½ teaspoon tabasco sauce

½ teaspoon salt

1. Cook same as No. 1.

Queso de Venezuela (Cheese Venezuela)

1 Edam cheese
1 chicken, 3½ to 4½ pounds
½ cup olive oil

1 small onion, minced
1 teaspoon salt
¼ teaspoon pepper

1 to 1½ cups boiled rice

1. Remove a small circle from top of cheese and take out soft inside cheese carefully, leaving rind whole and solid. Pour hot water over rind and soak for twenty-four hours.
2. Boil chicken in salted water until tender. Cool, and remove meat from bones. Cut in small pieces.
3. Heat oil in a frying pan until very hot, add onion, and cook until soft. Add salt and pepper.
4. Add chicken and cook for a few minutes, stirring constantly.
5. Add rice and mix well. Cook until hot through.
6. Drain cheese rind and fill with chicken mixture.
7. Place in a large baking dish. Bake twenty minutes, or until soft. (425°.)

Pescado (Fish)

Shrimp Pie
(Brazil)

1 cup butter
1 tablespoon lard
Salt

3 cups flour
4 egg yolks, beaten
Shrimps, well seasoned

1. Mix butter and lard with salt and flour. Add eggs and mix well.
2. Roll thin, and alternate layers of dough and shrimps in a buttered baking dish, finishing with dough on top.
3. Bake in a moderate oven until the crust is nicely browned. (450°.)

Escabeche
(Brazil)

Any fish for frying
French dressing

Seasonings: bay leaf, ginger, and other spices, lime juice

1. Fry fish.
2. Add seasonings to French dressing and pour over fish.

Vatapa
(Brazil)

1 onion, chopped
1 clove garlic, minced
2 bay leaves
2 cups water
½ pound any firm fish
Salt and pepper
1 pound fresh shrimps
2 tablespoons oil

Corn meal and flour mixed
  to thicken gravy
Peanuts
½ cup toasted ground
  almonds
½ pound dried shrimps
2 tablespoons milk of coconut

1. Put onion, garlic, and bay leaves in a pan of water on fire.
2. When it boils, add fish, salt, pepper, and bay leaves. Simmer until tender. Remove fish and add shrimps. When shrimps are cooked, remove them from saucepan. Strain juice through a cloth.
3. Thicken broth with corn meal and flour. Add oil, peanuts, almonds, dried shrimps, and coconut milk. Add shrimps, and fish with bones removed.

Cebiche
(Peru)

Fresh lime juice
Fillets of any fish
2 or 3 tomatoes, chopped
Small white onions, minced
  (equal to tomatoes)
1 chili pepper, minced

Finely chopped red or green
  pepper
1 clove garlic, minced
Parsley, minced
Brown sugar to taste
Salt and pepper

1. Pour lime juice over fish and let stand six hours. (Not cooked.)
2. Mix other ingredients and serve over fish.

Note: The fish may be cooked if preferred.

Arroz con Pescado (Fish and Rice)

1 cup rice
Butter for frying rice
1 tablespoon chopped onion

1 tablespoon butter
1 cup shredded fish
Salt and paprika

1. Boil rice twenty minutes in salted water. Drain and set aside to dry. Then cool.
2. When cold, fry in butter.
3. Fry onion in a tablespoon of butter and add fish.
4. Mix all together and add salt and paprika.

Pescado en Fuente (Fish-in-the-Fountain)
(Chile)

Slices of fish
Slices of tomato
Slices of onion, fried
Slices of boiled potato

Slices of hard-cooked eggs
Croutons of bread
Stock
Salt and pepper

1. Place fish, tomato, onion, potato, and eggs in layers. Season each layer. Place croutons on top.
2. Add a little stock and butter, if desired.
3. Bake slowly for one hour. (375°-400°.)

Pescado Cubano (Cuban Fish)

3 pounds fish
Mixture of nutmeg, flour, and salt
2 cups fresh corn cut from the cob
6 apples, cubed
1 quart onions, diced

1 pint diced white or sweet potatoes
1 quart tomato pulp
2 green and 1 red pepper, minced
2 cups diced bacon
Salt and pepper

1. Rub fish with nutmeg, flour, and salt. Put in a greased baking pan.
2. Mix other ingredients. Put half over fish. Bake for one hour.
3. Add rest of vegetables and bake another hour. Baste with oil if too dry. (375°.)

Portuguese Codfish
(Brazil)

1 pound salt codfish
Olive oil
2 onions, minced
2 cloves garlic, minced

1 cup tomato sauce
½ cup water
3 or 4 eggs, beaten
Minced parsley

1. Soak codfish overnight. Drain and boil for one and one-half hours. Cut in pieces.
2. Heat oil in a saucepan and brown fish on both sides.
3. Add onions and garlic, cook a few minutes, and then add tomato sauce and water. Simmer one-half hour.
4. When ready to serve, add eggs and parsley.

Arroz con Bacalao al Horno (Scalloped Rice with Codfish)
(Puerto Rico)

1 cup salt codfish	1 cup bread crumbs
1 cup rice	1 cup medium white sauce

1. Soak the codfish overnight. Drain, cover with fresh water, and boil one-half hour.
2. Boil rice in salted water until soft.
3. Place a layer of crumbs in bottom of a greased baking dish. Add half the rice, half the fish, and half the white sauce. Sprinkle with crumbs. Repeat.
4. Heat twenty minutes in a moderate oven. (375°.)

Bacalao Como la Criolla (Codfish Creole)

1 pound salt codfish	½ cup olive oil, or more
6 onions, chopped	1 tablespoon paprika
Chopped celery	Salt
Bay leaf	4 to 6 tomatoes

1. Soak codfish overnight.
2. Brown onions, celery, and bay leaf in oil. Add paprika, salt, and tomatoes.
3. Flake fish and spread a layer in a saucepan. Cover with vegetable mixture. Repeat until all ingredients are used.
4. Cover and cook over slow heat one hour or longer.

Pisto Manchego
(Cuba)

1 cup shrimps	1 cup tomato sauce
1 cup cooked green peas	1 cup chopped ham
1 cup diced cooked as- paragus	6 eggs, beaten
	Salt and pepper

Fat for frying

1. Mix the above and scramble in hot fat.
2. Serve for lunch or dinner, either alone or with cooked rice.

Paella
(Cuba)

2 cups diced chicken	Salt and pepper
1 pound pork, diced	1 cup rice
1 onion, minced	Saffron or curry powder
Sprig of parsley	Mixture of sea food

Water

1. Boil chicken with pork, onion, parsley, salt, pepper, and water to cover until tender. Strain.
2. Cook rice in broth and color with saffron or curry powder.
3. Mix chicken, rice, and sea food. Bake in a casserole for one hour. (400°.)

Brazilian Shrimps

1 onion, cut in strips	2 tablespoons flour
1 green pepper, cut in strips	1 tablespoon butter
2 cups tomato juice	1 teaspoon sugar
1 pound shrimps	Salt

1. Place onion and pepper in a saucepan with tomato juice.
2. Cook fifteen minutes and add shrimps.
3. Cream flour and butter. Add to tomato mixture, season with salt, and simmer until thick and smooth.

Curried Shrimps
(West Indies)

1 cup rice	1 tablespoon curry powder
1 small onion	1 teaspoon salt
2 tablespoons butter	1 cup stock
3 tablespoons grated coconut	1 cup shrimps
	1 tablespoon lemon juice

1. Boil rice in salted water until soft.
2. Slice onion thin and fry in butter.
3. Stir in coconut and curry powder, salt, and stock. Simmer one-half hour.
4. Add cooked shrimps and lemon juice.
5. Place rice on a serving dish and pour this mixture over it.

Entradas (Entrees)

Lentejas con Tomates (Lentils with Tomatoes)
(Brazil)

2 cups lentils
½ cup lard or olive oil
1 cup minced ham
1 cup sliced onions
2 cloves garlic, minced

1 cup tomato purée
1 tablespoon seasoning
(chili powder, cayenne, salt, pepper or coriander)

½ cup grated cheese

1. Wash lentils and boil in stock or water until tender.
2. Heat fat and fry ham, onions, and garlic until brown. Add tomato and seasonings. Cook three minutes.
3. Mix with lentils and put all in a casserole.
4. Sprinkle with cheese. Bake until cheese melts. (450°.)

Frituras con Pollo de Guatemala (Chicken Croquettes)
(Guatemala)

1 chicken, about 3 pounds
2 bay leaves
4 whole cloves
2 tablespoons minced onion
2 tablespoons minced parsley
1 pair sweetbreads

1 pint milk or cream
1 tablespoon butter
1 tablespoon flour
½ teaspoon nutmeg
⅛ teaspoon cayenne
2 eggs, beaten
Salt and pepper

Cracker crumbs

1. Unjoint chicken and cover with water. Add bay leaves, cloves, and one tablespoon each of parsley and onion. Cover and simmer until chicken is tender.
2. Clean sweetbreads well and soak fifteen minutes in cold water. Simmer for fifteen minutes. Dip in cold water and skin.
3. Chop sweetbreads and chicken. Measure two cups of each.
4. Make a sauce of one cup of milk, flour, and butter. Add the rest of the onions, parsley, and seasonings.
5. Add chicken and sweetbreads. Cool and form into croquettes.
6. Dip croquettes into beaten egg, roll in cracker crumbs, and allow to dry for one hour. Dip again in egg and crumbs.
7. Fry in deep hot fat until light brown. Drain on paper.
8. Garnish with parsley, water cress, or olives.

Un Pastelao de Carne (Lamb Pie)
(Brazil)

1½ pounds stewing meat (lamb)
Salt and pepper
4 tablespoons fat
8 small potatoes
2 onions, minced
1 bell pepper, chopped
1 teaspoon chili powder (optional)
4 tablespoons flour
¼ cup water
Biscuit dough

1. Remove skin and bones from lamb and cut in pieces. Season with salt and pepper.
2. Melt fat and brown lamb.
3. Add potatoes, onions, bell pepper, chile powder, and enough water to cover. Simmer slowly for two hours, or until meat is tender and vegetables well cooked.
4. Thicken gravy with flour blended with one-fourth cup of water.
5. Put in a buttered baking dish and cover with biscuit dough.
6. Bake in a hot oven for twenty minutes. (475°.)

Sopa (Cheese and Corn-meal Loaf)
(Paraguay)

1 can tomatoes (No. 2)
2 medium onions, chopped
4 tablespoons fat
1 teaspoon salt
Few grains pepper
1½ cups corn meal
⅛ teaspoon soda
1 teaspoon baking powder
1½ cups cheese
1 cup milk
3 tablespoons melted butter

1. Drain juice from can of tomatoes and reserve it.
2. Brown onions in fat and add tomato pulp. Cook five minutes.
3. Add juice, salt, and pepper. Heat to boiling point.
4. Make a dough of corn meal, soda, baking powder, cheese, milk, and melted butter. Add to tomato mixture. Pour into a loaf pan.
5. Bake in a slow oven one and a half hours, or until firm and brown. (350°-375°.)
6. Cut into slices to serve.

Albornia de Chayote

3 chayotes or squash
4 ounces ham or salt pork
1 onion, chopped
1 tomato, chopped
½ green pepper, chopped

1 clove garlic, minced
Pepper and paprika
Coriander leaves
1 teaspoon salt
¼ cup water

3 eggs

1. Wash chayotes and boil until tender. Peel and cut in cubes.
2. Grind meat and brown in a frying pan for five minutes. Add onion, tomato, green pepper, garlic, salt, pepper, paprika, coriander, and water. Cover and cook slowly for five minutes.
3. Add chayote and more water if necessary. Cook five minutes.
4. Add eggs, well beaten, and remove mixture from fire at once.

Sopón de Gandules (Pigeon Pea Chowder)

1½ cups pigeon peas
¼ teaspoon soda
¼ cup salt pork, cubed
1 cup fresh corn
1 cup potatoes, cubed
¼ cup onions, chopped

¼ clove garlic, minced
1 teaspoon salt
Pepper
3 cups milk
1 tablespoon butter
Crackers

1. Soak peas overnight. Drain. Add one quart of water and soda. Bring slowly to a boil. Boil five to eight minutes. Drain.
2. Remove skins and cook in fresh water until partly done. Add salt pork, corn, potato, onions, garlic, salt, and pepper. Cook until water is absorbed.
3. Add milk and butter. Heat and pour over hot crackers.

Pollo de Guatemala (Guatemala Chicken)

1 pound ground pork
1 onion, chopped
1 tomato, chopped
3 tablespoons chopped pickle

Garlic, minced
2 dozen raisins and almonds
Salt and pepper
1 chicken

1. Make a stuffing of pork, onion, tomato, garlic, pickle, almonds, raisins, salt, and pepper.
2. Stuff chicken. Rub breast with butter. Place in a roasting pan, and add a little water or stock. Roast until tender and uniformly brown, basting it occasionally. (450°-475°.)

Pollo Picante (Chicken Picante)
(Peru)

Fowl, cut in pieces	2 tablespoons lard
Salt	6 chili peppers
4 medium potatoes	2 tablespoons olive oil
2 onions, chopped	1 cup chopped cheese

1. Cover fowl with boiling water, add salt, and stew until nearly tender.
2. Add potatoes, cut in half. Stew for twenty minutes more.
3. A half hour before serving, fry onions in lard and add pulp of peppers. Bring all to a boil and add oil and cheese.
4. Stir until cheese is melted, and pour all over chicken. Bring to a boil, being careful not to burn.

Pavo de Guatemala (Turkey)
(Guatemala)

Turkey	2 slices boiled ham, diced
1 pound chestnuts	1 sausage, chopped
2 loaves stale French bread	1 tablespoon capers
½ cup tomato catsup	1 teaspoon chopped parsley
½ onion, grated	1 teaspoon chili powder
½ cup walnuts, chopped	1 tablespoon vinegar
½ cup white wine	1 teaspoon salt
½ cup ripe olives, stoned	1 tablespoon each raisins
4 eggs, beaten	and currants

1. Boil chestnuts twenty minutes. Shell, skin, and chop.
2. Grate bread.
3. Mix all ingredients together. Stuff turkey and roast it.

Pollo de Portola (Chicken Portola)
(West Indies)

1 fresh coconut	1 green pepper, chopped
2 ears corn	6 tomatoes, stewed
2 onions, sliced	1 clove garlic, minced
4 tablespoons olive oil	Salt and pepper
2 tablespoons diced bacon	1 spring chicken

1. Cut off top of coconut. Remove nearly all meat.
2. Cut corn from cob and add three tablespoons of coconut to it.
3. Cook onions in oil, and add bacon, pepper, tomatoes, garlic, salt, and pepper. Cook until it thickens. Strain into corn.
4. Add chicken cut in four parts. Then fill coconut shell. Using top as a cover, close tightly and seal with a paste to keep the flavors in.
5. Put coconut into a pan of water and cook in the oven for one hour. Baste frequently to keep coconut from burning.

Pollo y Legumbres (Fried Chicken and Vegetables)
(Costa Rica)

2 small spring chickens	8 strips lean bacon
4 cups boiling water	3 hearts lettuce, quartered
1 teaspoon salt	1 clove garlic, minced
12 small white onions	6 cloves
8 to 10 young carrots, halved lengthwise	4 egg yolks, well beaten
	Juice of 1 lemon

1. Place chickens in a saucepan, and add water and salt. Boil for ten minutes. Remove chickens and cut into serving pieces.
2. Parboil onions and carrots five minutes in boiling, salted water. Drain and wipe dry.
3. Fry bacon, and remove from pan. Add chicken, onions, carrots, lettuce, garlic, and cloves. Cook slowly until chicken is a golden brown and vegetables tender. Turn chicken several times.
4. Boil chicken stock down to two cups. Pour a little stock over egg yolks. Put in top of a double boiler, and add remaining stock and lemon juice. Cook until mixture thickens.
5. Arrange chicken on a hot platter, and place vegetables on top.
6. Pour sauce around chicken and vegetables.

Chicken with Green Corn
(Peru)

1 small chicken	1 large green pepper, chopped
½ cup water	
2 tablespoons butter	1 clove garlic, minced
1 large tomato, peeled and chopped	2 cups grated green corn
	Salt and pepper
1 onion, thinly sliced	Dash cayenne

1. Disjoint chicken and place in a saucepan. Add water and boil until chicken is nearly tender. There should be no water left.

2. Melt butter in a frying pan, add onion and garlic, and sauté until soft. Add tomato and green pepper, and cook for five minutes.

3. Add chicken, corn, salt, and pepper. Cook until chicken is tender.

Note: Canned corn put through a grinder may be substituted for green corn.

Pastel Español de Polli (Spanish Chicken Pie)

1 chicken	5 tomatoes
2 onions, minced	2 dozen ripe olives
2 green peppers, minced	1 clove garlic, minced
1½ tablespoons flour	7 ears corn
Salt and pepper	

1. Cut up and boil chicken until tender.

2. Fry onions and pepper in chicken fat. Add flour and blend.

3. Stew tomatoes and add olives and garlic.

4. Cut corn from cob and season. Put in a greased baking dish. Add chicken, then other ingredients, and cover with gravy made by thickening chicken broth.

5. Bake until brown. (400°.)

Fricassee de Pollos (Chicken Fricassee)

1 chicken	1 tablespoon chopped parsley
2 onions, chopped	1 cup tomato juice
2 cloves garlic, minced	2 tablespoons toasted bread crumbs
Lard	Salt, pepper, and Spanish sage
1 cup green olives	
6 stuffed olives	

1. Clean chicken and cut into small pieces. Fry in lard with onion and garlic until tender.

2. Add olives, parsley, tomato juice, bread crumbs, salt, pepper, and Spanish sage. Mix well.

3. Cook ten minutes, or until thoroughly heated.

Arroz con Pollo (Chicken and Rice) No. 1
(Cuba)

Diced bread
½ cup olive oil
2 cloves garlic
1 fat fowl
3 onions, chopped
4 tomatoes, chopped

1 tablespoon minced parsley
4 red chilies, chopped
Salt
¼ teaspoon saffron or
    curry powder
2 cups rice

Water, if needed

1. Brown diced bread in oil and put aside for a garnish. Then fry garlic a few minutes and discard it.
2. Clean chicken and cut it into joints. Place in oil for ten minutes, turning constantly.
3. Add onions, tomatoes, parsley, and chilies to chicken. Stir all carefully and cook ten minutes. Season with salt and curry powder.
4. Add rice and turn all into a casserole. Let simmer until rice is tender.
5. Lift chicken onto a platter and make a ring of rice around it. Garnish with croutons.

Arroz con Pollo (Chicken and Rice) No. 2
(Cuba)

1½ cups rice
¼ teaspoon saffron or
    curry powder
Chicken for frying

1 cup cooked peas
2 or 3 Spanish red or green
    peppers, thinly sliced
Salt

1. Cook rice in boiling, salted water with saffron or curry powder.
2. Fry chicken and mix it with peas and peppers. Season with salt.
3. Combine chicken mixture and rice. Put in a casserole or clay pot and heat thoroughly in oven. (400°.)

Note: This is the most popuar dish in Cuba, and is served almost every day.

Arroz con Pollo (Chicken and Rice) No. 3
(Cuba)

3 young chickens
Fat for frying
6 onions, chopped
4 cloves garlic, minced
3 tomatoes, chopped
1 green pepper, chopped
Broth

1 cup dry sherry or champagne
1½ pounds rice
Salt, pepper, saffron
Juice of 1 lime
Red pepper or pimiento for
    garnish

1. Disjoint chickens and fry with vegetables. Cook all thoroughly. Remove meat from bones.

2. Make broth of bones. Strain it into a frying pan.

3. Cook a short time and add sherry or champagne. Then add rice, chicken, salt, pepper, and saffron. Cook over a slow fire or in a casserole until rice is soft.

4. Serve in the casserole and garnish with peppers or pimientos.

Arroz con Pollo (Chicken and Rice) No. 4
(Nicaragua)

1 young chicken	½ pound rice
2 tomatoes, chopped	¼ pint capers
1 green pepper, chopped	½ pint olives
1 onion, chopped	1 pimiento, chopped

Salt

1. Boil chicken two hours with tomatoes, pepper, onion, and about one tablespoon of salt, in enough water to cover it.

2. Wash rice well and add it to chicken with capers, olives, and pimiento. Cook one-half hour longer, or until the rice is soft. Add more salt, if necessary. Let rice dry a few minutes before serving.

Arroz con Pollo (Chicken and Rice) No. 5
(Puerto Rico)

1 small chicken	1 Spanish sausage (chorizo)
1 quart water	
2 small cans tomato sauce	1 teaspoon salt
1 cup rice	⅛ teaspoon pepper
1 dozen olives	½ dozen asparagus tips
1 can artichokes	1 can pimientos

1 bunch parsley

1. Joint chicken and sear it well. Add water and cook for one-half hour.

2. Add tomato sauce, washed rice, olives, artichokes, sausage cut in half-inch pieces, salt, and pepper. Cook until rice is tender.

3. Serve in original earthenware dish or kettle. Garnish with asparagus tips, pimientos, and parsley.

Arroz con Pollo (Chicken and Rice) No. 6
(Argentina)

.1 chicken or 1 pound fresh
   pork
Salt and pepper
3 tablespoons salad oil
1 green pepper, cut in one-
   inch squares

1 small onion, minced
2 cloves garlic, minced
1 or 2 sprigs parsley,
   minced
2 tomatoes, cut in pieces
1⅛ cups rice

Pinch of saffron

1. Disjoint chicken or cut meat into small pieces. Sprinkle with salt and pepper, and fry in oil in a large kettle until partially browned.
2. Add green pepper, onion, garlic, and parsley. Let it cook for several minutes.
3. Add tomatoes and cook all about five minutes longer.
4. Stir in about two quarts of boiling water and let mixture cook gently until meat is almost tender.
5. Wash rice, and add it to chicken, stirring to prevent its sticking to the bottom of kettle. Season to taste. Add saffron, and continue cooking until rice is tender. The result should not be dry, but rather a soft mixture. If too dry, add a little boiling water before removing from the fire.

Note: Leftover chicken may be used. Canned tomatoes or canned tomato sauce may be substituted for fresh tomatoes.

Pato con Arroz (Duck and Rice)
(Peru)

1 duck
Butter
½ cup ground onion
Pepper, salt, coriander

2 tablespoons minced
   parsley
1 clove garlic, minced
½ cup rice

1. Fry duck in butter and add pepper, salt, and coriander. Cover with water and boil until tender.
2. Add rice and boil five minutes longer. Then simmer forty-five minutes.

Arroz con Frijoles (Rice and Beans)
(Panama)

½ pound beans
1 pound rice
1 to 2 cups tomato juice
½ tablespoon Worcester-
   shire

3 green peppers, sliced
½ pound frankfurters,
   diced and fried
Pimientos
Salt

1. Soak beans overnight. Drain, cover with fresh, salted water, and boil until beans are nearly tender.
2. Add other ingredients and water enough to cover. Stir well.
3. Ten minutes later stir again. Then let simmer slowly until beans and rice are soft.

Arroz de Cubana (Cuban Rice)

1½ cups diced cold meat	6 eggs, fried
1 cup brown sauce or gravy	6 bananas, fried
2 cups boiled rice	Potato chips

1. Arrange a border of rice on a platter and put meat in middle.
2. Top rice with fried eggs, and place bananas on meat. Put chips around edge.

Carbonada de Criolla (Creole Stew)
(Argentina)

1 pound beef or veal, cut in half-inch cubes	6 peeled tomatoes
Flour	6 sweet potatoes, sliced
Fat or oil	1 cup peas or corn cut from the cob, or both
2 onions	Halves of peaches (¼ amount of meat)
3 peppers	

Salt and pepper

1. Dust meat with flour and brown in fat.
2. Chop onions, peppers, and tomatoes. Fry in fat, putting the onion and pepper in first, then adding tomatoes.
3. Add potatoes, peas, and corn. When half cooked, add peaches. Season to taste with salt and pepper.

Carbonada (Browned Stew)
(Uruguay)

1 or 2 onions, sliced	1 cup tomato sauce
Olive oil	3 cups water or stock
¼ cup minced parsley	1 cup beef or lamb, cubed
½ cup minced celery	1 cup potatoes, cubed

1 cup rice

1. Fry onions in oil and add parsley and celery. Add tomato sauce and stock.
2. Add meat and potatoes, then rice. Do not stir while rice is cooking. Shake the pan instead. Cook until rice is soft. Add more stock or water as needed.
3. Serve as dry stew.

Carbonada (Browned Stew)
(Chile)

1 tablespoon colór	2 cups cold beef or mutton,
1 slice onion	cubed
1 red pepper, chopped	2 potatoes, sliced thick
Small squares pumpkin	2 cups stock or water
Salt and pepper	1 tomato, chopped

1. Heat colór and fry onion, pepper, pumpkin, and meat. Season.
2. Add potatoes and when slightly colored, add stock and tomato.
3. Cover closely and simmer until vegetables are cooked.

Charquican
(Chile)

2 cups leftover meat, or	½ cup each, peas, string
jerked or chipped beef	beans, tomato, squash,
1 onion, chopped	corn cut from cob
Sprig of parsley and mint,	Salt and pepper
minced	Broth

2 or 3 potatoes

1. Mix all ingredients together except potatoes. Add enough broth to simmer until vegetables are tender.
2. Quarter potatoes and boil separately. Then combine.

Chupe
(Peru)

2 onions, sliced	1 teaspoon minced parsley
1 tablespoon butter	1 tablespoon washed rice
4 or 5 tomatoes, cut in	Salt, pepper, sugar
pieces	1 cup cream or milk
6 medium potatoes, peeled	1 egg, well beaten
and quartered	4 tablespoons grated cheese

1. Fry onions in butter until brown. Add other vegetables and rice. Cook all about twenty minutes. Season.
2. Add cream, egg, and cheese. Allow them to boil up once. Serve.

Lomo (Loin of Pork)
(Peru)

Tenderloin of pork
Grated onion and garlic
Salt, paprika, thyme

2 tablespoons tarragon
vinegar
5 tablespoons oil

1. Marinate meat for several hours in a sauce made by combining other ingredients. Turn several times.
2. Broil meat.
3. Heat sauce and pour over meat and serve.

Pudín de Maiz (Corn Pudding)
(Chile)

1 pound ground meat
Cold boiled chicken
1 green pepper, chopped
1 onion, chopped
1 tablespoon colór
1 dozen seeded raisins
1 dozen ripe olives

2 hard-cooked eggs, quartered
8 ears corn
1 tablespoon lard
3 eggs
1 tablespoon sugar
1 boiled onion, cut in pieces

Powdered sugar

1. Fry meat, chicken, pepper, and onion in colór. Add raisins and olives. Put all in a pudding dish. Arrange hard-cooked eggs over this.
2. Grate corn and fry in lard, stirring until pasty.
3. Mix beaten egg yolks, sugar, corn, and boiled onion. Fold in stiffly beaten egg whites. Spread over meat topped with eggs in the pudding dish.
4. Bake twenty minutes. Sprinkle with powdered sugar. Bake ten minutes more. (400°.)

Empanadas (Turnovers) No. 1
(Chile)

2 cups cold meat, diced
1 small onion, chopped
1 green pepper, chopped
Lard
Brown gravy

1 dozen raisins
2 hard-cooked eggs, sliced
½ cup ripe olives
Piecrust
Powdered sugar

1. Mix meat, onion, and pepper, and fry in lard. Add gravy, raisins, eggs, and olives.
2. Make a rich pastry, using one well-beaten egg as part of moisture.
3. Roll out crust. Place filling on half of it. Wet edge of the pastry, fold over, and pinch well together. Bake thirty minutes. (475°.)
4. Dust with powdered sugar before serving.

Empanaditas (Little Turnovers)
(Chile)

Make crust and mixture as above, but form into rounds the size of a saucer. Pinch edges well together and fry in deep fat. Drain and serve with powdered sugar.

Note: Cheese or preserves may be used in place of meat.

Empanadas (Turnovers) No. 2
(Chile)

2 tablespoons olive oil	1 pound raw meat, diced
2 tablespoons minced onion	1 tablespoon flour
¼ teaspoon thyme	1 cup meat stock
¼ teaspoon summer savory	3 tablespoons lard
¼ teaspoon oregano	4 cups flour
¼ teaspoon sage	¾ teaspoon salt
⅛ teaspoon pepper	3 tablespoons ice water
½ teaspoon salt	2 hard-cooked eggs

Raisins

1. Heat oil in a saucepan, and add onion and seasonings. Cook two or three minutes.
2. Add meat and cook until browned.
3. Add flour, and then stock. Stir until smooth. Let simmer until meat is tender.
4. Heat lard to boiling point, and combine with flour and salt. Mix it to a dough with ice water. Roll out and cut into six-inch rounds.
5. Place a generous tablespoon of meat mixture on one half of each round. Add one slice of egg and one teaspoon of raisins. Moisten edges of pastry, fold, and pinch together.
6. Fry in deep fat until nicely browned.

Note: The turnovers may be baked in a moderate oven if desired. (375°.)

Tamales No. 1
(Argentina)

5 or 6 ears corn	2 or 3 large onions, chopped
1 cup sugar	2 or 3 tomatoes, chopped
1 cup flour	2 or 3 peppers, chopped
2 tablespoons beef stock	Mixture of butter and oil
2 tablespoons canned to-	Salt and pepper
mato paste	

1. Scrape corn from cob and chop fine. Mix well with sugar and flour. Add stock and tomato paste. Season.

2. Make a sauce of onions, tomatoes, and peppers, fried in butter and oil. Combine mixtures and cook one hour. Cool.

3. Take two whole smooth cornhusks. Overlap two broad ends, and fill with a spoonful of mixture. Roll, bind with raffia, and steam twenty to thirty minutes.

Tamales No. 2
(Costa Rica)

2 cups hot corn-meal mush
1 cup fat or lard
Well-seasoned boiled pork
   or chicken

Plantain leaves or corn-
   husks
Salt

1. Mix corn-meal mush, fat, and salt.

2. Dice meat and fry slightly. Add to corn-meal mixture.

3. Put enough for one tamale on a plantain leaf or husk, folding the ends and sides over. Tie tamale with a cord.

4. Cook one hour in boiling water. Cut cord and serve tamale on leaf or husk.

Tamales No. 3
(Ecuador)

1 cup corn meal
Salt
1/2 teaspoon sugar
2 tablespoons butter
2 cups boiling water
1 tablespoon melted butter
2 tablespoons white flour

2 tablespoons ground pea-
   nuts
1 cup cooked chicken, cubed
5 or 6 olives, minced
1 hard-cooked egg, chopped
2 tablespoons raisins
Cornhusks

1. Mix corn meal, salt, and sugar. Add butter and boiling water. Boil five minutes.

2. Make a sauce of melted butter, flour, peanuts, chicken, eggs, and raisins.

3. Spread paste on cornhusks and cover with sauce. Roll husks and tie tightly.

4. Steam for one hour.

Tamales No. 4
(Salvador)

Dry corn	Well-seasoned chicken or
Cinnamon and salt	pork (⅓ as much meat
Butter	as corn)
½ cup raisins	Cornhusks

1. Cook until tender as much dry corn as is needed for tamales. Drain.
2. Add cinnamon, salt, and butter. Cook over a slow fire until firm.
3. Place mixture on cornhusks, and cover with meat and raisins.
4. Tie husks together and put into a deep pan. Cook in boiling water for twenty minutes. Serve hot or cold.

Tamales No. 5
(Panama)

12 ears of corn	Fat
2 pounds pork, cut in pieces	2 large onions, sliced
Several tomatoes, cut in	1 green pepper, sliced
pieces	Salt and pepper

1. Grate corn and soak in barely enough water to cover for half an hour.
2. Fry pork, and add vegetables, salt, and pepper. Mix with corn.
3. Pour into a greased baking dish and bake until it sets. (400°.)

Tamales No. 6
(Venezuela)

1 chicken	1 can corn
1 loaf bread	Sugar to taste
1 cup milk	¼ cup butter, melted
2 eggs	Salt and pepper

1. Cut chicken into pieces and parboil it.
2. Break bread into pieces and soak it in milk.
3. Beat eggs and add corn. Then add bread, sugar, butter, salt, and pepper.
4. Put some of mixture in a baking dish, and then some chicken. Repeat until all ingredients are used, having corn mixture on top.
5. Bake until chicken is tender. (400°.)

Carne de Chile (Deviled Meat)
(Chile)

2 eggs, well beaten
1 tablespoon mustard
3 tablespoons flour
1 teaspoon olive oil
1 tablespoon vinegar

Salt and cayenne
Cold meat, sliced
Lard
Broth or hot milk
1 tablespoon butter

1. Make a batter of eggs, mustard, flour, oil, vinegar, salt, and cayenne.
2. Soak slices of meat in batter and fry in hot lard.
3. Pour remaining batter into hot milk or broth. Add butter. Heat sauce and pour over meat.

Guiso de Carne (Meat Stew)
(Guatemala)

1 pound beef or lamb, ground
2 medium onions, grated
1 teaspoon minced parsley
Bacon or sausage

Salt, saffron, allspice
Juice of orange or grapefruit
1 tablespoon colór

1. Mix meat and onions. Add parsley, salt, saffron, and allspice.
2. Heat colór in a frying pan and add meat mixture. Cover and simmer for about one hour.
3. Turn onto a hot platter and garnish with bacon or sausage.

Tortas de Ternera (Veal Pie)
(Peru)

½ cup almonds, blanched
1 pound veal, ground
1 hard-cooked egg, chopped
½ cup sliced olives

1 cup broth
Salt and pepper
1 tablespoon fat
1 tablespoon flour, or more

1. Pound almonds fine and add meat, egg, olives, and broth. Add salt and pepper and simmer for one hour.
2. Add flour and fat enough to make mixture quite thick. Cool.
3. Form into cakes, dust with flour, and brown in lard.
4. Serve with tomato or Spanish Sauce. (Pp. 38, 91.)

Cariucho
(Ecuador)

2 large onions, chopped	1 teaspoon paprika
2 tomatoes, chopped	3 tablespoons peanut butter
1 green pepper, chopped	2 cups milk
2 tablespoons lard or oil	2 pounds flank steak
Salt and pepper	4 large potatoes, boiled

1. Fry onions, tomatoes, and pepper in fat. Season with salt, pepper, and paprika.
2. Add peanut butter and milk, and simmer half an hour.
3. Season steak and bake in oven until well done. Remove to a platter.
4. Surround with sliced potatoes and cover with sauce.

Cazuela de Ave (Bird Pot)
(Chile)

1 chicken, jointed	½ cup green peas
2 or 3 potatoes, cubed	1 onion, chopped
½ cup green beans	1 tablespoon rice
1 cup cubed squash or pumpkin	Salt and cayenne
	1 hard-cooked egg, chopped

1. Parboil chicken, and fry it until tender.
2. Add vegetables, rice, salt, and cayenne to chicken stock and boil until tender.
3. Place chicken on a platter and pour over vegetable mixture.
4. Garnish with egg and parsley.

Puchero (Chowder) No. 1
(Argentina)

1 chicken or loin of rib or beef	1 onion, chopped
Few sausages	Few pieces squash or vegetable marrow
Salt	Few carrots, cut in slivers
1 stalk celery, chopped	1 very young cabbage, chopped
Few leeks, chopped	1 tomato, chopped
Minced parsley	1 green pepper, chopped
Peeled sweet and white potatoes, quartered	¼ cup rice

1. Cover meat and sausages with boiling, salted water and simmer a few minutes. Skim well and add celery, leeks, and parsley. Cook one hour.
2. Add other vegetables and rice, and cook until tender.

Puchero (Chowder) No. 2
(Argentina)

2 cups garbanzos or Spanish peas
2 onions, chopped
1 clove garlic, minced
Olive oil for frying
2 pounds of any stew meat
6 potatoes

A few chilies, chopped
Salt and pepper
Vinegar to taste, if desired
Any vegetables in season
Vermicelli or bread
Stock to cover

1. Soak garbanzos several hours or overnight. Drain.
2. Fry onions and garlic in olive oil. Then brown meat and add chilies, salt, pepper, and vinegar. Heat a few minutes.
3. Add other ingredients, except potatoes, and cook several hours. Add potatoes forty-five minutes before serving.

Note: Serve meat and vegetables separately.

Gaspado de Carador (Game Stew)

4 pieces rabbit
2 partridges
4 quail
Oil for frying
3 cloves garlic, minced
2 onions, chopped

2 bay leaves
1 carrot, diced
10 peppercorns
1 clove
Salt and pepper
4 pounds tomatoes

1. Brown meat in oil and add other ingredients, except tomatoes.
2. Fry tomatoes and press through a sieve. Add to meat mixture and simmer all until meat is tender.

Roasted Quail

12 quail
Salt and pepper
Bacon

Grape, or other similar leaves

1. Clean quail. Place liver inside.
2. Sprinkle with salt and pepper and wrap with bacon. Then wrap in vine leaves.
3. Cook in a slow oven thirty to forty-five minutes. (375°.)
4. Serve on vine leaves.

Costillas de Cerdo Especiales (Special Spareribs)
(Paraguay)

Spareribs
Vinegar
3 eggs
Salt and pepper

Parsley, minced
2 tablespoons bread crumbs
and flour
Fat for frying

1. Separate ribs and push meat to end of bone. Cover with vinegar, add salt and pepper, and let it stand for one-half hour.
2. Roast slightly on the broiler.
3. Beat eggs with parsley, salt, flour, and crumbs.
4. Dip ribs in batter and fry in hot fat.
5. Serve with potatoes, beans, or Spanish peas.

Carne Primera
(Cuba)

Meat (round steak)
Salt and pepper
Fat

Vinegar
Garlic

1. Slice meat very thin. Pound well.
2. Season and put in a deep dish. Cover with vinegar. Add garlic, and let stand two hours.
3. Fry in hot fat.

Cordero Asado (Lamb with Vegetables)

Roast of lamb
1 tablespoon butter
1 bay leaf
Salt and pepper

½ cup white wine
2 pimientos, chopped
1 clove garlic, minced
1 tablespoon minced parsley

1. Put lamb in a casserole with butter, bay leaf, salt, and pepper. Heat in oven and turn when brown.
2. Add wine and baste occasionally. Roast until done.
3. Just before serving, fry pimientos, garlic, and parsley. Add all juice from baking dish.
4. Pour over meat to serve.
5. Serve with string beans, eggplant, and potatoes.

Corona Asada (Crown Roast)
(Paraguay)

Meaty spareribs
2 cups bread crumbs
2 or 3 stalks celery, minced
1 onion, minced
2 sprigs parsley, minced

½ cup raisins
Salt, pepper, paprika, cloves
1 cup cooked rice
1 cup crushed pineapple, drained

2 carrots, minced

1. Have spareribs broken, but not separated. Fasten ends together.
2. Mix other ingredients as a dressing and fill center.
3. Bake two hours in a slow oven. (375°.)
4. Serve with candied or jellied sweet potatoes.

Chuleta (Pork Chops)
(Peru)

6 pork chops
Lemon juice

Salt and pepper
Grated cheese

1. Squeeze lemon juice on each pork chop. Sprinkle chops with salt and pepper. Let stand one-half hour.
2. Sprinkle with grated cheese. Bake until brown and well done. (400°.)
3. Serve with peas or beans.

Olla Podrida
(Uruguay)

2 or 3 carrots
2 medium turnips
2 onions
1 clove garlic, minced
½ tablespoon minced parsley

1 small beef round, ground
1 cup raw rice
Salt, pepper, cloves
3 medium potatoes, peeled and cut in quarters

1. Chop vegetables fine. Put all ingredients except sweet potatoes in a saucepan, add water to cover, and cook slowly for half an hour.
2. Add potatoes and cook for one hour longer.

Olla à la Española (Stew)
(Cuba)

1 small cabbage
1 cup cooked cowpeas
2 Spanish sausages, cut in pieces
6 strips bacon, diced

1. Shred cabbage, place in a saucepan. Add other ingredients, and cook very slowly for one hour. Serve hot.

Note: This dish is served at dinner in place of soup.

Cameroes
(Brazil)

1 cup rice
1 large onion, chopped
1 clove garlic, minced
½ pound tomatoes, quartered
½ pound, or more, sausages, cut in pieces
2 chili peppers, chopped
Salt, pepper, cayenne
2 tablespoons butter

1. Boil rice in salted water about fifteen minutes. Drain and let water run through rice.
2. Fry onion and garlic in butter. Add tomatoes.
3. Fry sausages and add other ingredients.
4. Mix all ingredients together. Place in a saucepan, cover, and cook thirty or forty minutes.

Pato de Lima (Fried Duck Lima)
(Peru)

1 young duck, disjointed
3 cups boiling water
¾ teaspoon salt
4 tablespoons butter
1 tablespoon chopped onion
2 tablespoons fresh peanut butter
Dash cayenne
1 sweet red pepper, minced (or 1 pimiento, minced)
1 teaspoon minced parsley

1. Place duck in a saucepan, and add water and salt. Boil for fifteen minutes.
2. Remove duck and dry with a towel.
3. Boil stock down to one cup.
4. Melt butter in a frying pan, and add onion and duck. Sauté over a slow heat, turning often, until tender and slightly browned.

5. Pour cup of stock into a saucepan, and add peanut butter, cayenne, red pepper, and parsley. Boil gently, stirring constantly, until thickened.
6. Arrange duck on a hot platter and pour sauce over it.

Note: A young chicken may be cooked in this same manner.

Rabbit Stew
(Panama)

1 large rabbit	1 can consommé
1 cup vinegar	1 cup red cooking wine
8 cups cold water	1 tablespoon mixed pick-
Browned flour	ling spices
½ pound fat salt pork	1 tablespoon Worcester-
24 small green onions	shire sauce
1 clove garlic, minced	1 tablespoon browned flour

2 tablespoons cold water

1. Cut rabbit into eight pieces. Place in a large bowl or crock and add vinegar and water. Let it stand for two hours or longer.
2. Remove meat, wipe it dry, and roll it in browned flour.
3. Fry out the salt pork in a saucepan, remove the pork, add the rabbit, and brown well.
4. Add onions, garlic, consommé, and wine. Simmer three hours. Then add spices and Worcestershire sauce.
5. Remove meat and thicken gravy with flour blended with cold water, using one tablespoon flour and two tablespoons water for each cup of liquid.
6. Return meat to gravy and let it stand in a warm place thirty minutes.

Legumbres (Vegetables)

Frituras de Lechuga (Lettuce Fritters)

2 heads lettuce	4 eggs
Salt and pepper	Oil for frying

1. Boil lettuce in salted water. Drain and cut into pieces.
2. Beat egg whites and drop in the yolks. Stir until well blended. Add lettuce, salt, and pepper.
3. Fry spoonfuls of lettuce and egg in boiling oil. Serve hot.

Torta de Plátanos (Banana Cake)

Several ripe bananas
Few drops mushroom
   catsup
Grated cheese
½ cup sour cream
Bread crumbs

2 tablespoons butter

1. Mash ripest bananas and flavor with ketchup.
2. Butter a baking dish and cover bottom with purée. Then sprinkle it with grated cheese.
3. Slice less ripe bananas over this, and then another layer of cheese.
4. Moisten crumbs with sour cream and spread on top. Dot with butter and bake thirty to forty minutes. (400°.)

Pudín de Papas (Sweet Potato Pudding)

1 slice pumpkin
2 ripe bananas
4 sweet potatoes
½ fresh coconut
1 teaspoon salt
1 cup melted sugar or sirup
2 tablespoons melted drip-
   pings or lard

½ teaspoon black pepper

1. Grate pumpkin, bananas, sweet potatoes, and coconut. Mix well and add other ingredients.
2. Bake in a well-greased baking dish thirty to forty minutes. (450°.)

Ajiaco
(Peru)

4 boiled potatoes
1 pint tomato sauce
2 thick slices stale bread
1 tablespoon olive oil
6 hard-cooked eggs
1 pound fresh cheese, cubed

1. Add sauce to potatoes while they are warm and not quite done.
2. Soak bread in water. Squeeze. Add to potatoes with oil.
3. Heat thoroughly and stir in cheese. If too thick add a little water. Heat until cheese is melted.
4. Pour on a platter and garnish with eggs cut in quarters lengthwise.

Calabazita (Little Squash)
(Chile)

2 pounds pumpkin or win-
   ter squash
1½ cups tomatoes
½ onion, chopped
3 sweet peppers, chopped
Fat
Salt and Pepper
1 egg, beaten

½ cup cheese

1. Peel pumpkin, remove seeds, and cut into eight pieces.
2. Place it in a saucepan with tomatoes, and heat.
3. Fry onion and peppers in fat and add to pumpkin. Add salt and pepper.
4. Cover and simmer until tender.
5. Just before serving, add beaten egg and cheese. Heat until cheese is melted.

Locro
(Chile or Peru)

1 slice onion, minced	6-inch square of pumpkin, cubed
1 sprig parsley, minced	
1 tablespoon colór	½ cup string beans, cut up
½ cup fresh corn	Stock or water
3 potatoes, sliced	Salt and pepper

1. Fry onion and parsley in colór. Add corn and cook a few minutes.
2. Add vegetables, and stock enough to moisten. Add salt and pepper.
3. Simmer until well cooked and blended.

Corn Mousse
(Argentina)

6 ears corn	1 tablespoon butter
1 cup thick white sauce	Salt, pepper, sugar, nutmeg
3 eggs, beaten	

1. Grate corn and add sauce, butter, salt, pepper, and sugar. Add eggs and beat well.
2. Put in a greased mold. Bake like a custard in a pan of warm water until set. (350°.)

Pudín de Maiz (Corn Pudding)
(Bolivia)

5 ears corn	4 tablespoons melted butter
3 eggs	Salt and pepper
¾ cup sweet milk	1 teaspoon paprika
Slices Swiss cheese	

1. Cut corn from cob and add eggs, milk, butter, salt, pepper, and paprika.
2. Turn half the mixture into a greased mold and cover with slices of Swiss cheese. Then pour on rest of mixture.
3. Set it in a pan of warm water and bake in a slow oven for forty to fifty minutes. (350°.)

Humitas de Choclo
(Chile)

5 ears corn

1 onion, minced

1 tomato, chopped

Parsley, chopped

Salt and pepper

Other seasonings, if desired

1. Cut corn from cob and add vegetables. Salt and pepper.
2. Boil in cornhusks, or bake in a buttered pan for about twenty minutes.

Frijoles Negros (Black Beans)
(Costa Rica)

2 cups black beans

Salt and pepper

3 onions, minced

1 red or green pepper, minced

Lard

Milk to cover

1. Pick over beans, and wash and soak in water overnight.
2. Drain, cover with fresh water, season, and boil until soft.
3. Fry onion and pepper in lard and add to beans.
4. Cover with milk and let come to a boil.

Frijoles de Lima (Lima Beans)
(Brazil)

2 cups fresh lima beans

2 heads lettuce, chopped

Spring onions

Olive oil

Salt and coriander seeds

Hot water

Eggs

1. Parboil beans and lettuce. Drain and add other ingredients, and boil slowly until beans are tender.
2. Serve with poached eggs on top, and a little sugar, if desired.

Frituras de Apio
(Puerto Rico)

2 cups cooked arracacha or celery root

2 tablespoons butter

1 teaspoon salt

Few grains cayenne

1 egg, beaten

1 teaspoon minced parsley

¼ teaspoon celery salt

1. Rice arracacha and add butter, salt, and cayenne. Cool.
2. Add egg, parsley, and celery salt.
3. Roll in flour and fry in deep fat. Drain.
4. Serve hot as main vegetable.

Malanga con Crema (Sweet Potato Custard)

3 cups mashed malanga or sweet potato
3 eggs
3 cups milk

2 teaspoons melted butter
1 teaspoon salt
1/8 teaspoon pepper
1/4 cup cheese

1. Line a buttered casserole with mashed malanga or sweet potato.
2. Beat eggs slightly. Add milk, butter, salt, pepper, and grated cheese.
3. Pour into a casserole and bake in a moderate oven until custard is set and nicely browned. (400°.)
4. Serve as main dish.

Yautia á la Crema (Sweet Potato Custard)
(Puerto Rico)

3 cups mashed yautia
3 eggs
3 cups milk

2 tablespoons melted butter
1/8 teaspoon pepper
1 teaspoon salt

1/4 cup grated cheese

1. Line a buttered casserole with mashed yautia.
2. Beat eggs slightly and add milk, butter, salt, pepper, and cheese. Pour into a yautia-lined casserole.
3. Bake in a moderate oven until brown and custard has set. (350°.)

Scalloped Yautia (Scalloped Sweet Potato)
(Puerto Rico)

2 tablespoons butter
2 tablespoons flour
1 cup milk

1 teaspoon salt
Dash of pepper
2 cups sliced yautia

1 cup buttered crumbs

1. Make a white sauce of butter, flour, milk, salt, and pepper.
2. Place a layer of yautia in a buttered casserole, and cover it with sauce. Repeat until all ingredients are used.
3. Cover with buttered crumbs.
4. Bake one hour. (400°.)

Habas al Horno (Scalloped Lima Beans)
(Puerto Rico)

1 cup milk	1 tablespoon onion juice
2 tablespoons flour	3 cups cooked lima beans
2 tablespoons fat	6 slices bacon
Salt and pepper	Pimientos

1 tablespoon minced parsley

1. Make a white sauce of milk, flour, fat, salt, and pepper. Add beans.
2. Place all in a buttered baking dish. Cover with slices of bacon.
3. Place in a hot oven until bacon is crisp. (475°.)
4. Garnish with pimientos and parsley.

Chauchas de Argentina

1½ cups cut string beans	2½ cups potatoes
Oil	1 tablespoon butter
Lemon juice	Salt

Slices red pepper

1. Cook beans in salted water. When tender, drain them. Add oil and lemon juice.
2. Make a potato purée, and add butter, salt, and red pepper.
3. Spread beans on a platter and pour purée over them.
4. Garnish with slices of red pepper.

Boniatos (Sweet Potato Fritters)

2½ cups sweet potatoes	1 tablespoon flour
2 eggs, beaten	Fat for frying
1 teaspoon baking powder	Powdered sugar

1. Cook potatoes in salted water, or bake in oven. Skin, and pass them through food chopper. Cool. Measure two and one-half cups.
2. Add eggs, baking powder, and flour. Mix well.
3. Cook a tablespoon at a time in fat until brown. Sprinkle with sugar.

Note: Pumpkin may be used in place of potato.

Mollete

1 cup milk	1 cup corn meal
2 eggs, beaten	1 cup flour
1 cup cold mashed squash	2 teaspoons baking powder

½ teaspoon salt

1. Mix milk, eggs, and squash. Beat well.
2. Mix dry ingredients and sift into squash to make a batter.
3. Make little cakes. Bake on both sides on a hot griddle.
4. Serve hot sprinkled with sugar.

Zapallitos de Milanesa (Milan Squash)

Small round squash   Bread crumbs
1 egg, beaten   Salt and pepper
                      Fat

1. Clean squash and cut into slices. Roll in egg and bread crumbs. Season with salt and pepper.
2. Fry in deep fat.

Chayote de Crema (Creamed Chayote)

3 chayote, squash, or cu-   1 teaspoon salt
  cumbers   1 teaspoon mace, cinnamon,
3 tablespoons butter   or curry powder
3 eggs   1 tablespoon grated green
3 teaspoons sugar   lime rind
                    ½ cup milk

1. Wash chayotes well. Steam or boil until tender.
2. Cut in half lengthwise and remove pulp. Mash.
3. To mashed pulp, add butter, one whole egg, and two beaten yolks, sugar, salt, spice, and rind. Add milk if too dry. Fold in stiffly beaten egg whites.
4. Refill shells and brown five minutes in a hot oven. (475°.)

Chayote Relleno con Queso (Chayote Stuffed with Cheese)

3 chayote, squash, or cu-   1 teaspoon salt
  cumbers   ¼ cup milk or water
1 cup grated cheese   ½ cup buttered bread
½ teaspoon minced parsley   crumbs
Dash of pepper   1 tablespoon butter

1. Wash chayotes well. Steam or boil until tender.
2. Cut in halves lengthwise and remove pulp. Mash.
3. Mix cheese and seasonings with pulp and add milk or water if dry.
4. Refill shells and cover with crumbs. Brown in a hot oven for five minutes. (475°.)

Chayote Rellenos (Stuffed Chayote or Squash)

3 chayote or squash
¼ cup cooked rice
¾ cup bread crumbs
1 egg, beaten

½ teaspoon salt
2 teaspoons lemon juice
3 tablespoons butter or
    bacon fat

Sliced bacon, if desired

1. Parboil chayotes, scoop out pulp, and mash.
2. Mix rice, crumbs, egg, salt, and lemon juice with pulp. Refill shells.
3. Top with bacon fat, or with sliced bacon.
4. Place chayotes in a baking pan, and add water to cover bottom of pan. Cover and bake for twenty-five to thirty minutes. (450°.)

Chayote Frito (Fried Chayote)

Sliced chayote
1 egg, beaten

Salt and pepper
Fat for frying

1. Slice chayote. This may be parboiled if desired.
2. Season egg and dip vegetable into it.
3. Fry in fat until brown.

Tomates Asados (Broiled Tomatoes)

Tomatoes
Fat or oil

Flour and corn meal, mixed
Salt and pepper

1. Wash tomatoes and cut in half crosswise.
2. Dip cut side in oil, then in corn meal, flour, salt, and pepper mixed together.
3. Place on the broiler, skin side down. Broil slowly until tomatoes are tender and nicely browned.

Ejotes Españoles (String Beans, Spanish Style)

2 cups string beans
½ onion, chopped
2 pimientos, chopped

1½ cups sauce (cream, to-
    mato, or béchamel)
Salt and pepper

1. Cook beans with onion until tender.
2. Add pimiento, sauce, and seasonings. Cook ten minutes longer.

Pasteles de Plátano (Banana Pie)

¼ cup fresh pork
½ cup ham or salt pork
1 small onion
1 green pepper
1 clove garlic
1 tomato
½ cup water
¼ cup raisins
1 dozen olives
¼ cup chopped blanched
   almonds

1 tablespoon capers
½ teaspoon wild marjoram
   leaves
½ teaspoon coriander
   leaves
½ teaspoon paprika
2 teaspoons salt
Pepper
6 green bananas
½ cup milk
Plantain or cabbage leaves

1. Grind meat and sauté five minutes. Grind onion, pepper, garlic, and tomato, and add to meat. Add water, raisins, capers, olives, almonds, and seasonings. Cook ten minutes.
2. Grate and mash bananas. Season with salt and add milk.
3. Divide into twelve parts and spread about one-half inch thick on the leaves.
4. Place some filling on each and fold into a package. Tie.
5. Steam two hours.

Savory Lentils

2 cups dried lentils
2 teaspoons salt
1 quart cold water

1 large onion, minced
½ cup olive oil or bacon fat
Few drops tabasco sauce

1. Pick over lentils, wash thoroughly, cover with water, and soak overnight. Drain.
2. Place in a saucepan, and add salt and water. Cover and simmer thirty to forty minutes, or until tender. Drain. Reserve one cup of liquid.
3. Cook onion in oil or bacon fat. Add lentils and cook fifteen minutes.
4. Add tabasco sauce and liquid. Heat and serve.

West India Pilau

3 green peppers
2 tablespoons butter

1 small onion, sliced
1 cup boiled rice

1 pint stock or gravy

1. Remove seeds and veins from peppers. Cut into pieces, and fry in butter. Remove from pan and fry onion.
2. Chop onion and peppers, and add rice and stock.
3. Place mixture in a baking dish. Heat in oven until very hot.

Alcaparrias (Dressed with Capers)

1 green plantain, or 2 bananas	3 tablespoons chopped beef
½ teaspoon salt	½ small onion, minced
2 teaspoons melted lard	½ tomato, minced
⅛ teaspoon paprika	½ clove garlic, minced
¼ pound yautia or sweet potatoes	¼ green pepper, minced
	3 olives, minced
	3 tablespoons capers

1. Wash and peel plantains. Cook in salted water for five minutes.
2. Grate and add salt, lard, and paprika.
3. Boil the sweet potatoes, mash, and add to grated plantains.
4. Sauté beef, onion, tomato, garlic, green pepper, olives, and capers.
5. Make plantain mixture into six balls. Make an indentation with the thumb, put meat mixture in center, and reshape the balls.
6. Cook in soup or sauté in fat. Serve with tomato sauce.

Note: Cheese may be used instead of meat mixture.

Mofongo

3 green plantains	3 tablespoons crisp pork rind or sausage
1 clove garlic, minced	
1 teaspoon salt	

1. Wash, peel, and roast plantains until tender.
2. Pound in a mortar, and add salt, garlic, and pork rind. Mix well.
3. Shape into a loaf or small cakes, reheat, and serve with meat.

Ensaladas (Salads)

Brazilian Salad
(Brazil)

1 cup seedless grapes	1 cup nuts, chopped
1 cup shredded pineapple	1 cup mayonnaise
1 cup minced apple	Juice of 1 lemon
1 cup minced celery	Lettuce
2 cups whipped cream	

1. Mix fruits, celery, nuts, mayonnaise, and lemon juice.
2. Serve on crisp lettuce.
3. Top with whipped cream. Garnish with chopped nuts.

Ensalada de Pimiento (Pepper Salad)
(Cuba)

1 cup shredded cabbage	2 cups corned beef
2 green peppers, chopped	Mayonnaise
2 large, cold, boiled po-	Seasonings
tatoes, sliced	Lettuce

3 hard-cooked eggs

1. Mix cabbage, pepper, corned beef cut in strips, potatoes, and mayonnaise. Add any other seasonings desired.
2. Serve on crisp lettuce. Garnish with hard-cooked eggs.

Ensalada de Puerto Rico (Puerto Rico Salad)

6 choice tomatoes	1 green pepper, shredded
¾ cup shredded cabbage	Salt, pepper, paprika
1 tablespoon minced onion	Mayonnaise

Lettuce

1. Scald, skin, and chill tomatoes. Remove pulp with a pointed spoon. Drain shells.
2. Mix cabbage, onion, pepper, seasonings, and mayonnaise.
3. Fill tomatoes, and top with mayonnaise and paprika.
4. Serve on lettuce leaves.

Ensalada Mixta (Combination Salad)
(Puerto Rico)

Plantains	Lettuce
Cooked vegetables	French dressing

1. Steam ripe plantains. Chill and dice or slice them.
2. Combine with cooked vegetables.
3. Serve on crisp lettuce with French dressing.

Ensalada de Bolivia (Bolivia Salad)

2 cups boiled potatoes, cubed	2 tablespoons shredded celery
3 hard-cooked eggs, chopped	½ tablespoon chopped chives
2 tablespoons pimiento, chopped	1 tablespoon vinegar
2 tablespoons chopped green pepper	French dressing
	Lettuce

1. Toss together gently, potatoes, eggs, pimiento, green pepper, celery, and chives.
2. Add vinegar to French dressing and pour over other ingredients. Let stand at least one hour.
3. Serve on crisp lettuce.

Escabeche
(Chile)

2 pounds white fish	Slices of orange
1 bay leaf	Bits of orange peel, cut thin
Sprig of thyme	1 green pepper, chopped
1 teaspoon grated onion	French dressing

Lettuce

1. Cook fish with bay leaf and thyme. Drain and cube.
2. Add other ingredients and let stand several hours.
3. Garnish with lettuce and serve.

Ensalada de Panama (Panama Salad)

Breast of fowl, cubed	1 banana, diced
3 slices pineapple, cubed	4 artichokes, chopped
1 grapefruit, diced	1 cup asparagus tips
1 avocado or alligator pear, diced	Seasoned mayonnaise
	Lettuce
1 orange, diced	Pimiento strips

Olives

1. Mix fowl, fruit, vegetables, and mayonnaise. Chill.
2. Serve on a platter bordered with crisp lettuce. Garnish with strips of pimiento and olives.

Ensalada de Chayote (Chayote or Squash Salad)
(Puerto Rico)

Chayote	Any desired seasoning
Mayonnaise	Lettuce

1. Boil the chayote in salted water until tender. Peel and slice lengthwise when cold.
2. Garnish with mayonnaise and seasonings.
3. Serve on lettuce.

Corazones de Palma (Hearts of Palm)
(Haiti)

Water cress
Hearts of palm (canned)
1 avocado
1 large tomato
Mayonnaise

1. Place water cress on individual salad plates.
2. Chop hearts of palm and cover water cress.
3. Put a slice of tomato on this.
4. Mix mayonnaise with mashed avocado and serve on salad.
5. Garnish with balls of avocado.

Ensalada de Pollo (Chicken Salad)
(Venezuela)

Cooked chicken
Oil and vinegar
12 stalks asparagus, cooked,
    or 1 can
Mayonnaise
½ cup mustard pickle
1½ cups cooked peas or 1
    can (No. 2)
Salt and pepper
Lettuce

1. Cut meat in small pieces. Add a little oil and vinegar to it.
2. Cut tips from asparagus and save for a garnish. Cut remainder of stalks in small pieces.
3. Mix mayonnaise with chicken, asparagus, peas, pickles, salt, and pepper.
4. Place chicken in a dish. Surround it with lettuce, and garnish with asparagus tips.

Salpicon
(Chile)

1 pint cold veal, lamb, or
    chicken
2 hard-cooked eggs, sliced
1 teaspoon onion juice
Few mint leaves, minced
2 heads lettuce, shredded
French dressing, well sea-
    soned
2 tablespoons chopped
    parsley

1. Cut up all ingredients and add French dressing. Toss until well mixed.
2. Serve on crisp lettuce.

Ensalada de Melón (Melon Salad)
(Brazil)

1 watermelon	Powdered sugar
Limes	Lettuce

French dressing

1. Cut watermelon in thick slices and remove seeds.
2. Cut into small triangles. To each cup of melon add juice of half a lime and three tablespoons powdered sugar. Chill one hour.
3. Arrange three triangles on individual lettuce leaves.
4. Serve with French dressing seasoned to taste.

Avocado
(Cuba)

Red pepper	Vinegar
Cinnamon	Avocados
Mustard	Lettuce

1. Mix red pepper, cinnamon, mustard, and vinegar.
2. Peel and cut avocados in half lengthwise. Place cut side down on a lettuce leaf. Make deep indentations with back of a knife and fill with mixture. Chill before serving.

Note: Avocados may be filled with commercial cocktail sauce.

Avocado y Tomate (Avocado and Tomato)

3 tomatoes	French dressing
1 large avocado	Lettuce or water cress

1. Peel and cut tomatoes in thick slices.
2. Peel avocado and slice.
3. Arrange shredded lettuce or water cress on individual plates.
4. Place alternate slices of tomato and avocado on lettuce.
5. Pour highly seasoned French dressing over salad.

Fruit Salad
(South America)

2 bananas, sliced	2 peaches, sliced
½ cup chopped Brazil nuts	2 pears, sliced
1 cup cubed pineapple	¼ cup mayonnaise
5 dates, cut fine	1 cup whipped cream

1. Mix above ingredients and serve on lettuce.

Ensalada de Tomates Amarillos (Yellow Tomato Salad)

6 yellow tomatoes
1½ cups cooked string
    beans
French dressing

2 tablespoons chopped red
    pepper
2 tablespoons chopped
    green pepper

Lettuce

1. Wash and peel tomatoes. Chill.
2. Marinate beans in French dressing. Chill.
3. Cut tomatoes in halves and arrange on lettuce.
4. Pile beans on tomatoes. Sprinkle red and green pepper on top. Serve with French dressing.

Ensalada de Plátanos con Saffron (Curried Banana Salad)

½ cup almonds
½ pimiento
2 teaspoons minced onion
2 bananas

2 tablespoons boiled rice
French dressing flavored
    with saffron or curry
    powder

Lettuce

1. Blanch and chop almonds and shred pimiento.
2. Add minced onion, sliced bananas, and rice.
3. Pour curry dressing over this.
4. Serve on crisp lettuce.

Ensalada de Avocado y Piña (Avocado and Pineapple Salad)

1 tablespoon gelatin
¼ cup cold water
1¼ cups boiling water or
    pineapple juice

½ bunch celery
6 maraschino cherries
2 slices pineapple
½ medium-sized avocado

1. Soak gelatin in cold water for five minutes, then dissolve it in boiling water or pineapple juice.
2. Dice celery, cherries, pineapple, and avocado.
3. Make a star of cherry and avocado in the bottom of the mold, and add a tablespoon of gelatin mixture.
4. When set, add remaining fruits in layers, then remaining gelatin.
5. Chill and unmold on lettuce.

Ensalada de Pescado Española (Spanish Fish Salad)

1 quart chopped celery	1 tablespoon minced green
2 cups flaked fish	pepper
1 tomato, cut small	Mayonnaise
1 tablespoon minced onion	Lettuce

1. Mince onion, pull water cress to pieces, and add olives, and mix well.
2. Serve on lettuce.

Ensalada de Bahia
(Brazil)

1 small onion	20 stuffed olives
1 quart water cress	French dressing

1. Mince onion, pull water cress to pieces, add olives, and mix well.
2. Serve with French dressing.

Ensalada de Plátanos (Banana Salad) No. 1

Bananas	Mayonnaise with cayenne
Walnuts or Brazil nuts, chopped	Lettuce

1. Cut bananas in slices, mix with nuts and mayonnaise.
2. Serve on crisp lettuce.

Ensalada de Plátanos (Banana Salad) No. 2

Bananas	Walnuts or Brazil nuts
Mayonnaise with cayenne	Lettuce

1. Cut bananas in half lengthwise. Dip in mayonnaise.
2. Chop nuts and roll bananas in them.
3. Serve on crisp lettuce.

Dulces (Desserts)

Pudín de Piña (Pineapple Pudding)

⅓ cup granulated tapioca
¼ cup sugar
¾ cup brown sugar
¼ teaspoon salt
1 quart milk, scalded

1 egg yolk, beaten
6 tablespoons melted butter
1 cup crushed pineapple
⅓ cup Brazil nuts, cut fine
1 egg white, stiffly beaten

1. Cook tapioca, sugar, salt, and milk in a double boiler fifteen minutes, or until tapioca is clear. Add egg yolk, stirring well.
2. Cook one minute and add butter. Cool.
3. Add pineapple and nuts, and fold in egg white. Chill.

Pudín de Plátanos y Nueces (Banana and Nut Tapioca)

¼ cup granulated tapioca
½ teaspoon salt
2 cups hot water
⅔ cup sugar

1 egg
3 tablespoons lemon juice
2 bananas, sliced
½ cup peanuts, chopped

1. Cook tapioca, salt, and water in a double boiler for fifteen minutes.
2. Add sugar, and then beaten egg yolk, stirring vigorously. Cook until thick.
3. Remove from heat, and add lemon juice, bananas, and nuts. Cool.
4. Fold in stiffly beaten egg white. Chill and serve with whipped cream, and garnish with chopped peanuts.

Pudín de Coco (Coconut Cream Tapioca)

1 quart milk
¼ teaspoon salt
4 tablespoons granulated
    tapioca
1 cup sugar

4 egg yolks
Meringue:
    ½ cup sugar
    4 egg whites
    ½ cup coconut

½ cup coconut

1. Scald milk in top of a double boiler. Add salt and tapioca, and cook fifteen minutes, stirring frequently.
2. Mix sugar, coconut, and egg yolks, slightly beaten. Combine with

tapioca mixture, stirring vigorously. Continue cooking until they are slightly thickened. Pour into a greased baking dish.

3. Beat egg whites until stiff, and fold in sugar. Pile lightly on top of tapioca mixture. Cover with coconut.

4. Bake in a slow oven about fifteen minutes, or until a golden brown. (350°.)

Pudín de Plátanos (Banana Supreme)

4 bananas	⅓ cup brown sugar
⅓ cup chopped nuts	⅛ teaspoon nutmeg
4 graham crackers, rolled	Whipped cream

1. Peel, scrape, and cut bananas lengthwise and crosswise into quarters.
2. Chop nuts very fine and blend with cracker crumbs, sugar, and nutmeg.
3. Roll bananas in mixture, and lay them close together in a buttered baking pan. Bake for twenty minutes in a moderate oven. (350°-375°.)
4. Serve with whipped cream.

Crema de Café (Coffee Mousse)

1 tablespoon gelatin	Crushed burnt-sugar al-
⅔ cup very strong coffee	monds or nut brittle
¾ cup sugar	or macaroons

3 cups whipped cream

1. Soften gelatin in cold coffee to cover it.
2. Cook remaining coffee with sugar to thread stage. Add softened gelatin, and stir it until dissolved. Strain and cool.
3. Fold in whipped cream and turn into molds. Freeze in the automatic refrigerator or with ice mixed with salt.
4. Unmold and garnish with crushed almonds, or nut brittle, or macaroons. Both nuts and macaroons may be used if desired.

Dulce de Leche (Caramel Cream)
(Argentina)

1 cup sugar	1 quart milk (sweet or
Grated lemon rind	sour)

Cinnamon sticks

1. Bring milk and sugar to a boil and then lower heat. Cook three hours, stirring occasionally. Test in cold water for a soft ball.
2. Add cinnamon and lemon rind toward end of cooking. To prevent curdling, stir vigorously when removing it from fire.
3. Serve on soda crackers or bread.

Note: A can of condensed milk may be boiled in the can for three hours.

Crema de Coco (Coconut Cream)
(Cuba)

2 fresh coconuts
1 cup coconut milk
Sugar sirup

Milk
3 egg yolks for each cup
of liquid

1. Grate coconut and let stand in coconut milk one-half hour. Squeeze through a clean bag until all juice is out.
2. To every cup of coconut milk, add a cup of sugar sirup (sugar and water cooked to the thread stage). Measure and add half as much cow's milk.
3. Stir in unbeaten egg yolks and heat all over the fire. Stir well and add vanilla.
4. Serve in parfait glasses or as a sauce for ice cream. If custard is used for ice cream, add coconut meat, cinnamon, and almond or lemon flavoring.

Dulce de Coco y Leche (Milk and Coconut Cream)
(Honduras)

3 cups sugar
1 quart milk

½ pound mashed or shredded fresh coconut

4 egg yolks, beaten

1. Boil sugar and milk, and when it becomes sticky, add coconut.
2. Add egg yolks and mix well. Heat and remove from fire.
3. Serve with powdered cinnamon and raisins.

Queso de Piña (Pineapple Cheese)
(Venezuela)

2½ cups sugar
14 eggs, beaten

1 fresh pineapple, grated, or one No. 2½ can grated pineapple

1. Melt enough sugar to coat a baking dish.
2. Grate pineapple and press out juice, or drain canned pineapple. Add juice to remaining sugar and boil until it threads. Cool.
3. Beat sugar sirup into eggs, add pineapple, and pour all into a baking dish.
4. Place in a pan of warm water, and bake in a slow oven until firm. (350°.) Chill.

Plátanos Helados (Frozen Bananas)
(Dominican)

6 large bananas
½ pound powdered sugar

1 quart water
Grated rind of 1 lemon

1. Slice bananas and cover with sugar. Let stand one-half hour.
2. Add water and lemon rind. Mix well and freeze.

Gisadas
(West Indies)

1 coconut, grated
1 egg, beaten
Coconut milk

Brown sugar to sweeten
Flavoring: nutmeg, cinnamon, or rosewater

Pastry

1. Mix coconut, egg, milk, sugar, and flavoring to a paste.
2. Make small tarts in muffin tins and fill with paste.
3. Bake about thirty minutes, or until nicely browned. (475°. Reduce to 400° after ten minutes.)

Crema de Café (Coffee Bavarian Cream)

1 tablespoon gelatin
4 tablespoons milk
½ cup powdered sugar

½ cup strong coffee
1½ cups whipping cream
Ladyfingers

1. Soak gelatin in milk for five minutes. Add softened gelatin and sugar to scalding coffee. Stir until dissolved. Allow to cool and start to set. Do not let it stiffen.
2. Whip cream and fold into coffee mixture. Stir until well blended and stiff.
3. Split ladyfingers and line a mold. Fill with cream. Chill in refrigerator.
4. Garnish with whipped cream and chopped nuts, if desired.

Pudín de Manzanas ó Zanahorrias (Apple or Carrot Pudding)

1 pound apples or carrots, grated
2 cups brown sugar

Grated rind of 1 lemon
12 egg yolks, beaten
Cinnamon

1. Mix all together and make in a buttered tin for one-half hour. (400°.)

Masamara Morada
(Peru)

3 or 4 ears of purple corn
Mixed fruits cut in ½-inch pieces (peaches, grapes, pineapple, etc.)

Sugar to taste
1 sweet potato or 1½ tablespoons constarch for each cup fruit

1. Cut corn from cob, cover with water, and boil to extract color. Strain.
2. Cook fruits in juice until tender. Sweeten to taste.
3. Grate sweet potato and wash several times to get out starch. Put in a bag; then wash starch and use it to thicken fruit juice. When cornstarch is used, mix it with a little cold water before adding.
4. Cook fifteen or twenty minutes.

Baked Quinces

10 or 12 large quinces   Sugar

1. Make a hole in center of each quince. Fill with sugar.
2. Bake until almost done. Add more sugar.
3. Bake until tender, spreading juice on top from time to time.
4. Serve with cream.

Manzanas de Cuba (Cuban Apples)

6 tart apples
Coconut
Blanched almonds, chopped
Jelly

½ cup sugar
1 cup water
1 tablespoon lemon juice

1. Pare and core apples. Steam until *almost* tender.
2. Place in a buttered pan. Fill cavities with coconut and almonds.
3. Make a thin sirup of sugar, water, and lemon juice. Pour over apples.
4. Bake in a hot oven until soft, basting often. (450°.)
5. Garnish with jelly.

Plátanos Frotados (Banana Whip)

1 cup banana pulp
Lemon juice

½ cup sugar
1 or 2 egg whites

1. Mix banana pulp and lemon juice. Add mixture to sugar and egg whites.
2. Beat until stiff, about ten to twenty minutes.
3. Serve in dessert glasses.
4. Garnish with sliced bananas and serve with cream or custard sauce.

Crema de Café Español (Coffee Spanish Cream)

½ cup milk
1½ cups coffee
1 tablespoon gelatin, soaked
   in coffee

3 eggs
5 tablespoons sugar
¼ teaspoon salt
½ teaspoon vanilla

Whipped cream

1. Heat milk, coffee, and softened gelatin in a double boiler, stirring until gelatin is dissolved.
2. Add beaten egg yolks, sugar, and salt. Cook five minutes.
3. Remove from fire. Cool slightly. Add vanilla and stiffly beaten egg whites. Pour into a mold and chill.
4. Unmold and serve with whipped cream.

Note: This will separate into clear and frothy layers.

Pudín de Datos (Date Pudding)
(Haiti)

½ cup walnuts or pecans,
   cut in pieces
12 dates, cut in pieces

5 eggs
1 cup sugar, or less
Whipped cream

1. Butter a deep cake pan. Place nuts and dates in bottom.
2. Beat egg yolks, add sugar, then fold in stiffly beaten egg whites. Pour onto nuts and dates.
3. Bake until ingredients hold together. (375°.)
4. When cold, crumble into pieces and serve with whipped cream.

Pudín de Patata (Sweet Potato Pone)

2½ cups grated raw sweet
   potatoes or yams
1½ cups molasses
1 cup melted butter
½ cup finely cut, preserved
   ginger
½ teaspoon salt

½ cup minced candied
   orange peel
½ tablespoon ginger
½ teaspoon allspice
½ teaspoon cloves
½ teaspoon mace
½ teaspoon cinnamon

1. Mix potatoes, molasses, and butter. Beat until well blended.
2. Add other ingredients, mix thoroughly, and pour into buttered baking dish.

3. Bake one and one-half hours, or until a knife inserted in center comes out clean. (350°.) Let cool in dish.
4. Serve with following sauce:

HONEY SAUCE

4 tablespoons butter	1 cup strained honey
4 tablespoons cornstarch	¼ cup water

1. Melt butter in a saucepan, add cornstarch, and blend.
2. Add honey and water. Cook five minutes.
3. Serve hot immediately, for sauce hardens when it becomes cold.

Torrijas
(Honduras)

1 pound sponge cake	3 cups boiling water
6 eggs	Cinnamon bark
Lard for frying	¼ cup Malaga wine
3 pounds sugar	Powdered cinnamon

1. Cut cake into one-fourth-inch slices.
2. Beat egg whites until stiff. Beat yolks, and fold into whites. Spread on both sides of cake slices.
3. Fry slices in deep fat until light brown. When fried, put them in a pan, using boiling water to remove lard. Change water when it becomes greasy.
4. Make a sirup of sugar and boiling water. Boil quickly at first, then lower heat and boil until slightly thick. While sirup is hot add some cinnamon bark.
5. Add wine shortly before removing sirup from fire.
6. Remove cinnamon bark and pour sirup over cake. Sprinkle cake with powdered cinnamon. Serve hot.

Note: This is a Christmas dessert.

Sopa Dourada (Golden Soup)
(Brazil)

Loaf of bread	Sugar for sirup
Butter	18 egg yolks

Cinnamon

1. Dice inside of a loaf of bread. Fry in butter and put into sugar and water sirup. Boil.
2. When sirup becomes thick, add egg yolks, stirring over a low fire. Mix well and sprinkle with cinnamon.

Peanut Cakes
(Brazil)

1 pound roasted peanuts
1⅓ cups sugar

2 cups flour, or more
4 eggs, well beaten

1. Mix all ingredients and knead well. Form into cookies. Place on a greased cooky sheet.
2. Bake in a hot oven until light brown. (475°.)

Glazed Squares
(Brazil)

2 cups sugar
1 pound roasted peanuts,
　chopped
1 pound shelled almonds,
　chopped

1 teaspoon ground cinna-
　mon
⅔ cup water
5 egg whites, beaten stiff
12 egg yolks, beaten

3 tablespoons flour

1. Mix sugar with peanuts, almonds, cinnamon, and water. Add eggs and mix well. Boil, stirring with a wooden spoon. Cook until mixture leaves the pan. Add flour mixed with a little water.
2. Heat mixture until dough leaves bottom of pan. Put it on a greased and floured cooky sheet, and press it to one-half- or one-fourth-inch thickness. Sprinkle with cinnamon.
3. Brown in a hot oven, and glaze it with one-half cup sugar mixed with one-fourth cup water. (475°.)
4. When dry, cut in squares.

Quesadilla de Arroz (Little Rice Cakes)
(Honduras)

1 pound butter
1 pound sugar
14 eggs

1 pound rice flour
1 teaspoon baking powder
½ teaspoon salt

1. Cream butter and sugar and add well-beaten egg yolks, beating until sugar is dissolved.
2. Gradually stir in flour, which has been sifted with baking powder and salt. Fold in stiffly beaten egg whites.
3. Pour dough into greased muffin tins until about three-fourths full.
4. Bake in a moderate oven. (400°.) Cake is cooked when blade of a knife comes out clean.

Currant and Almond Cake
(Guatemala)

1 cup butter or fat
1 cup sugar
10 eggs, well beaten
2 cups flour
3 teaspoons baking powder

½ teaspoon salt
½ cup currants
½ cup chopped almonds
½ teaspoon vanilla or grated orange rind

1. Cream butter and sugar, and add eggs. Mix well and add flour, which has been sifted with baking powder and salt. When well mixed, add other ingredients.
2. Bake in a loaf or sheet in a hot oven. (450°.)

Torta Rellena (Filled Cake)
(Paraguay)

½ cup butter
1 cup sugar
1 egg, beaten
1 teaspoon vanilla

2 cups flour
1 teaspoon soda
2 teaspoons cream of tartar
½ teaspoon salt

½ cup milk

1. Cream butter and sugar, and add egg. Mix well and add vanilla.
2. Sift dry ingredients and add alternately with milk.
3. Place a thin layer of dough in a baking pan, cover with filling, and put another layer of dough on top. Bake twenty to twenty-five minutes. (400°.)

FILLING

1 cup chopped raisins
½ cup sugar

⅔ cup water
1 tablespoon cornstarch

1. Mix and cook until thick.

Torto de Café (Mocha Layer Cake)

½ cup butter
1 cup brown sugar
2 eggs
2 cups flour
¼ teaspoon soda
½ teaspoon mixed spices

½ teaspoon salt
2 teaspoons baking powder
½ cup cold coffee
½ cup molasses
Whipped cream
Brazil nuts

1. Cream butter, add sugar, and blend thoroughly. Add beaten eggs and beat until smooth.
2. Sift dry ingredients and add alternately with coffee and molasses.
3. Bake in two layer-cake pans at 350° for twenty minutes, or until done. Remove from the pans and cool.
4. Ice cake with sweetened whipped cream flavored with coffee. Decorate with finely chopped Brazil nuts.

Torta de Crema de Plátanos (Banana Cream Cake)

Any sponge cake baked
in layers

Whipped cream

FILLING

1 cup banana pulp
Juice of ½ lemon or
orange juice

½ cup sugar
1 tablespoon butter

1. Press bananas through a sieve and add juice, sugar, and melted butter.
2. Cook together until thick. Cool.
3. Spread between layers of cake. Top with whipped cream.

Note: One egg and a tablespoon of water may be added to the filling.

Torta de Coco (Coconut Cake)

2 cups sugar
1 cup water
2 egg whites

2 cups coconut
1 teaspoon vanilla
Any layer cake

1. Boil sugar and water until it threads. Pour slowly onto stiffly beaten egg whites. Beat. When it begins to hold shape, add most of coconut and vanilla.
2. Spread between layers, and on top and sides of cake. Dust top and sides with remaining coconut.

Coffee Caramel Cake

1 tablespoon gelatin
⅓ cup sugar
⅓ cup black coffee
¼ cup milk

½ cup whipped cream
Layer cake
Chopped nuts mixed with
powdered sugar

1 egg

1. Soak gelatin in three tablespoons of cold water.
2. Heat sugar in a frying pan until brown, and pour on coffee.
3. When coffee clears, put it into the double boiler with milk and softened gelatin. Heat until gelatin is dissolved.
4. Beat egg yolk, and add a small amount of the hot mixture. Then pour into remaining mixture. Remove from heat. Stir as it cools.
5. Beat egg white stiff, blend with cream, and fold it into custard when custard begins to stiffen. Chill.
6. Spread it on cake.
7. Dust top with powdered sugar and chopped nuts.

Chipa
(Paraguay)

12 eggs	1 teaspoon salt
2 pounds shortening	2 cups milk
2 pounds cheese, grated	5 pounds mandioca flour
Anise flavoring	or corn meal

1. Beat eggs one by one into shortening. Add cheese, flavoring, and salt; then add milk and flour alternately.
2. Knead thoroughly and separate into desired sizes.
3. Place in bread pans and bake in a hot oven with a banana leaf, or other mild-scented leaf, on top.

Note: This is a native bread of Paraguay.

Tortillas (Pancakes)
(Ecuador)

1 cup flour	Cold water
1 teaspoon sugar	Butter for frying
Pinch of salt	Melted sugar
2 eggs, beaten	Quartered lemons

1. Mix dry ingredients, add eggs, and enough cold water to make a thin batter.
2. Fry in butter, and when done pour melted sugar over each. Make pancakes the size of a dinner plate. Serve with lemon.

Tortas de Frutas (Fruit Cakes)
(Panama)

Puff paste	Oranges
Sliced pineapple	Bananas
Sugar	1 or 2 lemons

½ cup nuts, chopped

1. Line a baking dish with puff paste.
2. Spread with a layer of sliced pineapple. Sprinkle with sugar.
3. Add a layer of oranges, sugar, bananas, and a few slices of lemon. Sprinkle with nuts. Lay strips of pastry at right angles.
4. Bake in a slow oven one hour or longer. (350°.)

Pastel de Plátano (Banana Pie)
(Guatemala)

1 teaspoon cinnamon
1 chili pepper, chopped, or mixed spices
1 cup seeded raisins, chopped
Pastry
6 bananas, cut in half lengthwise
½ cup chopped almonds
1 tablespoon melted butter
Sugar to sweeten
¼ cup sherry
4 egg whites

1. Mix cinnamon, chili pepper, and raisins.
2. Steam bananas and rub through a sieve. Add raisin mixture, almonds, butter, sugar, and sherry. Fold in stiffly beaten egg whites.
3. Make into a double-crust pie.
4. Bake one-half hour. (475°.)

Cajeta de Almendra (Almond Cakes)
(Chile)

2 cups sugar
1 cup water
½ to ¾ cup almonds or walnuts, chopped
5 egg whites

1. Cook sugar and water to thread stage.
2. Beat egg whites stiff. Beat in sirup a little at a time. Beat hard until mixture thickens slightly. Add nuts.
3. Pour into small paper cups and bake twelve to fifteen minutes. (300°.)

Camote y Piña (Sweet Potato Candy)

2 cups sugar
1 cup water
1 pound sweet potatoes
½ cup grated pineapple
Cinnamon to taste

1. Boil sugar and water to thread stage.
2. Boil potatoes, press through a sieve, and add to sirup. Cook until thick, stirring constantly.
3. Add pineapple and cinnamon, and cook a few minutes.
4. Serve in sherbet glasses.

Chayote con Jengibre (Gingered Chayote Chips)
(Puerto Rico)

3 chayotes	½ cup water
3 cups sugar	¼ cup canton ginger

2 lemons or limes, sliced

1. Wash chayotes with a brush, and boil until tender. Pare and cut thin, crosswise. Place them in a jar.
2. Boil sugar, water, ginger, and limes for ten minutes.
3. Pour over chayotes. Let stand several days.

Pelo de Angel (Angel's Hair)
(Puerto Rico)

Chayotes	Thick sugar sirup

1. Cut chayotes into thin strips and cook in sirup.
2. Serve cold with the sirup.

Sweet Pickle Chayote

3 chayotes	1 piece stick cinnamon
1½ cups vinegar	1 teaspoon whole allspice
1½ cups sugar	berries
¼ teaspoon whole cloves	1 tablespoon mustard seed

Dash red pepper

1. Wash chayotes and boil until tender. Pare and cut into eighths lengthwise. Place in a glass jar.
2. Boil for ten minutes the vinegar, sugar, and spices (which have been tied in a cheesecloth bag).
3. Pour over chayotes. Seal and set aside for several days.

Note: Small onions, string beans, or cauliflower may be added.

Amarillo con Canela (Golden Ball)

3 green bananas	½ cup sugar
3 tablespoons butter	1 teaspoon cinnamon
1 yellow lime	¼ cup water

1. Peel bananas and steam until tender.
2. Melt butter in a baking tin, cut bananas lengthwise, and lay over butter.

3. Squeeze lime juice over them. Sprinkle with sugar and cinnamon.
4. Add water and bake ten to fifteen minutes. (450°.) Baste frequently while baking.
5. Serve hot.

Dulce de Chayote (Preserved Chayote)

3 chayotes or melons	1½ cups sugar
¾ cup water	1 stick cinnamon

1 lime, sliced

1. Wash and peel chayotes. Cut in lengthwise slices.
2. Mix water, sugar, cinnamon, and lime, and boil five minutes.
3. Add chayotes and boil until tender.
4. Serve cold as a dessert.

Dulces de Coco y Almendra (Coconut and Almond Candy)
(Brazil)

1 cup milk	1½ cups sugar
1 cup chopped almonds	1 small coconut, grated

6 egg yolks

1. Bring milk to boiling point and add almonds, stirring constantly. Cook until dry.
2. Add sugar and coconut mixed with egg yolks. Stir over a slow heat until thick enough to be easily handled. Let stand one day.
3. Form into balls and roll in sugar.

Stuffed Prunes
(Brazil)

2 cups sugar	Sugar for filling
1 cup water	Cloves and stick cinnamon
2 pounds prunes	8 egg yolks, beaten
1 coconut, grated	1½ tablespoons flour

1. Make a sirup of sugar and water. Cook prunes in it until it becomes pasty. Remove prunes.
2. Cook sirup down and then return prunes. Boil lightly and then remove prunes and take out pits.
3. Measure coconut, use an equal amount of sugar, add spices, and boil to a paste. Add egg yolks. Then add this mixture to the sirup.

4. Stir constantly until mixture leaves sides of the pan. Add flour mixed with a little cold water. Stir quickly to prevent burning or lumping. Cool and form into balls.

5. Stuff prunes and roll in sugar.

Turron de Vino (Wine Candy)
(Chile)

1 cup sugar
½ cup wine

3 egg whites, beaten stiff

1. Boil sugar and wine to a sirup. Cook until it forms a soft ball.
2. Beat into egg whites.
3. When well mixed, boil over a moderate heat until thick.
4. Drop by spoonfuls onto a greased dish.

Creole Cookery

Even in the American home,
Are Spanish dishes—all our own.

Creole Cookery

Creole cookery, that delectable blend of French and Spanish tastes, began in America in an effective protest still known as the "Petticoat Insurrection."

French cuisine had attained a high point of perfection, and early French settlers in Louisiana introduced many new and tempting dishes. Side by side with this French influence upon the South was the Spanish.

The pepper-loving, garlic-using Spaniard modified his seasonings with pastes and soups which he borrowed from his neighbor, the Italian, and brought them with him to Louisiana. Hoosier and Kaintuck learned to enjoy the Mexican chili con carne. Cold-natured Yankees came to crave the red-hot tabasco sauce, and adapt their pies to the tropical fruits. Thus Louisiana became a genuine hodgepodge of everybody's taste, all seasoned with the Creole art in the hands of that master of the kitchen—the old "Mammy."

Who can forget the Southern fried chicken, candied yams, corn on the cob, watermelon, or any of the other tempting dishes that the old Mammy has added to the menu? How tempting her famous hot breads, and the dishes she has created from beans, rice, okra, bananas, pomegranates, and molasses!

The waters of the South, around New Orleans, supply an abundance and variety of sea foods unknown to any other city, and no wizard can compare with the old black Mammy in its preparation. She plays tricks on the crabs and oysters, and makes the turtle glad he was caught.

All the foods of the South are not included here—rather those that have been inherited and developed from the land across the sea—from France and Spain.

Appetizers

Crab Cocktail

1 crab
1 cup cream, whipped
¾ cup catsup

4 tablespoons Worcester-
   shire sauce
4 teaspoons lemon juice

Salt and pepper

1. Mix above ingredients and serve in cocktail glasses.

Melon Ball Cocktail

Melon balls
¾ cup grape juice or
   orange juice

Juice of ½ lemon
Sugar, if desired (pow-
   dered)

Mint leaves

1. Scoop out melon balls and pour strained juice over them. Chill.
2. Serve in cocktail glasses with mint-leaf garnish.

Cocktail Sauce

4 tablespoons tomato
   catsup
2 tablespoons chopped
   tomatoes

4 tablespoons mayonnaise
2 tablespoons chopped
   green peppers
2 tablespoons chili sauce

1. Mix well together.

Avocado and Shrimp Cocktail

Equal portions of diced
   avocado and shrimps

Cocktail sauce

1. Combine avocado and shrimps. Place in cocktail glasses.
2. Add sauce and serve.

Shrimp Cocktail

2 cups shrimps
1 tablespoon Worcester-
shire sauce
1 cup tomato catsup
1 tablespoon horse-radish

1 tablespoon vinegar
2 tablespoons lemon juice
3 drops tabasco sauce
2 teaspoons creole mustard
(prepared mustard)

Salt

1. Mix well and chill.

Note: Crab, oysters, or lobster may be used in place of shrimps.

Fruit Juice Cocktail

¼ cup sugar
1 cup pineapple juice
1 cup orange juice

2 tablespoons lemon juice
Crushed ice
Sprigs of mint

1. Boil sugar and pineapple juice together ten minutes. Chill.
2. Combine with orange and lemon juice.
3. Serve in cocktail glasses, half filled with crushed ice.
4. Garnish with mint.

Mixed Fruit Cup

1 cup strawberries
1 cup pineapple juice
2 tablespoons wine jelly

¼ cup orange juice
1 cup orange pulp
1 cup other fruit

Mint or cherries

1. Mix above ingredients, except mint or cherries, at least one hour before serving. Chill.
2. Serve in sherbet glasses with mint or cherry garnish.

Miscellaneous Appetizers

Clam juice, sauerkraut juice, tomato juice, orange juice, grapefruit juice, and grape juice may all be served as appetizers.

Soups

Tomato Soup

1 quart tomatoes or stock and tomatoes	1 sprig parsley, minced
	Salt and pepper
1 onion, chopped	1 tablespoon flour

1 tablespoon butter

1. Put tomatoes, onion, parsley, salt, and pepper on to cook.
2. Mix flour and butter and add to soup. Cook until onion is tender.

Oyster Soup

2 onions, chopped	Stock
1 stalk celery, diced	Rice
1 green pepper, chopped	3 tomatoes, peeled and quartered
Butter or oil	

1 pint oysters

1. Brown onions, celery, and green peppers in butter or oil. Add stock.
2. Add rice and quartered tomatoes to stock and boil thirty minutes, or until rice is soft. Season.
3. Poach oysters in their own juice and add to stock just before serving.
4. Serve with crackers.

Chicken Gumbo

½ boned, cooked fowl	2 tablespoons butter
1 carrot	2 tablespoons rice
1 turnip	2 quarts broth
1 small onion	4 tomatoes, peeled
½ green pepper	12 okras, sliced
1 leek	1 tablespoon salt

1. Cut fowl into small square pieces.
2. Dice carrot, turnip, onion, pepper, and leek, and brown them in butter.
3. Add rice and chicken bones, and moisten them with broth. Season with salt.
4. Cook thirty minutes and add tomatoes cut in quarters, okra, and chicken. Cook thirty minutes more.
5. Remove bones and serve hot.

Pendennis Turtle Soup

2 pounds veal bones
2 carrots, diced
2 onions, diced
2 tablespoons butter
3 tablespoons flour
2 quarts beef stock or water
1 small can tomatoes

1 small can tomato purée
Salt and pepper
6 whole cloves
½ cup sherry wine
2 cups boiled fresh turtle
    meat
1 lemon

2 hard-cooked eggs

1. Roast bones, carrots, and onions in butter until brown. Sprinkle with flour and brown again.
2. Place bones and vegetables in a saucepan and add stock or water, tomatoes, tomato purée, salt, pepper, and cloves. Boil two hours.
3. Add wine and strain through cheesecloth.
4. Add turtle meat cut in cubes, and lemon and eggs, also cut in cubes. Boil up quickly and serve.

Crab Soup

1 dozen crabs, or 1 pound
    crab meat
1 tablespoon butter
1 small onion, minced
Salt and pepper

2 cups milk
½ cup cream
½ teaspoon Worcestershire
    sauce
1 teaspoon flour

1 tablespoon sherry

1. Cook crabs about twenty minutes in boiling, salted water. Pick meat from shells.
2. Put crab meat in a double boiler, and add butter, onion, salt, and pepper. Simmer five minutes.
3. Heat milk and add crab mixture, then cream and Worcestershire.
4. Thicken with flour and add sherry.
5. Cook over a low flame for one hour.

Shrimp Gumbo

1 pound beef
½ pound ham (from
    knuckle)
2 tablespoons lard

1 pound shelled shrimps
4 dozen small okra pods
1 large onion, chopped
Red pepper and salt

1. Cut beef and ham into inch cubes and brown in lard.
2. Add shrimps, okra, and onion. Season to taste.
3. Let simmer over a slow fire about twenty minutes. Add water two inches above contents of kettle and let simmer two hours. Add more water if needed.

Note: Crab may be used in place of shrimps.

Sea Food Gumbo

1 quart shrimps or 1 cup
   crab, 1 cup shrimps, and
   2 dozen oysters
2 onions, minced
1½ quarts water or part
   oyster liquid
1 red bell pepper, minced
1 tablespoon butter

Seasonings: parsley, salt,
   thyme, bay leaves, pepper, and Worcestershire
   sauce
2 cups okra, sliced
½ cup cooked rice
3 large tomatoes, cut in
   pieces

1 tablespoon flour

1. Cook fish with one onion, salt, and water.

2. Brown other onion, and bell pepper, with butter. Then add flour and stock from fish. Season.

3. Add okra, rice, tomatoes, and fish. Let simmer a short time before serving.

Black Bean Soup

2 cups dried black beans
Cold water
½ pound salt pork
1 onion, minced
4 stalks celery, diced

1 carrot, diced
Salt and pepper
Other seasonings as desired
   (cloves, mace, lemon, or
   wineglass of sherry)

Lemon

1. Soak beans overnight in two quarts of water.

2. In the morning add two more quarts of water, salt pork, onion, celery, and carrot. Cook until beans are soft.

3. Remove salt pork and cut it into pieces. Press beans and vegetables through a sieve, saving all the liquid. Season and combine ingredients.

4. Thicken, if desired, with one tablespoon flour and two tablespoons water which have been well blended. Serve with lemon.

Sauces

Creole Sauce

1 onion, chopped
2 green peppers, chopped
1 tablespoon oil
1 clove garlic, minced
1 tablespoon flour

6 tomatoes, peeled and
    crushed
Salt and pepper
6 canned mushrooms, sliced
½ teaspoon minced parsley

½ teaspoon chopped chives

1. Heat onion and pepper in oil.
2. Add garlic, flour, and tomatoes. Season.
3. Add mushrooms, parsley, and chives. Cook twenty minutes, stirring occasionally.

Note: This sauce can be used on meats, eggs, fish, and fowl. Chopped ham is often added to the sauce.

Creole Dressing

1 clove garlic
6 tablespoons salad oil
2 tablespoons vinegar
1 teaspoon salt

Dash of cayenne pepper
2 teaspoons minced parsley
2 teaspoons minced onion
2 teaspoons tomato catsup

1. Rub surface of bowl with garlic.
2. Combine two tablespoons of oil with vinegar. Gradually beat in rest of the oil.
3. Add seasonings and flavorings. Chill.

Raisin Sauce

1 cup raisins
5 cloves
1 cup water
¾ cup brown sugar

1 teaspoon cornstarch
Salt, pepper, and Worcestershire sauce if desired
1 tablespoon butter

1 tablespoon vinegar

1. Simmer raisins, cloves, and water about ten minutes. Add sugar, cornstarch, salt, and pepper, which have been mixed together.
2. Stir until slightly thickened, and add butter and vinegar.

Note: This sauce is used for baked ham.

Shrimp Sauce

1½ cups chopped shrimps
3 tablespoons lemon juice
1½ cups white sauce

Parsley, minced
2 hard-cooked eggs, minced
Salt and pepper

1. Soak shrimps in lemon juice for one-half hour. Then add them to white sauce.
2. Add parsley, hard-cooked eggs, and seasonings. Heat and serve.

Note: This sauce is used for fish.

Mushroom Sauce

1 cup mushrooms or 1 me-
  dium-sized can
4 tablespoons butter

3 tablespoons flour
1 cup rich milk or thin
  cream

1. Heat mushrooms in butter. Add flour and brown slightly.
2. Add cream and cook until it thickens.

Note: This sauce is used for steak or chicken.

Fish

Spanish Oysters

2 or 3 green onions and
  tops, chopped
1 tablespoon butter
2 tablespoons flour
1 can tomatoes (No. 2)
Few drops Worcestershire
  sauce

Salt, pepper, cayenne
Few sprigs parsley, minced
2 pickles, sliced
1 tablespoon chopped green
  peppers
1 tablespoon chopped celery
3 dozen oysters

1. Fry onions in butter, and add flour. Blend and add tomatoes, season-ings, and other ingredients except oysters. Simmer thirty minutes.
2. Add oysters and heat until edges curl.

Note: Mushrooms may be added if desired.

Oysters Louisiane

1 dozen oysters
3 tablespoons butter
2 teaspoons minced onion
2 tablespoons chopped red
  pepper

3 tablespoons flour
Salt, pepper, cayenne
½ cup grated Parmesan
  cheese

1. Parboil oysters in their own liquid for ten minutes. Remove oysters and place in a casserole.
2. Add enough water to liquid to make one and one-half cups.
3. Melt butter, add onion and red pepper, and fry until soft. Add flour and blend. Gradually add liquor, stirring constantly. Bring to a boiling point and season. Pour over oysters.
4. Sprinkle with grated cheese, place in a hot oven, and bake until thoroughly heated. (450°.)

Chesapeake Oyster Loaf

1 loaf French bread
Butter
2 dozen oysters

½ cup cream
1 tablespoon minced celery
Salt and pepper

2 drops tabasco sauce

1. Cut top crust from bread and scoop out the inside.
2. Butter one third of portion taken out and toast it in oven.
3. Fry oysters in butter a few minutes, and add cream, celery, seasonings, and toasted bread.
4. Fill hollowed loaf with this mixture and cover with top crust. Place in a baking pan and bake twenty minutes. (375°.) Baste frequently with oyster liquid.
5. Slice and serve hot.

Shrimp Creole

1 small onion, minced
1 green pepper, minced
1 tablespoon oil
1 teaspoon flour
2 tomatoes, peeled and diced

1 clove garlic, minced
Salt and pepper
24 shrimps
¼ cup tomato sauce
1 tablespoon sherry

1. Cook onion and pepper in oil for ten minutes.
2. Add flour, tomatoes, garlic, salt, and pepper. Cook twenty minutes.
3. Add shrimps, tomato sauce, and sherry. Cook fifteen minutes.

Shrimp Balls

1 pound shelled shrimps
Salt, pepper, cayenne
1 teaspoon each, minced green onion tops, green pepper, and parsley

1 teaspoon butter
1 cup toasted bread crumbs
1 tablespoon lard
2 tablespoons flour
2 to 3 cups water

1. Chop shrimps and add seasonings.
2. Melt butter, add bread crumbs and shrimps. Shape into cones or balls.
3. Fry in deep fat.
4. Melt lard in a saucepan, add flour, and brown. Add water and cook until thickened. Add balls. Cook fifteen minutes.

Note: Boiled rice may be substituted for crumbs.

Shrimp Pie No. 1

3 slices bread (½ inch thick)
1 cup milk
2 cups shrimps
2 tablespoons melted butter

Mace, nutmeg, salt, and pepper to taste
2 tablespoons sherry
1 teaspoon Worcestershire sauce

1. Soak bread in milk and mash with a fork.
2. Add shrimps, butter, and seasonings.
3. Bake in a buttered casserole in oven for twenty minutes. (375°)

Note: Serve with green salad.

Shrimp Pie No. 2

1 onion, chopped
1 green pepper, chopped
1 tablespoon butter
2 cups shrimps

4 slices stale bread
1 can tomatoes (No. 2)
2 or 3 hard-cooked eggs, chopped

Salt and pepper

1. Fry onion and pepper in butter until brown. Add shrimps and seasonings.
2. Mix bread and tomatoes. Add to first mixture. Cook for twenty minutes.
3. Add eggs and place in a buttered casserole.
4. Bake fifteen minutes in a moderate oven. (375°.)

Shrimp and Corn Pie

2 cans corn

2 eggs, beaten

1 tablespoon melted butter

½ cup milk or tomato juice

1 cup shelled shrimps

Salt and pepper

1. Mix all together and pour into a buttered casserole.
2. Bake one-half hour. (300°.)

Shrimps and Hominy

2 cups shrimps

½ cup butter

Salt and pepper

2 cups cooked hominy

1. Melt butter in a saucepan, and add shrimps, salt, and pepper. Cook ten minutes.
2. Serve hot with hominy.

Eggplant Stuffed with Shrimps

1 large eggplant

2 onions, chopped

1 clove garlic, minced

1 tablespoon butter

1 pound shrimps, chopped

1 cup buttered crumbs

1 teaspoon chopped green pepper

1 teaspoon minced parsley

Salt and pepper

1. Cut a piece from top of eggplant. Remove pulp, being careful not to break shell. Boil pulp in a very little water until tender. Mash.
2. Fry onions and garlic in butter, and add shrimps, pulp, crumbs, green pepper, parsley, and seasonings.
3. Fill eggplant shell and bake twenty to thirty minutes. (400°.) Mixture may be baked in a buttered baking dish, if desired.

Note: Ham, bacon, or sausage may replace shrimps.

Crab Stew

Meat of one large crab

½ glass sherry

1 onion

1 sweet pepper

1 tomato

Pinch of rosemary

1 clove garlic

1 teaspoon butter

1 teaspoon flour

2 tablespoons cream

Salt, pepper, paprika

Worcestershire sauce

1. Soak crab in sherry for two hours.
2. Chop onion, pepper, tomato, and rosemary. Mash garlic, and add butter and flour. Mix well and add cream and seasonings. Heat in a saucepan, and add crab and sherry.
3. Cook over a slow fire eight minutes. Add a little Worcestershire sauce.
4. Serve on toast or crackers.

Deviled Crab

1 dozen fresh crabs (2 cups crab meat)
¼ teaspoon each, mustard, nutmeg, mace
2 cloves

1 tablespoon melted butter
1 egg yolk, beaten
½ cup sherry
1 egg white, beaten stiff
Cracker crumbs

Salt and pepper

1. Mix crab meat, seasonings, butter, and egg yolk.
2. Add sherry, then egg white.
3. Fill crab shells or a buttered baking dish. Sprinkle with crumbs.
4. Bake for one-half hour at 350°.

Stuffed Crabs

2 tablespoons butter
1 cup sliced mushrooms
1 tablespoon flour
½ cup cream

1 pound cooked crab meat
Juice of ½ lemon
1 teaspoon capers
1 teaspoon chopped parsley

2 egg whites, beaten stiff

1. Melt butter and add mushrooms. Cook until tender. Take mushrooms out of pan.
2. Add flour to butter, blend well, and add cream.
3. When thick, add other ingredients in order given.
4. Fill crab shells, or place in a buttered casserole.
5. Bake for twenty minutes in a 350° oven.

Soft Clams, Louisiana

48 clams with shells
Salt and pepper
1 green pepper

4 stalks celery
8 slices of bacon
Bread crumbs

1. Wash and clean clams. Place each one in a half shell. Season with salt and pepper.
2. Chop pepper and celery and sprinkle over the clams.
3. Cut each slice of bacon in six pieces and place a piece on each clam.
4. Sprinkle with bread crumbs.
5. Bake for fifteen minutes. (400°.)

Creole Chowder

3 or 4 slices bacon
1 onion, chopped
1 bell pepper, chopped
2 cans tomato sauce

2 cans minced clams
Salt and pepper
Potatoes
Cracker crumbs

1. Cut bacon into small pieces and fry. Remove bacon, and put some of it in bottom of a casserole. Fry onion and green pepper.
2. Add tomato sauce, minced clams, remainder of bacon, salt, and pepper.
3. Pare and slice potatoes and place in a casserole. Season well.
4. Pour tomato mixture over potatoes and sprinkle with cracker crumbs.
5. Cover and bake in a moderate oven for two hours. (375°-400°.)

Bluefish, Creole

3 pounds bluefish or any
    large white fish
1 teaspoon salt
Pepper

½ teaspoon paprika
Melted butter
Creole sauce
Bread crumbs

Lemon

1. Season fish with salt, pepper, and paprika. Brush with butter. Bake for twenty-five minutes. (400°.)
2. Pour on creole sauce and sprinkle with bread crumbs. Bake fifteen minutes. Serve with lemon.

Escalloped Fish

2 pounds tenderloin of fish
    (trout, redfish, or snap-
    per)
2 tablespoons butter
1 tablespoon oil
1 dozen oysters

½ green pepper, chopped
Minced parsley
Salt, pepper, cayenne
½ cup toasted bread
    crumbs
6 strips bacon

1. Boil fish until tender. Shred and place in a baking dish. Pour olive oil over it and dot with butter.
2. Put on a layer of oysters, green peppers, parsley, salt, pepper, and cayenne. Repeat until all ingredients are used.
3. Spread crumbs on top and lay strips of bacon over all.
4. Bake twenty-five minutes. (350°.)

Miscellaneous Entrees

Corn Creole

½ onion, chopped
½ green pepper, chopped
1 pound ground meat
  (beef)
1 tablespoon shortening
  or oil

1 can corn
1 can tomato sauce
½ cup corn meal
2 cups milk
Salt and pepper
1 egg, well beaten

Olives

1. Cook onion, pepper, and meat in fat in a frying pan until brown.
2. Remove from heat and add corn, tomato sauce, corn meal, milk, salt, and pepper. When well mixed, add egg and olives. Mix all thoroughly.
3. Bake in a buttered casserole for forty-five minutes. (400°.)

Liver à la Créole

1 pound calf's liver, cut in
  inch cubes
Salt and pepper
2 small onions, thinly sliced

1 tablespoon minced parsley
Deep fat for frying
Lemon slices
Few sprigs parsley

1. Sprinkle liver with salt and pepper, and cover with onion and parsley. Let stand two hours.
2. Fry in deep fat for one minute. (390°.) Drain.
3. Place on a hot platter and garnish with lemon and parsley.

Creole Beef Stew

1½ pounds lean beef
Potatoes, peeled
2 cups tomatoes
1 large onion, chopped
1 green pepper, chopped
1 cup string beans

1 cup corn, cut from cob
2 carrots, sliced
Flour
1 tablespoon minced parsley
1 teaspoon Worcestershire
  sauce

Salt and pepper

1. Place beef in a casserole and surround with as many potatoes as needed.
2. Mix tomatoes, onion, pepper, beans, corn, and carrots. Pour over potatoes. Season with salt, pepper, Worcestershire sauce, and parsley. Partly cover meat and vegetables with water. Place lid on casserole and put in a slow oven. (350°.) Bake until meat is tender. Add more water if necessary.
3. Remove meat to a hot platter and garnish with vegetables.
4. Thicken gravy with flour. Just before serving, add parsley and Worcestershire sauce.

Casserole of Beef

2 pounds round of beef	¾ cup bread crumbs
2 onions	1 teaspoon salt
1 large carrot	⅛ teaspoon cloves
1 slice salt pork	¼ teaspoon pepper
1½ cups green peas	2 cups tomatoes

1 cup water

1. Trim most of fat from meat and cut into small cubes.
2. Chop onion, carrot, and salt pork. Add peas, bread crumbs, salt, pepper, and cloves. Put a layer of mixture into a casserole, then a layer of meat. Repeat until all ingredients are used.
3. Mix tomatoes with water and pour over all.
4. Cover closely and bake very slowly for three hours. (350°.)

Entrecotes (Creole)

2 tender sirloin steaks	Garlic
1 tablespoon oil	Salt and pepper

Creole sauce

1. Rub meat with oil and garlic. Season with salt and pepper.
2. Arrange on a broiler and broil eight minutes on each side.
3. Serve with Creole sauce. (P. 221.)

Texas Hash

2 cups rice	2 pounds round steak,
4 quarts boiling water	ground
4 small onions, sliced	½ teaspoon pepper
1 quart tomatoes	2 teaspoons salt

1. Cook rice in boiling, salted water until soft. Drain.
2. Cook remaining ingredients together for twenty minutes.
3. Combine rice and meat mixtures, and bake twenty minutes in a hot oven. (475°.)

Creole Pork Chops

6 pork chops	1 tablespoon minced parsley
2 tablespoons flour	2 tablespoons minced green
1 tablespoon fat	onion tops
2 tablespoons minced green	1 tablespoon red pepper
peppers	pulp
2 tablespoons minced onion	1 bay leaf
Salt and pepper	

1. Roll chops in flour and fry in fat.
2. Remove chops, add a cup of water and seasonings. Simmer all until gravy is thick.

Jambalayah No. 1

1 pound fresh pork	3 quarts beef broth or hot
2 onions	water
2 sprigs thyme	1½ cups rice
2 sprigs parsley	Salt and pepper
1 bay leaf	¼ teaspoon cloves
1 tablespoon butter	½ teaspoon chili powder
1 pound ham	and cayenne

1. Cut pork in small pieces. Mince onions and herbs and brown in butter.
2. Chop ham and add to the mixture. Cook five minutes.
3. Add broth or water, and when it boils, add rice.
4. Season to taste. Boil half an hour, or until rice is soft.

Jambalayah No. 2

1 to 1½ cups cold chicken,	1 large onion
veal, or lamb	1 green pepper
1 cup boiled rice	1 large stalk celery
1½ cups stewed tomatoes	Salt and pepper
Buttered crumbs	

1. Mix chicken, rice, and tomato, and cook ten minutes.
2. Chop onion, green pepper, and celery, and add to other mixture. Season.
3. Place in a buttered baking dish, and cover with crumbs. Bake one hour. (375°.)

Chicken Cutlets

Chicken cut in pieces   Bread crumbs
Melted butter   Halves of tomatoes
1 egg, beaten   Mushroom purée
                Cooking wine

1. Dip pieces of chicken in melted butter, then in egg and crumbs.
2. Fry in butter.
3. Arrange on halves of tomatoes, which may be sautéd, if desired.
4. Pour mushroom purée over cutlets. Purée may be flavored with cooking wine if desired.

Chicken Custard

1 cup strong chicken broth   3 egg yolks, well beaten
1 cup thin cream   Salt to taste

1. Scald broth and cream and pour over egg yolks. Season.
2. Cook in a double boiler until thick, stirring constantly. Or bake in a slow oven in custard cups set in a pan of warm water. (325°.)

Chicken Pie

1 or 2 frying chickens   Rich pastry
Salt and pepper   Flour

1. Cut chickens into pieces. Cover with boiling water, season, and cook until tender.
2. Line sides of a baking dish with pastry. Put in a layer of chicken. Dust with flour. Add rest of chicken.
3. Pour enough broth over chicken to moisten.
4. Cover with pastry. Prick holes in pastry to let out steam. Or, arrange chicken and pastry in alternate layers, with pastry on top.
5. Bake until brown. (400°.)

Mock Terrapin Stew

2 fricassee chickens   2 cups milk, scalded
¼ pound butter   6 egg yolks, well beaten
2 tablespoons flour   Salt and pepper
                1 large glass cooking wine

1. Disjoint chickens, place in a saucepan, cover with boiling water, and simmer until tender.
2. Remove meat from bones and dice.
3. Melt butter in a saucepan, add flour and blend, add scalded milk, and remove from fire. Add egg yolks, salt, and pepper. Place over a low heat. Do not allow to boil.
4. Add chicken. Just before serving, add wine.

Chicken Cakes

1 cup chopped boiled breast
of chicken
2 eggs
1 tablespoon cream

Salt and pepper
Butter
½ cup minced celery
1 cup white sauce

1. Mix chicken, one well-beaten egg, cream, salt, and pepper. Make into small flat cakes.
2. Beat second egg slightly. Dip cakes in egg and fry in butter until browned on both sides. Remove to a hot platter.
3. Add celery to white sauce and pour over cakes.

Roast Squab with Rice Pilau

4 squabs
6 slices bacon
¾ cup chopped celery
1 onion, minced

2 cups rice
4 cups chicken stock
4 eggs
Salt and pepper

Mustard pickle juice

1. Dress squabs and clean thoroughly.
2. Dice bacon and fry until crisp. Remove bacon, add celery and onion to bacon fat, and fry until soft.
3. Boil rice in chicken stock until tender. Add bacon, celery, and onion. Add well-beaten eggs and season with salt and pepper.
4. Stuff squabs with rice mixture.
5. Make four mounds of remaining mixture, and put in a roasting pan. Lay a squab on each mound.
6. Bake in a hot oven for twenty-five minutes, basting frequently with mustard-pickle juice. (450°.)

Baked Ham

1 ham
¼ cup vinegar or fruit
juice

Cloves
½ cup water
1 teaspoon dry mustard

Brown sugar

1. Trim ham. Cover with cold water, and boil for two or three hours. If very salty, change water once. Remove skin, stick with cloves, and place in a roasting pan.
2. Mix vinegar or fruit juice with water and mustard. Pour over ham and use for basting. Bake slowly two hours or longer, depending on size of ham. (350°.)
3. Cover with brown sugar and bake very slowly for an hour or longer.

Broiled Ham

1 slice ham   1 cup water
1 cup milk

1. Trim ham and soak in water and milk for an hour, or longer.
2. Wipe well and place on a broiler rack under a slow heat. Broil slowly. When cooked and slightly browned, remove to a hot platter.

Stewed Tripe

½ green pepper, minced   ½ clove garlic, minced
2 small onions, sliced   ½ teaspoon minced parsley
2 tablespoons oil   Salt and pepper
4 tomatoes, peeled and   1½ pounds honeycomb
   crushed   tripe
½ teaspoon sugar

1. Cook pepper and onion in oil. Add garlic, tomato, parsley, salt, pepper, and sugar. Mix well and cook thirty minutes.
2. Heat tripe in oil. Season and add the above sauce.
3. Mix well and cook until blended, twenty to thirty minutes.

Stuffed Cabbage

1 medium cabbage   ¼ cup minced ham
1 dozen small sausages or   1 tablespoon butter
   oysters, minced   ¾ clove garlic, minced
½ cup buttered bread   1 teaspoon each, minced on-
   crumbs   ion, parsley, red pepper

1. Quarter cabbage, tie in a cloth, and boil one hour.
2. Mix other ingredients and fry in butter.
3. Open cabbage leaves and put stuffing between them. Tie up again and cook two hours in boiling water with a piece of red pepper.
4. Serve with cream sauce.

Creole Eggs

1 dozen hard-cooked eggs   1 can tomatoes (No. 2½),
1 onion, chopped   strained
2 tablespoons butter   1 cup chopped celery
1 cup chopped green pep-   1 small can mushrooms
   pers   Salt, pepper, cayenne
2 to 3 tablespoons flour   Worcestershire sauce
1 cup white sauce

1. Chop egg whites and mash yolks.
2. Brown onion in butter. Add peppers, and then flour. Blend well and add tomato juice, celery, and mushrooms. Season with salt, pepper, and cayenne. Simmer twenty minutes.
3. Add white sauce and blend well.
4. Pour into buttered ramekins. Place in a hot oven until nicely browned. (475°.)

Fromage Fondue Creole

2 tablespoons butter
2 tablespoons flour
½ cup thin cream
3 egg yolks, well beaten

Salt and pepper
$\frac{1}{16}$ teaspoon nutmeg
1 cup grated Parmesan or
    Gruyère cheese

3 egg whites, stiffly beaten

1. Melt butter in a saucepan, add flour, and blend. Add cream. Cook, stirring constantly, until smooth and well blended. Remove from fire.
2. Stir in egg yolks, salt, pepper, nutmeg, and cheese.
3. Fold in egg whites.
4. Pour into small pudding or soufflé dishes, well buttered, and bake about twenty-five minutes, or until nicely browned. (350°.)
5. Serve at once or mixture will fall.

Vegetables

Creole String Beans with Tomatoes

3 pounds string beans
1 medium onion, minced

6 tomatoes
Salt and pepper

½ cup butter

1. Cook beans, onion, and tomatoes, peeled and quartered.
2. Add seasoning, but no water. Cook until beans are tender.
3. Add butter fifteen minutes before serving.

Succotash

Corn, fresh or canned
Equal quantity of green
    lima beans

Milk
Salt and pepper
Cracker crumbs

1. Mix corn and beans. Season and place in a baking dish. Cover with milk.
2. Cover with cracker crumbs and bake for twenty minutes in a hot oven. (475°.)

Note: String beans may be used for lima beans, or tomatoes may be added.

Baked Tomatoes with Okra

1 tablespoon chopped onion	Canned or fresh-cooked
1 tablespoon chopped green	okra
pepper	2 tablespoons sugar
1 tablespoon butter	Salt and pepper
1 can tomatoes	1 cup bread crumbs

1. Cook onion and pepper in butter for five minutes.
2. Add tomatoes and okra; then salt, pepper, and sugar.
3. Put alternate layers of vegetables and bread crumbs in a baking dish, having crumbs on top.
4. Dot with butter and bake for fifteen minutes in a hot oven. (475°.)

Squaw Corn with Apples

2 cups diced bacon	Salt and pepper
1 can corn	Brown sugar

Apples

1. Fry bacon. Add corn and seasonings. Cook for fifteen minutes, stirring frequently.
2. Peel apples and cut into quarters or eighths. Sprinkle with brown sugar and cook in bacon fat in another pan until tender. It is possible to push corn aside and cook apples at the same time.

Tomatoes Louisiana

6 tomatoes	2 tablespoons chopped ham
Salt and pepper	1 tablespoon chopped onion
1 teaspoon sugar	1½ cups broth
4 tablespoons rice	2 tablespoons butter

2 tablespoons grated cheese

1. Wipe tomatoes. Cut a thin slice from top, and scoop out centers. Season them with salt, pepper, and sugar.
2. Mix rice, ham, onion, and broth. Season. Boil twenty minutes.
3. Add butter and cheese. Mix well and fill tomatoes. Baste with melted butter.
4. Place in a baking dish, cover, and bake for fifteen minutes, or until tender. (450°.) Do not overcook, or tomatoes will lose their shape.

Corn Fritters

¾ cup flour
1 teaspoon salt
1 teaspoon baking powder
Pepper or paprika

1 cup corn (fresh or
  canned)
1 egg, beaten
4 tablespoons milk

1. Sift dry ingredients and add to corn. Add egg and milk.
2. Sauté or fry in deep fat, using a large spoonful for each fritter.
3. Drain on absorbent paper. Serve with sirup.

Candied Sweet Potatoes

Sweet potatoes
½ cup sugar

¼ cup hot water
3 tablespoons butter

1. Wash and cook potatoes in boiling water until tender. Drain, peel, and cut in two lengthwise. Arrange in a baking dish.
2. Make a thin sirup of sugar, water, and butter.
3. Pour sirup over potatoes. Bake for thirty minutes. (400°.) Baste occasionally.

Note: Carrots may be candied in this same manner.

Apple Fritters

2 eggs
1 cup milk
2 tablespoons sugar
2 tablespoons melted butter
¼ teaspoon salt

Dash of cinnamon
2 cups flour
2 teaspoons baking powder
4 apples, chopped fine
Fat for frying

Powdered sugar

1. Beat eggs into milk, and add sugar, butter, salt, and cinnamon. Mix them thoroughly.
2. Sift flour and baking powder. Add to egg and milk mixture. Add apples.
3. Fry batter by spoonfuls in deep fat.
4. Sprinkle with powdered sugar and serve hot.

Creole Banana Fritters

2 egg yolks	2 egg whites
1 cup flour	Bananas
1 tablespoon melted butter	Fat for frying
2 tablespoons lemon juice	Powdered sugar

1. Beat egg yolks and work in flour. Add butter and lemon juice. Add water enough to make a thin batter. Fold in stiffly beaten egg whites.
2. Peel and cut bananas in half lengthwise. Dip into batter and fry in deep fat.
3. Dust with powdered sugar. Serve hot.

Green Beans

2 quarts string beans	Salt and pepper
6 or 8 slices bacon	Water

1. Wash and string beans. Put in a kettle.
2. Add other ingredients and cover with water. Cook until tender. The beans should be almost dry when done.

Fried Okra

Tender okra	1 egg, beaten
Salt and pepper	Cracker crumbs
Deep fat	

1. Boil okra in salted water ten minutes. Drain and season.
2. Roll in egg, then in cracker crumbs.
3. Fry in deep fat until brown. Drain on paper.

Southern Squash

Squash, Hubbard or banana	Cinnamon, nutmeg, and salt
Sugar	Butter

1. Cut squash into pieces suitable for serving.
2. Sprinkle with sugar, cinnamon, nutmeg, and salt. Dot with butter.
3. Bake one and a half hours, or until tender. (400°.)

Eggplant à la Créole

1 cup spaghetti	2 tablespoons butter
1 eggplant	1 green pepper
4 tomatoes	Salt and pepper
1 cup grated cheese	1 cup cream

1. Cook spaghetti in boiling, salted water until tender. Drain.
2. Peel eggplant and slice thin. Put half in a casserole. Sprinkle with salt and pepper.
3. Peel and slice tomatoes and put half of them over eggplant. Next put a layer of spaghetti, using all of it. Cover with half the cheese and dot with butter. Add another layer of tomatoes, cover with chopped green pepper, and another layer of eggplant sprinkled with salt and pepper. Sprinkle on remaining cheese.
4. Pour cream over all and bake one and one-half hours. (400°.)

Peppers à la Créole

Minced cold meat	½ cup butter
Bread crumbs	Milk
Onions	Bell peppers
Tomatoes	Stock
Mushrooms	Tomato sauce

Boiled rice

1. Take equal parts of cold meat, crumbs, onions, tomatoes, and mushrooms. Chop all together. Stew in butter and enough milk to moisten for fifteen or twenty minutes.
2. Fill peppers with this mixture. Place in a baking dish, and surround with stock flavored with tomato sauce. Garnish with boiled rice.
3. Bake thirty to forty minutes. (400°.)

Okra Pilau No. 1

6 slices bacon, diced	2 cups raw rice
2 cups okra, cut in pieces	4 cups water

Salt and pepper

1. Brown bacon and remove from fat.
2. Fry okra in bacon fat over a slow fire.
3. Add rice, cold water, and seasonings. Cover and steam forty minutes, until rice is tender. Add bacon.

Okra Pilau No. 2

4 slices bacon, diced
1 onion, chopped
1 tablespoon chopped green
   pepper
2 cups tomatoes

2 cups okra, sliced thin
Salt and pepper
2 cups raw rice
1 teaspoon salt
2 quarts water

1. Fry bacon and remove from pan.
2. Add onion and pepper and brown. Add tomatoes and okra. Season. Simmer fifteen minutes.
3. Boil rice in salted water about twelve minutes. Drain and add to tomato mixture.
4. Cook for fifteen or twenty minutes. Add bacon and serve.

Okra and Corn

4 slices salt pork
2 green peppers, sliced
2 cups okra, sliced

2 tablespoons flour
⅔ cup milk
3 cups corn

Salt

1. Fry salt pork and add peppers and okra.
2. Cover with flour, stir well, and add milk and corn. Season.
3. Cook until peppers are tender.
4. Serve on toast.

Sweet Corn New Orleans Style

1 apple
¼ cup sirup
2 tablespoons chopped red
   pepper

1 tablespoon butter
1 cup corn pulp
½ cup cream
1 teaspoon salt

⅛ teaspoon pepper

1. Peel and slice apple. Stew gently in sirup.
2. Melt butter in another saucepan, add red pepper, and sauté lightly.
3. Add corn, cream, and salt and pepper. Cook ten minutes.
4. Place apple slices on a platter and pour corn over them. Serve at once.

Creole Tomatoes

2 cups canned tomatoes or   Salt and pepper
    6 fresh tomatoes   1 cup cracker crumbs
¼ cup chopped onion   1 tablespoon butter
½ cup chopped celery   1 cup canned mushrooms

1. Cook tomatoes, onion, celery, salt, and pepper until celery is tender.
2. Add crumbs, butter, and mushrooms. Put in a baking dish.
3. Bake about one-half hour, or until brown. (400°.)

Stewed Cucumbers

2 large cucumbers   ½ cup vinegar
½ cup water   2 tablespoons butter
1 medium onion, chopped   Salt and pepper

1. Cut cucumbers in one-quarter-inch slices. Add water and onion and simmer twenty minutes. Drain.
2. Add vinegar, butter, salt, and pepper, and cook three minutes.
3. Serve with tomato, cheese, or highly seasoned white sauce.

Salads

Okra Salad

1 teaspoon sugar   2 cups okra
4 tablespoons French   2 quarts water
    dressing   1 teaspoon vinegar

1. Remove stems, and wash, and cook okra in boiling, salted water for twenty minutes. Add vinegar and sugar, and boil thirty minutes. Drain and chill.
2. Serve with French dressing.

Stuffed Tomatoes

6 tomatoes   ¾ cup shrimp or crab
1 cup diced celery   Mayonnaise
½ cup minced olives   Seasoning
                        Lettuce

1. Peel tomatoes and scoop out pulp. Sprinkle tomato cups with salt, and invert.
2. Mix other ingredients and fill tomatoes.
3. Serve on lettuce with a garnish of mayonnaise.

Crab or Shrimp Louis

Lettuce   Chives, chopped
2 hard-cooked eggs, sliced   Crab meat or shrimps

Dressing:
   ½ cup French dressing   1 teaspoon Worcester-
   ½ cup chili sauce   shire
   Salt and pepper   2 tablespoons mayonnaise

1. Arrange lettuce leaves, and some shredded or sliced lettuce on individual plates.
2. Arrange hard-cooked eggs and chives on lettuce.
3. Mix ingredients for dressing.
4. Place crab or shrimps on lettuce, or in the dressing.
5. Pour dressing over all.

Tomato with Crab

2 tablespoons gelatin   2 tablespoons onion juice or
1 cup cold water   ¼ cup minced onion
2 cans tomato soup   2 tablespoons vinegar or
2 packages cream cheese   lemon juice
½ cup celery, cut fine   Crab meat
                        Mayonnaise

1. Soak gelatin in cold water five minutes.
2. Heat soup. Add softened gelatin and cheese. Stir until well blended. Cool.
3. Add vegetables and lemon juice and place in molds.
4. Garnish with crab meat when turned from molds. Serve with mayonnaise.

Jellied Vegetables in Tomatoes

8 medium-sized tomatoes
1 package lemon jello
1 pint tomato juice (made from centers)
½ teaspoon salt

2 cups mixed cook vegetables (peas, celery, carrots, beans)
Lettuce
Mayonnaise

1. Wash tomatoes, remove a thin slice from tops, and scoop out centers.
2. Place tomato shells upside down and set in a cool place until ready to fill.
3. Dissolve jello in boiling tomato juice, add salt, and chill.
4. When slightly thick, add vegetables and fill tomatoes with mixture. Chill.
5. To serve, cut each tomato into quarters, using a sharp knife dipped in hot water.
6. Serve on crisp lettuce leaves. Garnish with mayonnaise.

Shrimp and Tomato Gelatin

1 onion
1 can tomatoes
1 tablespoon vinegar
2 teaspoons sugar
Salt, pepper, cayenne
1½ cups hot water

1 box gelatin
½ cup cold water
¼ cup celery
4 hard-cooked eggs
2 pounds shrimps
Few sprigs parsley

1. Chop onion and cook with tomatoes, vinegar, sugar, seasonings, and hot water.
2. Soak gelatin in cold water and pour boiling mixture over it. Stir until gelatin is dissolved.
3. Chop celery, eggs, shrimps, and parsley, and put in a mold (or individual molds). Add gelatin mixture.
4. Set in icebox to congeal.

Tomatoes Stuffed with Peanuts

6 tomatoes
1 pound peanuts
Olive oil

Mayonnaise
Lettuce
Paprika

1. Cut a slice from tops of tomatoes and scoop out centers. Sprinkle tomato cups with salt, invert, and place in the icebox.
2. Shell peanuts, chop, and fry in a little olive oil until delicately browned. Cool.
3. Chop centers of tomatoes, and drain. Mix with nuts and a little mayonnaise. Fill tomatoes with mixture.
4. Place each tomato on a crisp lettuce leaf, and top with mayonnaise. Sprinkle with paprika.

Melon Salad

Melon balls
Orange juice
1 cup other diced fruit, if
  desired (orange, pine-
  apple, strawberry)

French dressing made with
lemon or orange juice
instead of vinegar

1. Soak melon balls in orange juice for thirty minutes.
2. Add other fruits and arrange all on lettuce.
3. Pour French dressing over all.

Cole Slaw

Cabbage, shredded

Dressing:

½ cup milk
1 tablespoon cornstarch
2 egg yolks

½ teaspoon salt
Pepper
4 tablespoons vinegar

1 tablespoon butter

1. Heat milk and add cornstarch, which has been mixed with a little cold water.
2. Pour over beaten egg yolks and add other ingredients. Heat but do not boil. Cool.
3. Add dressing to cabbage.

Note: For variation, any one or more of the following may be added: 1 chopped onion; 4 tablespoons minced celery; 1 cup chopped tongue or ham; 1 chopped red or green pepper; ½ cup grated pineapple; ½ cup peanuts; ½ cup raisins.

Cinnamon Apple Salad

Prepare cinnamon apples
  (see Cinnamon Apples,
  p. 248)

Lettuce
Cream cheese
Chopped nuts

Mayonnaise

1. Place apples on lettuce leaves.
2. Garnish with cream cheese balls, nuts, and mayonnaise.

Hot Breads

Buttermilk Biscuit

1 quart flour	2 teaspoons salt
1 teaspoon soda	6 or 8 tablespoons lard
2 cups sour buttermilk	

1. Sift flour, soda, and salt. Cut in lard.

2. Add buttermilk. Knead lightly and roll out one-half inch thick. Shape with a buscuit cutter. Place in a greased pan.

3. Bake in a hot oven for ten to fifteen minutes. (450°.)

Iron Spider Corn Bread

1 cup corn meal	2 cups sour milk or butter-
1 teaspoon soda	milk
1 teaspoon salt	2 tablespoons shortening,
2 eggs, well beaten	melted

1. Mix dry ingredients and add milk and eggs. Add melted shortening.

2. Beat all thoroughly and put into a greased skillet.

3. Bake for twenty minutes. (400°.)

Sally Lunn

1 pint milk	2 eggs, beaten
2 tablespoons butter	2 tablespoons sugar
½ teaspoon salt	Flour to make a thick
½ yeast cake	batter (3 or 4 cups)

1. Scald milk and add butter, salt, and sugar. Let stand until tepid.

2. Dissolve yeast cake in one-fourth cup warm water.

3. Add milk and yeast to eggs; then add flour. Mix well. Let rise.

4. Beat down with a heavy spoon. Let rise again and beat down, repeating three or four times. Pour into greased bread pans and let rise to double its size.

5. Bake in a moderate oven for forty-five minutes. (350°-400°.)

Southern Johnnycake

1 egg, well beaten
½ cup sour cream
1 teaspoon soda

1 cup flour
½ cup sugar
1 cup buttermilk

1½ cups corn meal

1. Mix in order given. Pour into a greased baking pan.
2. Bake in a moderate oven for twenty-five to thirty minutes. (400°.)

Virginia Spoon Bread

1 cup white corn meal
1 teaspoon salt
½ teaspoon soda
1 cup sweet milk

1 cup sour milk or buttermilk
2 eggs, well beaten
1 tablespoon fat, melted

1. Mix dry ingredients, and add milk and eggs. Beat well.
2. Melt fat in a pan or casserole. Pour in mixture and bake in a hot oven. (450°.)

Southern Corn Bread

2 cups corn meal
½ cup flour
1 teaspoon salt
½ teaspoon soda

2 teaspoons baking powder
1½ cups sweet buttermilk
1 egg, well beaten
4 tablespoons fat

1. Mix dry ingredients. Add buttermilk and egg.
2. Melt fat in a pan and add to dough.
3. Pour into a greased baking pan.
4. Bake in a moderate oven for forty-five minutes. (375°.)

Note: Crackling bread may be made from this recipe by substituting one cup of cracklings for fat. (Cracklings are the residue of pork fat after it has been rendered.)

Crisp Corn Bread or Hoecake

Hot water or milk   Corn meal
Salt

1. Make a thin batter of milk and corn meal. Add salt.
2. Pour batter one-fourth inch thick in a greased baking pan.
3. Bake in a very hot oven. It should be very crisp. (475°-500°.)

Popovers

2 cups flour	2 cups milk
2 or 3 eggs	2 tablespoons melted
½ teaspoon salt	butter

1. Put flour in a bowl. Make a well in the center and drop eggs and salt into it. Add milk and beat with a rotary beater.
2. Add melted butter and beat again.
3. Bake thirty minutes in hissing-hot, well-greased iron pans, or earthenware cups.

Waffles

1¾ cups flour	2 eggs
3 teaspoons baking powder	2 tablespoons butter, melt-
½ teaspoon salt	ed (3 tablespoons for
1 tablespoon sugar	electric iron)
1 cup milk	

1. Mix and sift dry ingredients.
2. Add milk gradually, then egg yolks, well beaten.
3. Add melted butter and fold in stiffly beaten egg whites.
4. Bake on a hot waffle iron.

Note: Three tablespoons of corn meal may be substituted for an equal amount of flour.

Beaten Biscuit

3 cups sifted flour	¾ teaspoon sugar
½ teaspoon salt	⅓ cup lard
½ cup milk	

1. Sift dry ingredients and blend with lard. Add milk enough to make a stiff dough. Use more or less milk as needed.
2. Place on a floured board and beat with a rolling pin until dough blisters and is smooth. Roll to one-half-inch thickness.
3. Cut with a biscuit cutter and prick with a fork.
4. Bake in a medium oven for thirty minutes. (375°-400°.)

Southern Desserts

When we think of the desserts of the South we cannot forget the watermelon or the ice cream and ices. But here are a few characteristic desserts you can make.

Ambrosia

6 oranges
½ cup powdered sugar

½ cup grated coconut
Cherries

1. Peel and slice oranges. Cut slices into quarters.
2. Arrange in a serving dish. Sprinkle with sugar and coconut.
3. Garnish with cherries.

Spiced Gingerbread

¾ teaspoon soda
1 cup sour milk
½ cup molasses
1 egg, well beaten
2 cups flour
2 teaspoons baking powder

½ cup sugar
½ teaspoon salt
¾ teaspooon ginger
1 teaspoon cinnamon
½ teaspooon nutmeg
¼ cup fat or butter

1. Mix soda with sour milk and add to molasses. Add egg.
2. Sift dry ingredients and combine mixtures. Melt butter, add, and beat batter vigorously.
3. Pour into a buttered, shallow pan and bake for twenty-five minutes in a moderate oven. (375°.)

Soft Gingerbread

1 cup boiling water
2 teaspoons soda
1 cup molasses
2 eggs, well beaten

2½ cups flour
1 teaspoon each, cinnamon, cloves, ginger
½ cup sugar

½ cup butter or drippings

1. Mix by same method as for Spiced Gingerbread above.

Strawberry Shortcake

2 cups flour
4 teaspoons baking powder
½ teaspoon salt
4 tablespoons shortening
2 or 3 tablespoons brown
    or white sugar

¾ cup milk
Butter
Strawberries
Sugar for berries
Whipped cream

1. Make a biscuit dough of flour, baking powder, salt, shortening, sugar, and milk. Form into two rounds, dotting butter on one round and covering with other one. Bake for fifteen to twenty minutes. (450°-475°.)
2. Reserve nicest berries for top. Mash other berries and sweeten with sugar. Let stand a short time.
3. Split cake. Put part of mashed berries between two layers, and the rest on top.
4. Spread whipped cream over this and garnish with selected berries.

Note: These may be made in individual sizes, if desired.

Heavenly Hash No. 1

Sliced pineapple or oranges
Orange ice cream or ice

Candied cherries, orange
    peel, ginger

Nuts

1. Arrange sliced fruit in individual dishes.
2. Put a round scoop of ice cream or ice on the fruit.
3. Chop nuts, cherries, orange peel, and ginger, and sprinkle over top.

Heavenly Hash No. 2

2 cups whipped cream
½ pound marshmallows
Maraschino cherries

½ pound blanched almonds
Ladyfingers or macaroons
Candied fruits, if desired

1. Sweeten and flavor whipped cream. Add mashmallows cut in small pieces. Chill.
2. Line a bowl with crushed ladyfingers or macaroons.
3. Mix almonds and cherries into cream and turn into the bowl. Chill.

Apples à la Créole

1 cup granulated sugar

1 cup water

6 apples

1 tablespoon gelatin, soaked
in ¼ cup cold water

1 cup brown sugar

1 tablespoon butter

½ cup cream

¾ cup chopped nuts

1 cup whipped cream

Chopped nuts for garnish

1. Boil granulated sugar and water for ten minutes.
2. Peel and core apples. Cook in the sirup until tender, keeping them whole. Remove apples.
3. Add softened gelatin to sirup. Stir until dissolved.
4. Cook brown sugar, butter, and cream together to soft-ball stage. Add nuts.
5. Put apples in a serving dish and fill centers with nut mixture. Pour sirup around apples and set to cool.
6. Garnish with whipped cream and chopped nuts.

Cinnamon Apples

2 cups sugar

½ cup red cinnamon can-
dies or fruit coloring
and cinnamon

1 cup water

Ice cream

Apples, cut in halves or
quarters

1. Make a sirup of sugar and water. Add candies.
2. Cook apples in sirup without stirring. Simmer until tender. Chill.
3. Serve with a scoop of ice cream.

Creole Baked Apples

Apples

½ cup sugar

½ cup water

1 tablespoon lemon juice

½ teaspoon butter

Marmalade

Whipped cream

1. Peel and core two apples. Bake until tender, but not broken.
2. Fill centers with marmalade and serve with following sauce and whipped cream.
3. SAUCE: Boil sugar, water, lemon juice, and butter for ten minutes. The sauce may be cooked with apples.

Chess Pies

½ cup butter
2 eggs or 1 white and 3
    yolks

1 cup sugar
1 cup chopped nuts
1 cup chopped raisins

1 teaspoon vanilla

1. Cream butter and sugar. Add beaten egg yolks.
2. Add stiffly beaten egg white, nuts, and raisins.
3. Put in individual, unbaked pastry shells. (Muffin tins will do.)
4. Bake in a hot oven (400°) until it sets, then lower temperature to 350° until brown.
5. Serve with whipped cream or meringue.

Pecan Pie

3 eggs, well beaten
1 cup brown sugar
1 cup dark table sirup

1 tablespoon flour
1 tablespoon butter, melted
1 teaspoon vanilla

¾ cup pecans, chopped

1. Place all ingredients, except pecans, in a bowl. Mix well, and add pecans.
2. Put mixture into an unbaked pie shell and bake in a slow oven about thirty minutes. (350°.)
3. Serve with whipped cream.

Raisin Pie

1 cup seeded raisins
2 cups water
1½ cups sugar
4 tablespoons flour

1 egg, well beaten
Juice of 1 lemon
2 teaspoons grated rind
Pinch salt

1. Soak raisins in water for three hours.
2. Mix sugar, flour, and egg. Then add other ingredients.
3. Cook over hot water for fifteen minutes, stirring occasionally. Cool.
4. Pour into an unbaked pie shell. Cover with narrow strips of pastry, crisscrossed.
5. Bake in a hot oven (475°) for twenty minutes; then reduce temperature to 375° and bake pie ten minutes longer.

Louisiana Molasses Custard Pie

1 cup molasses	¼ teaspoon soda
1 cup sugar	2 egg yolks
1 cup buttermilk	Flavoring: cinnamon and
2 tablespoons flour	vanilla

Rich piecrust

1. Mix molasses, sugar, buttermilk, flour, soda, and well-beaten egg yolks. Cool in a double boiler until thickened, stirring constantly. Add flavoring. Cool.
2. Pour into an unbaked pastry shell. Bake at 475° for ten minutes; then reduce temperature to 400° and bake until crust begins to brown.
3. Cover with meringue and finish baking at 300° for about fifteen minutes.

MERINGUE

2 egg whites   4 tablespoons sugar

1. Beat egg whites until stiff and dry; add sugar gradually, beating constantly.

Old-fashioned Indian Pudding

⅓ cup yellow corn meal	½ teaspoon salt
1 cup cold water	½ cup molasses
2 cups scalded milk	½ teaspoon ginger
½ cup sugar	1 teaspoon cinnamon
2 eggs	½ cup milk

1. Combine corn meal and water and add all but one-half cup of hot milk.
2. Combine all other ingredients with corn-meal mixture and bake one hour. (300°.)
3. Pour on other half cup of milk and bake two hours longer. Do not stir.

Note: Two cups of quartered apples may be added to this.

Molasses Cookies No. 1

1 cup butter	1 teaspoon cinnamon
1 cup sugar	1 teaspoon ginger
2 eggs	1 teaspoon nutmeg
¾ cup molasses	1 teaspoon caraway seed
2 cups flour	1 teaspoon soda in butter-
½ teaspoon salt	milk

3 tablespoons buttermilk

1. Cream butter and sugar, add unbeaten eggs and molasses, and beat well.
2. Mix and sift dry ingredients, and add alternately with milk.
3. Add more flour, if needed, to make dough stiff enough to roll.
4. Roll thin, and cut and place on greased cooky sheet.
5. Bake in a moderate oven for ten to twelve minutes. (400°.)

Molasses Cookies No. 2

1 cup shortening	2 cups flour
1 cup sugar	1 teaspoon soda
½ cup molasses	Salt and spices

½ cup hot water

1. Cream shortening and sugar, add molasses, and mix well.
2. Sift dry ingredients, and add alternately with water.
3. Add more flour, if necessary, to make dough stiff enough to roll.
4. Roll thin, cut, and place on a greased cooky sheet.
5. Sprinkle with sugar. Bake in a moderate oven for ten to twelve minutes. (400°.)

Cherry Log Cake (Jelly Roll)

3 eggs	1 teaspoon baking powder
1 cup sugar	½ teaspoon salt
3 tablespoons cold water	Powdered sugar
1 cup flour	Jelly

1. Beat eggs and sugar until thick. Add cold water alternately with dry ingredients, which have been sifted together.
2. Pour into a greased shallow pan and bake for twelve minutes in a moderate oven. (375°.)
3. Turn onto a cloth sprinkled with powdered sugar. Trim crusts, spread with jelly, and roll.

Yam Puff

4 large yams	½ cup sugar
½ cup butter	1 teaspoon salt
2 eggs, beaten	2 teaspoons baking powder

Marshmallows

1. Boil yams until soft. Peel, mash, and add other ingredients, except marshmallows.
2. Mix well and put in a buttered baking dish. Dot with butter.
3. Bake in a moderate oven for fifteen to twenty minutes. (400°.) Place marshmallows on top and return to oven to brown.

Mammy's Sweet Potato Pudding

3 medium sweet potatoes   1 cup sugar
3 eggs, well beaten   1 tablespoon butter
2 cups milk   1 teaspoon vanilla

1. Grate potatoes and add other ingredients.
2. Pour into a buttered baking dish and bake one hour in a moderate oven. (350°-375°.)

Sweet Potato Pone No. 1

1 cup butter   ½ cup milk
1 cup sugar   1 teaspoon ginger
2 cups grated sweet potato   Grated rind of 1 orange

1. Cream butter and sugar; then add sweet potato and milk. Beat well.
2. Add other ingredients.
3. Bake in a shallow, greased pan in a slow oven thirty to forty minutes. (350°.)

Sweet Potato Pone No. 2

2 cups grated raw sweet   ½ cup sugar
   potatoes   1 teaspoon grated orange
½ cup maple sirup   rind
2½ teaspoons powdered   ½ cup butter, melted
   ginger   Hard sauce

1. Mix ingredients well. Pour into a buttered baking dish.
2. Bake one and one-half hours. (325°.)
3. Serve with wine-flavored hard sauce.

Sweet Potato Pone No. 3

1 cup grated raw sweet   ½ cup sugar
   potato   ¼ cup molasses
2 eggs, beaten   ½ cup milk
               ½ tablespoon ginger

1. Mix sweet potato and eggs; then add other ingredients.
2. Place mixture in a buttered baking dish.
3. Bake one hour at 350°.

Miscellaneous

Miscellaneous

━━━━━━━━━━━━━━━━━━━━━━━━━━━━━━━━━━━

Canapés

Smoked Sturgeon Canapé

½-inch slices stale white bread
Butter
Anchovy paste

French mustard
Sturgeon or sardines
Chopped olives
Pimiento

Parsley

1. Cut bread into one-half inch slices. Trim off crusts and cut slices in triangles. Fry a golden brown in butter.
2. Spread with anchovy paste and French mustard.
3. Arrange sturgeon or sardines over canapés. Sprinkle with chopped olives and pimientos. Garnish with parsley.

Cheese Canapés

12 thin slices bread or crackers
1 can sandwich spread

2 tablespoons grated cheese
2 tablespoons bread crumbs
2 tablespoons butter

1. Spread hot buttered crackers or circles of bread with sandwich spread.
2. Sprinkle with grated cheese, and then with the bread crumbs. Dot with butter and brown in the oven.

Lobster Canapé

Bread or rolls
Butter
Hard-cooked eggs

Lobster meat
Cream
French mustard

Salt, pepper, cayenne

1. Slice rolls, or cut circular pieces of bread. Sauté in butter.
2. Force egg yolks through a sieve and mix with lobster. Moisten with melted butter and cream. Season with salt, pepper, and cayenne.
3. Spread meat on bread and garnish with egg whites, cut in strips or rings.

Relishes

Spanish Pickles

8 quarts green tomatoes, sliced
4 onions, thinly sliced
1 cup salt
1 pound brown sugar
½ ounce cloves

4 green peppers, finely chopped
½ ounce allspice berries
½ ounce peppercorns
½ cup brown mustard seed
Cider vinegar

1. Arrange tomatoes and onions in alternate layers in a large dish. Sprinkle each layers with salt. Let stand overnight.
2. In morning, drain and put in a preserving kettle. Add other ingredients, using enough vinegar to cover all.
3. Heat to boiling point and boil one-half hour.
4. Pour into jars and seal.

Mango Chutney

4 pounds green mangoes
½ pound salt
3 pounds brown sugar
1 pound almonds

½ pound green ginger
2 pounds raisins
2 ounces garlic, minced
2 ounces chilies, chopped

1 pint vinegar

1. Peel and grate mangoes. Mix with salt and sugar. Let stand overnight.
2. Blanch almonds and pound to a paste. Scrape and slice ginger.
3. Mix all ingredients. Put into wide-mouthed bottles and let stand in sunlight for two weeks.

Oyster Pickles

1 cup olive oil
½ cup vinegar
2 teaspoons salt
3 chilipepines, chopped
1 clove garlic, minced
2 peppercorns

2 tablespoons sweet mar-
joram
6 dozen oysters
1 cup oyster liquor
Lemon slices
Sliced chili pepper

1. Mix oil, vinegar, salt, chilipepines, garlic, peppercorns, and marjoram. Bring to a boil and boil two minutes.

2. Add oysters and liquor. Boil until oysters are plump. Add more oyster liquor if too tart.

3. Serve with liquor. Garnish with lemon and chili pepper.

Green Tomato Pickles

4 quarts green tomatoes
12 large onions
½ cup salt, or less
¼ cup ground mustard
2 tablespoons black pepper
2 tablespoons ground all-
spice

1 teaspoon ground cloves
4 green peppers, chopped
fine
1 red pepper, chopped fine
¼ pound white mustard
seed
1 pound brown sugar

2 quarts vinegar

1. Slice tomatoes and onions very thin. Place in a large dish in alternate layers. Sprinkle each layer with salt. Let stand twenty-four hours. Drain.

2. Put into a preserving kettle and add other ingredients. Boil down until the consistency of catsup, or about two and three-quarter hours.

3. Seal in jars.

Confitura de Tomate (Tomato Jam)

4 cups strained tomato pulp
4 cups sugar

1½ tablespoons brandy or
rum

1. Place all ingredients in a saucepan over a slow fire. Simmer until they are the consistency of jam.

2. Pour into jars and seal.

Red Pepper Catsup

24 red bell peppers
24 green bell peppers

8 onions, chopped
2 cups vinegar

1. Remove seeds and veins from peppers and cut in large pieces.
2. Add onions and vinegar. Simmer until peppers are soft. Strain.
3. Pour into small bottles. Seal.

Cucumber Relish

12 medium-sized cucumbers
½ cup salt
½ cup white mustard seed

⅛ cup black mustard seed
2 tablespoons celery seed
½ cup olive oil

Vinegar

1. Peel and slice cucumbers.
2. Mix salt, mustard seed, celery seed, and olive oil.
3. Place a layer of cucumbers in a jar, and sprinkle with mixture. Repeat until jar is full.
4. Cover with vinegar and seal.
5. Let stand several days before using.

Creole Sweet Pickled Figs

2 quarts figs
Salt
1 quart boiling water
2 teaspoons whole mace

2 sticks cinnamon
1 tablespoon whole cloves
1 pound sugar
1 quart vinegar

1. Place a layer of figs in a jar. Cover with a layer of salt. Repeat until all figs are used. Cover with cold water and let stand overnight.
2. In the morning, wash figs, cover with clear water, and let stand two hours. Drain.
3. Pour on boiling water. Let cool.
4. Tie spices in a cloth, place in a kettle, and add sugar and vinegar. Boil and skim.
5. Add figs and scald. Let mixture stand twenty-four hours.
6. Reheat, place in jars, and seal.

Preserves and Candy

Orange Marmalade

6 oranges   1 lemon

1. Wash and dry fruit. Cut into quarters without peeling. Cut each quarter into thinnest slices possible. Discard all seeds. Add three cups of water for each cup of fruit and let mixture stand overnight.
2. Heat slowly to the simmering point. Cook four to six hours, or until tender.
3. Let orange mixture stand overnight a second time.
4. Measure, reheat, and when boiling, add an equal measure of sugar.
5. Cook rapidly until mixture jells when tested on a cold dish, or at 218° on a sugar thermometer.

Orange Peel Candy

Orange peels   Coloring added to sirup,
Thick sugar sirup   if desired
                 Granulated sugar

1. Cut orange peel lengthwise into strips. Cover with cold water and bring to a boil. Cook thirty minutes and drain.
2. Add fresh water and simmer three or four hours, or until soft and transparent. Discard water.
3. Cook orange peel in sirup, allowing it to boil down until very little sirup is left. Add more water and cook down again. Repeat until thoroughly candied.
4. Sprinkle sugar on brown paper and roll strips of orange peel in it so that they will not stick.

Note: This is not as Spanish as it is suitable.

Index

Printed in the United States
133428LV00002B/56/A